DANGEROUS DESIGNS

In late-1990s Britain, the salwaar-kameez or 'Punjabi suit' emerged as a high-fashion garment. Popular both on the catwalk and on the street, it made front-page news when worn by Diana, Princess of Wales and Cherie Booth, the wife of UK Prime Minister Tony Blair.

In her ethnography of the local and global design economies established by Asian women fashion entrepreneurs, Parminder Bhachu focuses on the transformation of the salwaar-kameez from negatively coded 'ethnic clothing' to a global garment fashionable both on the margins and in the mainstream. Exploring the design and sewing businesses, shops and street fashions in which this revolution has taken place, she shows how the salwaar-kameez is today at the heart of new economic micro-markets which themselves represent complex, powerfully coded means of cultural dialogue and racial politics. The innovative designs of second-generation British Asian women are drawn from characteristically improvisational migrant cultural codes. Through their hybrid designs and creation of new aesthetics, these women cross cultural boundaries, battling with racism and redefining both Asian and British identities. At the same time, their border-crossing commercial entrepreneurship produces new diaspora economies which give them control over many economic, aesthetic, cultural and technological resources. In this way, the processes of global capitalism are gendered, racialized and localized through the interventions of diasporic women from the margins.

Parminder Bhachu is Professor of Sociology at Clark University, Massachusetts, USA. She was formerly Henry R. Luce Professor of Cultural Identities and Global Processes, and Director of the Women's Studies program. She is author of *Twice Migrants* (1985), and is co-editor of *Immigration and Entrepreneurship* (1993) and *Enterprising Women* (1988).

'Parminder Bhachu is the most authentic and imaginative intellectual of the diaspora that I have come across.... on the cutting edge – a sophisticated analyser of the multilayered identities and cultural locations that also occupy my films in the global diasporic arena ... the first academic to take me and my films seriously ... in all their complexities ... and wears great salwaar-kameezes too.'
Gurinder Chadha, director of *Bend it like Beckham, Bhaji on the Beach* and *What's Cooking?*

'This is such a smart, engaging, eye-opening book. Parminder Bhachu takes you inside the east London shop of Bubby Mahil and from there, amid patterns and customers and fax machines, you begin to see the globalized market in fashion and identities in a totally fresh way. Thanks to this innovative ethnography, we think new thoughts about defiance in the face of anti-Asian racism, entrepreneurial innovation from the cultural margins, and women's agency against the global odds.'
Cynthia Enloe, author of *Bananas, Beaches and Bases: Making Feminist Sense of International Politics*

'In my view, she is one of the most gifted writers working on the issues of diasporic cultures, ethnicity and cultural hybridity ... Her new book ... provides insights into the complexities of globalisation and the ways in which Asian women have been proactive agents within the micromarkets of the fashion industry.'
Les Back, Goldsmiths College, University of London, author of *Out of Whiteness* and *New Ethnicity and Urban Culture*

'Parminder Bhachu's *Dangerous Designs* is a revelation. Bhachu's Asian women are designing and stitching together both clothes and a new culture more in touch with our new capitalist global world than the traditional Anglo- and Indian elites who foolishly thought they were the center of a modern culture in which the center no longer holds.'
James Paul Gee, Tashia Morgridge Professor of Reading, University of Wisconsin-Madison

DANGEROUS DESIGNS

Asian women fashion
the diaspora economies

Parminder Bhachu

Routledge
Taylor & Francis Group

NEW YORK AND LONDON

First published 2004
by Routledge
2 Park Square, Milton Park, Abingdon, Oxon OX14 4RN

Simultaneously published in the USA and Canada
by Routledge
711 Third Avenue, New York, NY 10017

Routledge is an imprint of the Taylor & Francis Group, an informa business

© 2004 Parminder Bhachu

Typeset in Goudy by Wearset Ltd, Boldon, Tyne and Wear

Library of Congress Cataloging in Publication Data
Bhachu, Parminder.
Dangerous designs : Asian women fashion the diaspora economies /
Parminder Bhachu
p. cm.
Includes bibliographical references and index.
1. Fashion–Asian influences–History–20th century. 2. Costume
design–Asian influences–History–20th century. 3. Women fashion
designers–Asia–History–20th century. 4. Suits (Clothing) I. Title.
TT504.B43 2003
391'.2–dc21
2003046893

British Library Cataloguing in Publication Data
A catalogue record for this book is available from the British Library

ISBN 0–415–07220–4 (hbk)
ISBN 0–415–07221–2 (pbk)

DEDICATED TO MY SWEET MOTHER,
MERI PIARI MAMA

CONTENTS

CONTENTS

ILLUSTRATIONS

ACKNOWLEDGEMENTS

I dedicate this book to my mother without whose help and love nothing would have been possible for me. She got me to wear the Punjabi salwaar-kameez suits with cultural confidence and ethnic defiance in the 1970's by sewing them for me collaboratively, according to my own styles and design codes. She later also taught me to stitch these clothes proficiently for myself, making me a participant in the very suit economies I capture in this book. She was able to persuade me to remain culturally and sartorially confident in the overtly racist terrains of late 1960s/early 1970s London. This period was culturally barren, in British Asian terms, for young Asians like myself in their teens and early twenties, growing up in predominantly white areas of London. We had almost no Asian friends, nor were we from the directly migrant Indian and Pakistani home-orientated communities who returned to the subcontinent regularly for cultural reinforcement. In these racially and culturally harsh landscapes, our mothers played a central role in giving us a sense of ethnic pride and a sense of ourselves on our own terms – a confidence which spilled into other dimensions of our lives.

My brother, Binny Bhachu, has been my link to the larger world of design and fashion since I was a child. His professional training is in these fields and his own very striking hybridized style, a product of the multiple sites where he has lived in Europe and Africa, gave me exposure as a young person to these diasporically mediated and innovative worlds of fashion in which design-conscious turban-wearing Asian men like himself were influential trend-setters. I thank him for making me aware of these interesting worlds which I have since made my own in my academic and personal domains.

I could not have written this book without the help of my close friend of many years, Sasha Josephedis. I live in Massachusetts, USA. She lives in London, UK. Sasha acted as my writing coach and therapist – and for no charge! She is an anthropologist with multiple skills. For two years, whilst I was working intensively on this book, she monitored my time and she helped me think through its central themes and organize the material. She disciplined me to adhere to my writing schedule and attend my yoga classes. She remained on my case relentlessly and prevented my desire for 'writing delinquency' on many occasions. She did all this transatlantically. She is my genuine and precious friend to whom I owe much.

A Senior Simon Fellowship, awarded to me by Manchester University in Britain for the year of 1996, allowed me to conduct intensive ethnographic fieldwork on the diaspora fashion economies and entrepreneurs I write about here. I would like to thank Professor Roger Ballard for acting as my academic host and friend at Manchester University, and the Department of Religion and Theology for facilitating the Fellowship.

Ivan Light at UCLA is another treasured colleague whose specialism of migration and entrepreneurship, and whose theoretical frameworks on ethnic business, have benefited my work. I developed the embryonic themes of this book during an exciting fellowship year at UCLA during 1990–1, for which he invited me and during which time we collaborated on a book on a related topic.

Clark University, my academic institution and my home base, allowed me a semester without teaching commitments to finish this book. My colleagues there have helped me considerably in thinking through its themes. My thanks are due to Jody Emel and Sandy Azar for being such wonderful friends and colleagues in this enterprise and many other ongoing ones. In particular, I would like to thank my pal and mentor Cynthia Enloe, who has been an exceptionally caring intellectual supporter and a very dear friend. She is a bountiful goddess and I have been a happy beneficiary of her largesse for many years. She has made so much more possible for me in many domains of my life than I could have imagined for myself. Marcia Butzel acted as a sounding board and often put up with my long telephone conversations discussing drafts of the book. Fern Johnson has been another dear colleague and supporter of my work: I thank her for her many thoughtful comments on this book. Thanks too to my fellow anthropologist Sarah Michaels for being such a supportive colleague and, in addition, for introducing me to Jim Gee. Now at the University of Wisconsin, Madison, Jim urged me to read about the new capitalist processes and about market trends that dominate current global economies. He was and remains a real inspiration for me, believing in my work from the start and helping to place it within the broader intellectual frameworks he himself writes about innovatively and the economic and social trends he continuously monitors.

John Stone at Boston University, a fellow migrant from London, has been an encouraging and confidence-inspiring colleague who has always made me feel that the 'world is my oyster'. I am grateful for his help in reading earlier drafts of this book.

My thanks to my sweet friend of old, Jane Singh at the University of California, Berkeley, who made me focus on the politics of the fashion entrepreneurs, consumers and producers of the suit economy about whom I write here. She also made me think historically about the politicized diasporic aesthetics which have been innovatively reproduced by second-generation hybridizing agents in London. Jane invited me to present parts of this book twice at conferences on the diaspora at Berkeley, enabling me further to refine my ideas.

John Solomos and Les Back have both discussed my work and given me feedback on various phases of this book. They are my long-term friends from my

London days, who have remained my close colleagues, despite my translation to the USA. Both have been my staunch supporters and true friends who have stood by me at the critical turns in my career. Les found the picture used for the cover of this book. He also suggested its title. I am also grateful to Les for introducing me to Judith Barrett, whose editorial help and insightful comments have helped me finish this book.

Michael Keith at Goldsmiths College, University of London, negotiated the picture permission with the artist, Lorraine Leeson, who created the photomural which constitutes this book's paperback cover. She collaborated on this with Asian women from the East End of London through the former community arts co-operative called 'The Art of Change' of which she was a member. I thank both the artist for allowing me to use her work and also Michael for facilitating this permission.

It was fun to share my research with my friend Shaista Faruqi-Hickman who acted as my fieldwork-buddy on various occasions. She made incisive observations about fashion and design trends from the perspective of a transnationalized cosmopolitan British Asian. She is a woman who herself engages in a hybridized style of her very own. She is also an astute decoder of the fine gradations of social class aesthetics as played out in the clothes of women from multiple class locations in the overlapping circles that are at the same time 'ethnic', 'English', 'subcontinental', etc.

Finally, my research would not have been possible at all without the help of the fashion entrepreneurs, the seamstresses, the personnel, the consumers, and especially, my favourite people, my Punjabi women friends, the 'older and old' *masis* at Sikh temples: these wonderful and brave 'honorary aunts' are the heroines of my tale, and populate this complex and multifarious economy. I thank each and every one of them for giving me their precious time, despite their hectic and demanding schedules, and for sharing their experiences with me. I hope that I have captured their lives and experiences appropriately in this book.

INTRODUCTION

In her smart east London shop, Bubby Mahil drew as she listened to her customer, a young Gujarati Muslim woman. The designer captured in the sketch's rough lines the shape of neckline and collar, length and style of top, skirt and dupatta, and noted down colours, fabrics and embroidery. Through the eloquent lines of the sketch emerged a new formula for fusion bridal wear – a bit of salwaar-kameez, a bit of lengha, a bit of sari, with influences of the traditional European white bridal outfit. Once the customer had gone, Bubby elaborated the sketch, faxed it to her production site in India and made several follow-up phone calls to check details. The outfit would be ready for the customer to collect from the shop within two weeks, price £250.

In those few lines of the sketch, an eloquent expression of diasporic hybridizing and improvisational aesthetics, I was witnessing the actual process by which the new is produced, what Bernstein calls 'a recovery of something not yet spoken, of a new fusion' (Bernstein 1996). This moment for me embodied so many of the issues with which I had been grappling in thinking and teaching about cultural identities and global processes: racialized subjectivities, reflexive modernities, the dynamics of cultural production for people who move and migrate, the phenomenon of time-speed-space compression that defines global communications (see, for example, Giddens 1991, Lash and Urry 1994, Beck et al. 1994). Complex, culturally mediated design processes were reflected in how Bubby engaged with her customer, both in her design and its method of production. Her subsequent narrative of growing up in east London as a British Asian of East African Asian descent revealed how her experiences had politicized her and galvanized her into developing the hybrid style that captured her local contexts and expressed her identities as she constructed them.

This moment in Bubby's shop highlighted, too, features distinctive of the new capitalism. I do not think Bubby herself was aware of the extent to which her commercial style was in tune with these new capitalist processes, in particular, the detailed, collaborative customization of the product to construct/express the identity of the client:

1

The new capitalism, is ... about *customization*: the design of products and services perfectly dovetailed to the needs, desires, and identities of individuals on the basis of their *differences*. These differences may be rooted in their various sub-group affiliations or in their unique individuality.

(Gee 1996:43)

Crucially, Bubby is not just making clothes, but is co-constructing an identity with her clients. Within the new capitalism, material objects matter more for what they *signify* than their actual content:

... objects ... are progressively emptied of material content. What is increasingly produced are not material objects, but *signs*.

(Lash and Urry 1994:4)[1]

These signs, argue Lash and Urry, are of two types: post-industrial or informational goods, with a primarily cognitive content; or what they call postmodern goods, with a primarily aesthetic, content. The latter comprise objects whose prime function is aesthetic, such as pop music and film, but also material objects in which an 'increasing component of sign-value or image [is] embodied' (ibid.). It is into the latter category that Bubby's clothes fall. What makes her goods distinctive is her individual design input but this is a specific instance of a more general phenomenon:

The specific labour process is becoming less important in its contribution to value added, and the 'design process' is progressively more central ... The increased R&D [research and design] intensity is often importantly aesthetic in nature, as in the case of clothes, shoes, furniture, car design and so on.

(Lash and Urry 1994:15)

In commercial terms, Bubby's operation is small, local, with no 'middleman' between herself and the customer. This is another significant factor in the success of a new capitalist enterprise:

Only the businesses that are lean and mean, i.e., have no non-value-adding people close to the customer (i.e., local and global in effect, even if huge and global in reality) will succeed.

(Gee 1996:29)

In Bubby's co-constructed design process, all the value is added by the customer (who is in fact paying) and the vendor (who is making the profit herself). There is no intermediary. At the same time, she is part of the community in which she is selling, i.e. local, while global in her production processes (the clothes are manufactured on the subcontinent). Such localism is something to which large global corporations increasingly aspire – 'globalized localization' (Urry 1990:17): they seek to be perceived as local in order to maintain their markets. Corporations such as Nike and Reebok are having to pay more attention to the micro-communities of people who consume their products, as consumers become increasingly sophisticated about what they want and how they are being sold products. People now buy goods and services through word of mouth and their informal networks. Marketing talk is of the 'buzz of the market', developing marketing strategies that initiate a 'buzz' which then sells the product.[2]

Bubby, fortuitously, is precisely in tune with this current market moment:

> In the developed world today, economic survival is contingent on selling newer and ever more perfect(ed) customized (individualized) goods and services to niche markets – that is, to groups of people who come to define and change their identities by the sorts of goods and services they consume ... The winners design customized products and services on time/demand faster and more perfectly than their global competition does or they go out of business.
>
> (Gee et al. 1996:26)[3]

So Bubby has created a market from the margins, in which she collaborates with her customers to co-construct clothes that incorporate their design inputs within her distinctive style. It is this negotiative sensibility that gives her an advantage in creating these new economic domains, market sites that have emerged through the politicized cultural identities that she has had to construct and which are encoded both in her sartorial and commercial styles. Her openness to new ideas is part of her diasporic inheritance as a product of a multiply-migrant community, whose members developed their improvisational, collaborative aesthetics on the margins in Britain and in previous sites, where they had to struggle to constitute their ethnic identities. The aesthetics of having to maintain cultural confidence and negotiate cultural forms in locations of disadvantage have made Bubby open to capturing the new.

But Bubby, of course, is just part of the story of a dynamic British Asian, women-led fashion economy. Their hybridizing aesthetics represent dynamics similar to many facets of black cultural production and have much in common with other forms produced by people on the margins who draw from a range of sources in highly politicized, hostile landscapes (Ogren 1989, Gilroy 1993a and 1993b, Mercer 1994, Rose 1994, Tulloch 1999). Such cultural production constitutes a crucial form of resistance, often characterized by a negotiative aesthetic – which is all that you have when you are on the margins. When you do not have classificatory systems and vocabularies of command, your strength lies in your ability to improvise. Your weak power location forces you to improvise and to innovate.[4] Music yields the most widely appreciated examples, perhaps, from jazz to hip-hop and, within the Asian diaspora with which I am concerned here, bhangra and its subsequent reworkings.[5] This diasporic Punjabi music has combined multiple influences to create a new British Asian form that has a local specificity but which has also resonated within the many other diasporic and homeland sites to which it has travelled and where it has been further rearticulated. In common with other diasporic cultural forms – including fashion – it has combined many forms, a bit of this, a bit of that, to create a new form.

The Asian diaspora within Britain, which has given rise to the fashion economy with which this book is centrally concerned, consists both of people who are direct migrants from the subcontinent; and also multiple migrants, the twice- and thrice-migrant who have been to other destination economies, principally in East Africa, before migrating to Britain. The latter are experienced at the game of migration. They lack the desire of many direct migrants all over the world to go back 'home' to their countries of origin and to keep strong connections with their countries of origin. Multiple migrants do not have a myth of return and tend to be orientated to settling in their destination countries right from the point of entry (see Bhachu 1985, 1993a, 1993b, 1996). Such multiple migrants are already familiar with reproducing the cultural bases and managing their minority status in new settings. They already know what it is to struggle to constitute their ethnic identities, to manage their minority status and assert their cultural agendas. The diasporic stitching economy constitutes an essential part of this, the culture of sina-prona (literally, 'sewing and beading'), of improvisational patterning. In East Africa and, initially, in the UK, this was a need-based economy, in which such skills were critical if you wanted your children, yourself and your men to be clothed and the home to have cloth on the beds and on the table. I have already pointed out how Bubby draws on this cultural inheritance in her work, and it is a theme to which I shall return throughout the book.

What I want to do is to explore the transformations in cultural and consumer domains which have taken place under my eyes since arriving in London from Kenya as a teenager in the 1960s. Immigrants and their second-generation progeny have successfully fought for and forged their own cultural spaces and identities, while Asianizing cultural and commercial influences have diffused into mainstream British life and 'made it hip to be Asian'; we think of cultural producers such as: Gurinder Chadha (film director), Kulwinder Ghir (comedian), Bhajan Hunjan (artist) and Hardial Rai and Parv Bancil (playwrights). There is nothing facile about these emergences. They are the products of many years of politicking and cultural struggle. I am curious, therefore, about the processes of locally generated inputs that are recoding and reimagining previously denigrated domains of immigrant consumption and culture. What are the cultural struggles behind these transformative cultural and commercial dynamics? Who are the entrepreneurial agents who are making these commercial impacts? What are the cultural agendas and biographical experiences behind the creation of these new markets? And what part do global communications and technologies of transfer play in the whole process? What part are these cultural/commercial agents playing within the new capitalism?

My focus, in looking for answers to these questions, is the fashion economy of formerly 'ethnic clothes', in particular the Punjabi or salwaar-kameez suit, which has moved into mainstream consumer arenas (as I initially explored in Bhachu 1997). I examine the political subtexts involved in establishing these diaspora fashion markets, which have recoded European and transnational cultural and consumer spaces, despite the odds, both racial and commercial. I examine the innovative role of Asian women as cultural and commodity brokers, whose diaspora voices define these new consumer spaces through style and design. These spaces are products both of the battles of Asian women to assert their diasporically produced, British Asian cultural contexts; and of complex negotiations of identity. The women's command over economic resources, design expertise and modern communication technologies to rapidly transfer commodities is transforming transnational economic and cultural realms. At the same time, these new identity dynamics have initiated new ways of being British. Newspaper and magazine photographs of well-known British white women wearing the suit, such as Cherie Booth QC (in a design by Bubby Mahil), Jemima Goldsmith-Khan and the late Princess Diana, have familiarized it much beyond the circles in which it was otherwise worn. British black women in marginal communities had in fact worn the suit for a long time before its uptake by mainstream fashion and design agencies. These dynamics represent a 'buying into' and subscription to the identity scripts that Asian women are generating. British Asian women fashion entrepreneurs have started new national and transnational rhythms of fashion. Global connectors par excellence, their entrepreneurial skills are creating 'female aesthetic communities' (Goldstein 1995), which have important political and economic consequences in global markets. At one level, what is happening to these entrepreneurial designing women is quite specific to them, but it is also typical of our global world.

Their markets are complex mechanisms of multiple exchanges and cultural dialogues of identity, sartorial subversions, nation-making and political struggles, both in collusion with – and resistance to – capitalist processes. Asian women are using the market in innovative and disruptive ways, not just as mechanisms of economic exchange, but as potent instruments of their own transformative cultural and consumer politics which are, in turn, recoding British social landscapes. They are reshaping and contesting mainstream capitals and establishment conventions through their highly politicized cultural agendas encoded in their culturally tempered commercial sites. These pioneering women on the margins are redefining markets through their clothes-as-cultural-texts. They are politicized micro-marketers from the margins who engage in culturally mediated commerce in globalized, localized arenas.

Their market advantages are several. First, in terms of both gender and race, their politicized sensibilities as cultural workers on site participating in their own commercial arenas enable them to respond accurately and rapidly to the desires of their customers. Such responses are key requirements of the new capitalism (Gee *et al.* 1996): and are in contrast, as I shall show, to the elite India- and Pakistan-based entrepreneurs who entered the suit market during the 1990s when the foundation of this commerce had already been established by the locally raised British Asians. Their second market advantage comes from their ease of access to cheap sites of production via the technologies of global communications.[6] Third, it seems that the most cutting-edge of the designers benefit also from their diasporic inheritance as members of a multiply migrant community whose aesthetics are both improvisational and collaborative. Thus, their position of racial and cultural disadvantage in fact accords them a stance of advantage in their contemporary landscapes of reflexive modernity. Their collaborative aesthetic – of negotiating with customers to produce a product, of niche marketing that pays heed to the voices of their customers, of co-constructing – fits the current market moment. They have created their new markets by their negotiation of the disequilibrium in dissonant terrains. As Lester Thurow points out, writing about quite different market contexts, 'Disequilibrium conditions create high-return, high-growth activities. The winners … have the skills to take advantage of these new situations' (Thurow 1999:33).[7]

In this book, then, through my examination of this particular fashion economy, I present a narrative of cultural identities and global processes. It is a story of the connections that Asian women are making through their cultural and commercial activities constructing new local, national and international landscapes. It is about women connecting the globe from the margins and the networks they are generating in a fashion economy. I am examining the continuous and multiple stitching of the ruptures of diaspora communities which are on the margin. The book is thus both a cultural biography of that fashion economy and at the same time an ethnography of globalization. I narrate the stories of immigrant women and their second-generation daughters who have maintained their cultural systems, including the ethnic clothes, despite the racial and commercial odds. British-raised and British-born Asian women have redesigned and recontextualized the sartorial economies of their mothers into the commercial landscapes of the market. Their fashion economy has grown out of politicized cultural terrains negotiated through a multiplicity of identities and biographical trajectories of movement and location. Their clothes are texts that have recoded this erstwhile denigrated economy. It includes both fashion entrepreneurs – designers and marketers – and also the domestically based diasporic seamstresses. I explore the cultural and commercial connections that are producing niche markets mediated through dialogic cultural and identity texts. These innovative market circuits disrupt and subvert established sartorial economies.

I suggest that markets are complex mechanisms of cultural and commercial exchange, and are much more than straightforward sites of economic transactions. I point out that capitalist processes are not devoid of the gendered and racialized cultural inputs of people on the margins who are asserting their subaltern voices in the market. Whilst colluding with capitalist processes, they are also transforming them.

Throughout, I write as an active participant in the diasporic fashion economy I describe, currently based in the USA and previously in the UK and East Africa (Tanzania, where I was born, and Kenya and Uganda where I was raised). Like the seamstresses I describe in Chapter 10, I sewed from a young age. As I describe in Chapter 1, I was inducted into the sewing and suit economy in London by my mother. I am both a consumer of suits and also a domestic producer of them for myself. Over the past decade, I have become a chronicler and an academic conceptualizer of the various narrative threads and trajectories of this clothes economy.

The book falls into four main parts. In the first, 'Travels of the suit', I explain how immigrant women kept the suit economy alive and how their daughters now wear it with increased cultural confidence, as expressed also in musical forms, such as bhangra (Chapter 1); I examine the general phenomenon of ethnicized consumption within Britain, particularly in terms of food, before looking at how the suit has also entered the British mainstream (Chapter 2). In the second part, 'Design narratives', I present the work of two British Asian designers, Geeta Sarin (Chapter 3), and Bubby Mahil (Chapter 4); and contrast their aesthetics and style of working with three subcontinental fashion entrepreneurs/enterprises, Ritu Kumar (Chapter 5), Libas and Yazz (Chapter 6). In Part III, 'Suit marketers', I deal with the retail of ready-made suits: first in a chainstore, Daminis (Chapter 7), second through Komal Singh's catalogue and whole-sale enterprise, Bombay Connections, and third in Mala Rastogi's boutique, Creations (Chapter 8). Finally, in the fourth part, 'Sewing cultures: sketching and designing', I examine the sewing cultures of home-based seamstresses, describing in detail the culture of sina-prona and the democratizing influences of both patterns and sewing machines (Chapter 9), before presenting the sewing biographies of four domestic seamstresses (Chapter 10) and my conclusion.

Part I

TRAVELS OF THE SUIT

1

CULTURAL NARRATIVES OF
THE SUIT

Movements in the suits and movements of suits

The salwaar-kameez or Punjabi suit has traditionally been worn by women of North India and Pakistan and their diaspora overseas. These women were Hindu, Muslim and Sikh, originally sharing a regional territory and a common cultural base. While many women of all religions do also wear the sari in these areas, and some historically have worn only the sari, it is the suit that is seen as a distinctively Northern form of dress. It consists of three separate parts: kameez (shirt), salwaar (trousers) and chuni or dupatta (scarf or stole).

The suit appeared first in Britain from the mid-1960s onwards, a time of rapid growth of Asian communities as family groups consolidated themselves. Although Indian women had been a presence in Britain since the 1890s (Bhachu 1993a, 1993b), they had not previously constituted a critical mass and, publicly at least, had worn the sari in preference to the suit. Until the 1990s, then, the Punjabi suit was considered to be exclusively the dress of North Indian and Pakistani immigrant women. These immigrant clothes represented British Asians, who were not wanted on the British scene and were not welcome as citizens: they had been recruited as labour migrants (whom Britain was forced to accept because there were labour shortages after the Second World War) and because they were people resident in British colonies, with long-standing British citizenship rights and passports. The suit represented a threat; the colonized had come to the land of the colonizers. In Britain, local white people often referred to it derogatively either as a sari or a pyjama- or night-suit. It was negatively coded, the highly charged clothing of marginal women, of newcomers who refused to assimilate the sartorial styles of the local white Europeans.[1] These women were considered by the local white population and also by many Asians who had adopted an assimilationist stance as not being in tune with the times. They were classified as orthodox women who were rigid in maintaining their 'backward' cultures, when they should, as seen from the outside, have been adopting local styles. There were many racial slurs levelled against them. They were taunted and labelled 'Pakis', regardless of whether they were Pakistanis or not, whether locally born or not, or from the earlier diaspora communities with children who had never been to the subcontinent.

Modifications of the suit have always been made when worn in diaspora settings and in some cases women have had to give up wearing it completely. In the early days of settlement in the new locations, there is no reinforcing critical mass of suit-wearing women who can buoy up each other's sartorial confidence. For example, photographs taken in the 1920s in Vancouver (Canada) and California, the earliest centres of Punjabi settlement in North America, show Punjabi women wearing dresses which were long and modest, reaching just above the ankles, together with a headscarf, a short chuni, tucked inside the neckline or collars of their dress. Some also wore boots with these long dresses. I am told that stones were thrown at them by white racists for their different looks and sartorial styles. They had to adapt their clothes to be able to live their lives as safely as they could in overtly racist landscapes. Wearing a suit became a symbol of defiance for some North Indian and Pakistani women in the same way that the turban was for Sikh men. I now explore some of these narratives of 'suit defiance' in relating the movement of the suit from negatively coded 'ethnic clothing' to a global garment, fashionable both in the margins and within the mainstream.

Negatively coded suit stories of 1960s and 1970s Britain

My mother was told when we arrived in London in the late 1960s that she should give up wearing the suit. Already fifty years old, she had started work in an electronic components factory making coils and circuit boards in south London. She was advised by her Punjabi friends to wear flared trousers with a short kameez, as commonly adopted by other suit-wearing women, to avoid the 'night-suit' jibes of local white people. This modified version of the suit would be worn to work with a short chuni or a longer woollen one in the cold weather: the flared trousers were also worn at home with the longer chuni that is worn with the classic suit. Punjabi Sikh women even wore similar modified outfits at the temple though I want to reiterate that many adhered to the classic suit styles and saris for community functions and social occasions like weddings. My mother, however, refused to modify her style even at work, wearing suits in the classic styles she had always worn and stitched for herself (see Figure 1.1).

By the 1970s, suits were worn increasingly by Punjabi women. Younger women tended to wear it stylishly for special social functions rather than as everyday wear. Always a supremely fashion-focused garment, adapted and interpreted according to local and international fashion trends all the time, the relative length of the kameez, the volume of material in the salwaar and the width of ponchays (trouser cuffs) changed continuously throughout the decade. In the 1960s and early 1970s, there was no concept of 'ready-made' and the suits were made either by women themselves, buying material locally in Britain, or they had the suits made by Indian or Pakistani tailors when they went to visit the

Figure 1.1 The heroines of my tale – older women wearing classically styled suits in a south London Sikh temple.

subcontinent. The women who had their suits made in this way tended to make far less design input. This is not to say that they did not wear inventive suits, because Indian and Pakistani tailors are attuned to fashion trends and create suits that are both elaborate in their embellishment and complex in their construction. However, there tended to be a greater amount of standardization of these suits, according to what was in vogue in India and Pakistan at the time. In addition, the design uptake of current trends was inevitably slower.

The most innovative suits were worn by women who either sewed themselves or who had access to good sewers, often from their own backgrounds. Although India-produced suits were made of lovely fabrics and colours with inventive embroideries to which diaspora women did not on the whole have access (unless they visited the subcontinent regularly), British Asian design interpretations were much more fashion-focused and responsive to local trends. It was, above all, the multiply-migrant East African Asian women who had the sewing expertise to put their local design exposures and personal inventiveness into practice with great speed. Direct migrant women simply did not have the same sewing tradition, coming as they did from service economies of long-established professional sewing personnel, tailors and embroiderers, accustomed to meet their clothing demands. The multiple migrants, however, from East Africa, where there had been no comparable service economy, had grown up within the culture of sina-prona, where all clothes (and sheets, tablecloths, etc.) were home-made. The girls and women were systematically trained both at home by older female relatives and in local sewing schools. For them, an improvisational, hybridizing aesthetic was, of necessity, already in place. They further elaborated their skills in Britain because there was, as in the East African case, a need to do so. Surjeet, a multiply-migrant seamstress whose story I shall return to in Chapter 10, says that if she sees a suit on someone in the shop, she can make a copy of it in three hours from start to finish, including doing the hemming and putting on the buttons. This fast design uptake simply did not exist in the fashion economies of non-sewing women. But during the 1960s and 1970s there were few tailors and seamstresses who were 'sewing for money'. People made their own clothes but few sewed for others beyond their own family and kinship circuits.

By the late 1970s, however, this situation was changing. Many more seamstresses and tailors emerged as the Asian community established itself, ethnic confidence increased and more and more women started wearing suits. Crucially, many women now worked outside the home for wages. While lacking the time to sew themselves, instead they had their own money to spend according to their personal choices. The commodities they purchased encoded their cultural expressions and embodied their identities (see also Bhachu 1985 and 1991), and none more so than the suit.

The other dynamic for the growth of the ready-made suit market was the change taking place within the rituals of the traditional wedding, in particular a significant increase in wedding-gift exchange and elaborations in the wedding process. The increase in wedding-gift exchange was itself primarily the result of women participating directly in the labour market: the dowries of brides were elaborated because of their increased command of cash as waged workers, the elaborations taking the form of the bride's personal accessories and clothing, including, of course, suits (see Bhachu 1985 for a London-based analysis of this). At the same time, the actual process of the wedding also became more complicated, with many more ritual and social functions connected to it, each requiring a different and often new outfit[2] (see Bhachu 1985, 1986, 1993a, 1993b).

The women who had kept the suit economy alive were often working-class immigrant women, and in particular the older ones who, like my mother, adhered to the styles that they had always worn. These staunchly Punjabi women from different religious backgrounds really did maintain the form they migrated with. They were and have remained confident about what they wore. In turn they socialized their daughters into this suit economy and so produced a new generation of hybridizing women from among whom would subsequently emerge fashion entrepreneurs such as Geeta Sarin and Bubby Mahil – pioneering, pathbreaking commercial agents in the public suit economy. Their stories will be central to Chapters 3 and 4.

14

My suit narrative

My own story of suit wearing serves as an example of being socialized by a woman who, as I have already shown, made few concessions to the local economy in which she was situated, despite pressures on her 'to wear the trousers' as she puts it. It also illustrates well the East African Asian hybridizing and improvisational aesthetic and the design process of negotiation and co-construction.

I had started wearing a suit in Kenya in my early teens, but only rarely. Most girls wore frocks or dresses derived from the fashions of the time. During the early 1960s, my generation of girls and young women wore the New Look frock and versions of the 'twist dress'. We wore the New Look frock with a salwaar and chuni in the temple and at other times without the salwaar. I also wore the kurta and choost pyjama, the leg-hugging trousers which have folds of fabric at the ankle (the type of straight leggings worn by Indian Prime Minister Nehru). These were much in fashion in the mid- to late 1960s and were worn with high-neck kameezes made with long zips on the front opening. The zips had big plastic rings on the top, picking out colours from the kameez print. This interpretation of the kameez reflected the 'pop culture' style of the 1960s that was in vogue for young people of that generation – an example of the hybridizing aesthetic that British Asian women have elaborated in Britain in the 1980s and 1990s and which is played out in the new markets of the suit.

I moved to Britain with my parents in the late 1960s when I was fourteen. I went to local schools in south London in, essentially, very white suburbia. While a schoolgirl, I mostly wore standard school uniform and the clothes in vogue amongst my peer group. Then, when I was twenty-one, my mother made me some Punjabi suits which I wore at my sister's wedding. My mother chose the material for these and made them up according to the fashion then current. They suited me and I liked wearing them. However, I wore them just for the wedding and a few other functions. A year or so later, she made me suits, the materials for which I chose and which she sewed for me according to the styles I liked wearing. She took me to the material shops I liked going to in central London, places like John Lewis, the department store on Oxford Street, and also Liberty's, which specialized in William Morris and Paisley prints, fabrics with art deco motifs and tana lawn cottons. Of course at the time, I had no idea who William Morris was, nor of Liberty's oriental imperialist history. (Liberty's began trading in commodities 'from the Orient' in 1875, selling the goods brought back from India by the East India Company and from other Asian locations. Subsequently, it also specialized in products of the Arts and Crafts movement and art deco artefacts – see Adburgham 1975.) I simply liked their fabrics and bought them in their bi-annual sales. My mother would encourage me to select bold, clearly printed fabrics in vibrant colours. I was not clear or confident about my print choices then and would attempt to go for nondescript mish-mashed prints and colours. She had bold visual sense and was good at choosing fabrics that worked well in suits. She taught me a lot about mixing prints and colours that flow well in the suit silhouette, which has much combinational freedom because of its three separate parts. I am reminded of Sonia Delaunay's early twentieth-century 'simultaneous clothes' inspired by the Modernist art movement, whose bold designs (made up of geometric patterns, circles within circles, concentric discs and prisms) flowed together in simple lines, enhancing the body's movements.[3] My mother educated me into a colour and print palette that enabled the suit silhouette to flow similarly, a pedagogy of the suit economy in which she was experienced.

She also taught me how to cut and make a suit. At first, I would just make bits of the suit. Later, by my mid-twenties, I could cut and sew them completely. She told me continually that this was a skill I would need all my life in whichever country I was going to live. I had to master this skill of making a 'basic suit', she said. I have a large hardcover notebook of cutting instructions, measurements and fabric requirements, complete with pleat and dart information. I interpreted these early suits of the mid- to late 1970s using my own accessories, shoes, handbags, etc. She made me many more suits in later years, and others I made myself, until I started getting them made by seamstresses.

Our mother–daughter negotiations over details of collars, necklines and cuffs crucially enabled us to create styles that fitted my subcultural and subclass sartorial idiosyncrasies. I sat with her all the time as she sewed, drawing sketches for her and showing her magazine pictures. She succeeded in getting me to wear a suit in a mainly white British context in which there were few other Asian women. She used cloth, thread and seams to connect me with a Punjabi dress form and also my 'Punjabiness'. 'You should wear our Punjabi dress with pleasure,' she told me. 'All cultures have their own dress which they wear in this country and in their own countries. You should remain strong in yourself. You should not live with fear. You should be strong in your culture. You should wear the Punjabi dress of your culture.'

It was soon afterwards that I started connecting with other Punjabis as a graduate student and also acquired a more proficient understanding of the Punjabi language which I learnt to read and write more fluently. Also, being at the School of Oriental and African Studies at London University, I was inducted into the South Asian scene much more. I was also doing my Ph.D. on a multiply-migrant British Punjabi community, preparing to do ethnographic fieldwork.

Soon after completing my Ph.D., when I started my first job in an academic research unit, I began to wear the suit more than any other clothes. I was working in the race and ethnic relations field and had been politicized by all its academic and policy machinations. My understanding of the operations of the race relations bodies and their personnel had grown dramatically from my research experiences. I understood more closely the mechanics of knowledge production and race-related policy making in these politically charged fields. For many people in this area, studying British Asian and Black communities was an academic game which they got into and out of depending on academic fashions. Their locations were and remain very different from those of us who were from the communities being studied and had lived our lives in difficult terrains that we were continuously struggling to navigate. I was angered by the liberal stances of articulate anti-racist sounding people who were actually quite racist in their day-to-day interactions with some of us junior ethnic researchers and in their conceptualizations of community dynamics. In this phase, my constant wearing of the suit became an ethnically defiant gesture on my part, in the face of the racism within this field and my increased abilities to decode the politically correct anti-racist public rhetoric spouted by the seemingly liberal theorizers and practitioners.

My mother's sartorial and cultural interventions had come at a crucial moment of my life; her negotiations and her co-construction of the suit on my terms, being sensitive to my clothing styles, were critical in connecting me to my cultural base during a time that was difficult for us as recent migrants into an often hostile culture. The expression of overt ethnic registers like the suit was just not commonplace amongst young Asian women except within community social gatherings. I have worn the suit ever since, thanks to an astute and loving mother. She not only taught me how to make a 'basic suit' that I can elaborate on and sew in multiple ways, a sartorial template, but also gave me a template of cultural confidence, of learning to be myself on my terms regardless of the terrain.

I, too, as an adult have become a multiply migrant, now living and working in Massachussets, USA, where I find myself doing similar cultural work and engaging in the same negotiating aesthetics and sensibilities practised within the community contexts that produced me. These diasporic databanks constitute my inherited baggage in constructing a life for myself as a new migrant, a new US citizen, producing my US–British–East-African Asian home. So much of this production of a cultural life in the US incorporates 'bits and bobs' transmitted to me by a savvy, culturally confident, negotiating mother, who inducted me into these economies, in part at least, through the suit as a expression of cultural pride.

A narrative of suit defiance

A further narrative of cultural pride and sartorial defiance that I want to relate concerns the 1980s pre-professionalization and pre-mainstreaming contexts of the suit. Rani Singh was raised in a neighbouring area of Southall, west London. She therefore had easy access to what constitutes the Punjabi capital in England and to suit-wearing women. After she finished school and college, in the early 1980s she got a job with a bank. As a young woman in her twenties, she would attend Christmas and New Year office parties in a Punjabi suit even though she was told often by her Asian and white friends alike that this was not suitable garb for such functions. This was a time when local white people would still openly taunt suit-wearing women about their 'Paki clothes' and make all kinds of racist comments about 'curry bums in pyjamas'. It was commonplace for Punjabi women themselves to reject the suit: the cultural landscape was too negatively charged and difficult to negotiate; the suit was too clear an ethnic marker which they found hard to recode in a hostile climate. Rani told them she was proud to be a Sikh and that she 'didn't care what people thought'. She recounted to me how she told her office crowd:

> My father and brothers wear turbans. My mother has always worn a salwaar-kameez. And I am going to wear my lovely suits. I am not afraid of what goras [white people] or apnay [our people] say about our clothes. Why should you be afraid to wear the dress of our cultures? They wear the dresses of their cultures. They did not wear Indian clothes when they went to India. They do not give up wearing their clothes and wear the clothes we have, do they? Why should I give up our clothes! Why should I give in to their teasing? You have to be strong in yourself.

She made a point of wearing a different suit at every party and at any office social function, 'to show them that they could not force me into doing things I didn't agree with and didn't want to do'. She remained defiant. Times have changed so much since that she now wears suits all the time in the public spaces of the bank as do the cashiers at the public counters. She herself is in a senior position as the manager of a local bank branch and can take a lead sartorially and otherwise.

I relate this narrative of sartorial defiance to emphasize that the suit was so negatively coded that it was rejected by many younger Asian women who did not have the ethnic confidence to wear it. Although there were some who wore the suit stylishly and were role models to the younger women, they did not represent a 'young critical mass'. How precisely the suit became also a phenomenon of youth culture I shall relate in the section which follows.

Diasporic rhythms and the rhythms in the suits

In the mid- to late 1980s in Britain, something very exciting started happening – bhangra music started developing in Southall and in Birmingham which is in the Midlands. This was Punjabi music which was being mixed with Western instruments, with American Black music, with English pop music, with North African rhythms, with all kinds of different influences. This music was being created as something that was British and Asian. It was the coming together of all these forces that created something that I completely identified with ... I remember the first time walking through Leicester Square in London in the heart of the West End. There are very big discos there,

there is the Hippodrome and ... the Empire Ballroom. I remember walking through there and seeing lots of Indians hanging around. I made my way into the hall, I was absolutely amazed to see about 1,000 young Indians dancing madly to this band on the stage. This is something I had never seen ever in my life beyond, say, Indian weddings where there would be a handful of people and your parents would be forcing you to stand up there and dance. To see young people doing it themselves and enjoying it and smiling and laughing and at the same time taking a pleasure in creating new cultural forms. Around that time I got very much back into my own clothes. I used to mix them with leather jackets or denim, and young Sikh boys often used to go to the do's not cutting their hair but putting it back into pony tails or leaving them open and of course when they went back home, they would put their turbans back on. We all found that we were getting back into our language ... It was that getting back into Punjabi I think that opened the doorway in so many ways. It was at that moment for me that a British Asian identity was formed.

(Gurinder Chadha, Diasporic film director, in her Henry R. Luce lecture at Clark University, April 1995)

In the early 1980s, it was the emergence of bhangra music that brought young people together and was significant in bringing young women into suit wearing and so reconnecting them to their 'cultural roots'.

I want to emphasize in this section the interconnections between diasporic musics, the performative expressive forms; and the cultural and commercial dynamics of the suit economy. Both are highly politicized sites of cultural production. The music and clothes economies are parallel markets which draw on each other though, in this case, the music was definitely a precursor to the popularity of the suit amongst young people in their twenties and thirties.

Bhangra is a diasporic Punjabi fusion sound rearticulating Indian Punjabi harvest music. Its interpreters are local British Punjabis who have produced an internationally influential diaspora dance music which itself reflects the influences of other musical sources, in particular black dance music genres (Sharma et al. 1996). In turn bhangra has inspired further permutations, such as bhangramuffin and raggamuffin, a blended, fused dance music which has subsequently been rearticulated and reblended in multiple contexts both within and outside Britain. The development of these musical styles was a formative moment of the crystallization of young British Asian identities that was at the same time absolutely critical to their reconnection with the suit on their own terms in their own terrains in combinations that reflected their syncretic aesthetics.[4]

Crucially, the music created public sites for the expression of the overt symbols of young British Asians' ethnicities, especially clothes (including turbans and suits) and language, as highlighted by Gurinder Chadha at the start of this section. Sharma et al. further develop this point, arguing that the 'cultural spaces created by Bhangra [were] a means for Asian youth to assert their "Asianness" and locate themselves firmly in their contemporary urban surroundings' (1996:34). The politically charged terrains of club and concert venue were appropriated and translated into positive coding through the sheer numbers of young Asian people who participated. Thus they came to constitute a critical mass which in itself buttressed their confidence even further, not only giving them platforms for expression but also sites for networking and further cultural production.

This is not to say that all British Asian young people responded to bhangra in the same way. Not all of them had the same level of exposure to it. Some were and remain ambivalent about the music, perhaps not making the same cultural connections as those on whom its impact was transformative. Just as British Asians are located in many cultural and class contexts and all the subclasses and subcultures within these broad categories, so their consumption habits are equally varied. Raminder Kaur and Varinder Kalra, in describing the diversification in the bhangra sounds and the accompanying scenes, state that there were, '. . . complaints about Bhangra's untrendiness, linguistic barriers and lack of "socially meaningful" lyrics . . . In addition, there was ambivalence towards the distorted and essentialist view that Asian youth should have some kind of "natural" affiliation towards Bhangra' (1996:226).

At the same time there were also many other expressive forms derived from bhangra available to young people and which were recontextualized in the same landscapes that influenced bhangra music.

The point that I want to emphasize here, however, is that the music, the sounds and the dance, not just of bhangra but of its other, related forms, served to reconnect young Punjabi women to the suit. Together, these cultural forms – music, dance and clothes – gave expression to a developing British Asian identity:

> Bhangra . . . the music, the clothes and dances are the medium through which the otherness of British/South Asian experience is articulated . . . it is both a form of cultural resistance and an affirmation of the lives we lead . . . it is perceived as something distinct belonging to us . . . It is a definite break from tradition, but its reference points are rooted in tradition.
>
> (Music journalist Dil Neiyyar, quoted in Sharma *et al.* 1996:6)

The link between the music and the clothes is further emphasized by fashion retailers actually in the business of selling the suits (by this time we are into the ready-made economy with which I shall deal more fully in Chapters 7 and 8).[5] Harjit Samra says young women are continuously in his boutique, Sheba, on Southall Broadway, to buy an outfit for a bhangra function that they are attending over the weekend or during the week. He stresses the link between the wearing of the suit and a strengthening of cultural identity:

Suits have made the culture strong, designer outfits have brought the culture back. They have made a bigger contribution to making the culture stronger than religion, because in religion people are always fighting. There is always fighting at the gurdwara.

(Harjit Samra, interview with the author, 1996)

Komal Singh, of the wholesale retailers Bombay Connections, points out that the link is partly practical:

The bhangra thing and the salwaar-kameez are very connected, absolutely. What happened with bhangra was that people could dance to their own music. They could wear their own clothes because you can't actually wear a skirt and dance to bhangra in a skirt. You can but it does not work well. It's not that much fun. A lot of the leg movements require you to have a suit.

(Komal Singh, interview with the author, 1996)

Bhangra and dress are thus two intimately connected dialogical processes. To dance bhangra and giddha fluidly and fluently, a salwaar-kameez or a version of the suit is essential wear to facilitate the ankle-flicking movements and footwork and also the body movements. There is a fit between the rhythms in the clothes and the rhythms of the dance movements. Both music and dress are also governed by the same combinational aesthetics and sensibilities of the multiple migrant within the diaspora. So, the salwaar-kameez is itself transformed as a result of being worn in a new context, as Komal Singh again points out:

You see up to a thousand teenagers [at the Hammersmith Palais] and lots of them will be wearing Western clothes and a lot of them will be wearing salwaar-kameez. Now the salwaar-kameez is adapting itself and it's becoming more and more modern. If someone can wear a small halter top and a skirt underneath, they are now wearing a salwaar-kameez in a similar way, also ghagras and shararahs. Everything can be worn like that.

(Ibid.)

The processes are connected once more when Komal Singh attributes the increasing awareness and consumption of the suit beyond ethnic circuits to the musician Apache Indian who, in making it into the national charts, encouraged a bigger population of Asians and non-Asians than ever before to dance to bhangra and post-bhangra, bhangramuffin and ragga-bhangra musics (which combine bhangra with black musics). Apache's music was influential and affirming, having made it into the bigger mainstream arenas and thus reaching audiences far beyond the previous Asian-specific bhangra conduits. He illustrates supremely well my thesis that the general aesthetic of immigrants is that of negotiation and improvisation to formulate their cultural frames. His music in Britain has the specificity of a young Punjabi man raised in multi-ethnic working-class Birmingham in the British Midlands. His music combines reggae and Punjabi sounds with Jamaican and Punjabi patois. He has topped both the reggae and bhangra charts in the UK while also playing to packed stadia in India. He is famous and controversial in the international South Asian diasporas whilst at the same time being authenticated by African Caribbean diasporic communities.[6] His music is for me a reflection of the improvisational aesthetics of so much of diasporic cultural production demonstrated by second-generation British Asians. They have an edge in creating new forms by combining elements that are present in their contexts and which they negotiate anew. These combinational abilities give them their eloquence in cultural and commercial economies to capture new trends and create the emergent forms. This is reflected in the recent suit and music trends.

Clubwear meets the suit

Jasmeet, a Punjabi Londoner now in her early thirties, is subscriber to many forms of music, having come of age at a time when bhangra was already fully fledged, in fact was declining in its impact with the emergence of other influential diasporic Asian musics. She has worn the suit to bhangra functions, both at community social events like wedding receptions and family functions, as well as public events, primarily for young people, like those at the Hippodrome, the Hammersmith Palais and other major venues in Southall and Birmingham. She also goes to rave clubs where she wears a different interpretation of the suit. She wears much more leather for the rave events, she says, but always includes some Punjabi element like a shawl or a chuni, or she combines a leather jacket with a salwaar-kameez mostly in 'techno colours' – vibrant electric limes, deep pinks.

Another more recent music movement, post-post-bhangra, led by renowned music producer Talvin Singh's Soundz of the Asian underground, is initiating a new trend among suits that is connected with club culture: a novel music trend relating to a novel suit trend. Bashir Ahmed, a London-based British Asian designer trained at the prestigious Saint Martin's School of Art and Design, promotes his new collection of cyber suits using Talvin Singh's music and the club culture around the underground form. His suit collection is interpreted in vibrant electric colours – midnight blues, lime greens, silver, deep fucshia, wine and maroon – fabrics such as PVC, nets, stretch cottons and taffetas. In an article in *Eastern Eye*'s magazine section headlined 'It's about clubwear meeting the shalwaar kameez ...', he describes the location of his work and the sensibilities from which he produces it. He states:

> The real energies which trigger movement and change collect momentum on the street. This is where the Asian experience finds itself in London. This experience is just one arm of the larger network, that of

global consciousness ... The situation is unique, in that for the first time all the wheels are in motion at the same time with the force of three generations behind them. Look at the music scene ... The freshest, newest, most innovative music in clubland is the 'Soundz of the Asian underground'. This is where the artist Talvin Singh has the likes of Jarvis Cocker, David Bowie and Bjork hanging out at his club Anokha. The future is in an eclectic mix of cross-cultural dressing, derived from the real life, from the roles we play on a global adventure. The destination is somewhere in the future. It's about the clubwear meeting the shalwaar-kameez. It's about harmony and balance under contradictory influences and finding rhythm and rhyme amidst chaos. This is the aesthetics behind my work.

(*Eastern Eye* 17 July 1998)

The suit is taking another journey, 'a global adventure', to quote Bashir Ahmed. While in the case of bhangra, the music attracted young Asians to the clothes, in Bashir Ahmed's case he is using a British Asian music that is globally popular to encourage young people ito wear clothes that he has designed. The clothes are deliberately being connected with a music form as a marketing tool. Perhaps for the young, this connection will develop further and be linked in future with varieties of club cultures: for sure, the permutations will merge, submerge and diverge as Asians and non-Asians mix and combine forms to create new musical and sartorial aesthetics.

Conclusion

These dance and clothes products emerged from complex cultural dynamics, which were constantly negotiated expressions of identity. These combinational forms were intimately tied up with and produced through the multiplicity of influences on young people – some inherited, others they were exposed to in mixed peer groups of Asian, black and white British; and all the musical traditions that these peer groups were connected with and produced. These fusion forms are reflected in the commercial and cultural aesthetics that centrally determine the market. Thus, the market reflects the cultural politics and the cultural products that emerge from the expressive economies of migrants and their locally produced progeny.

It is the music, bhangra dance music in particular, that connected young Asians with their clothes and their language, in a heightening of cultural awareness on their terms. These dialogically produced aesthetics are the very stuff of diasporas. The continual negotiation of sensibilities and expressions affirm the identities of diasporic Asians. The market is thus as much a means of cultural – as of economic – exchange.

In the following chapter on ethnicized consumption, I describe the Asianization of British and some transnational consumer dynamics. I tell the story of the movement of the suit beyond ethnic circuits, its appropriation by and impact on mainstream design circuits, on leading fashion icons, on the haute couture agencies and street fashion companies. I discuss the hybridities, the interpretive modes of younger second generation women who have translated the suit through to their subcultural and street styles. These are the sartorial contexts, fashion trends and popular cultural mores that have produced second-generation fashion entrepreneurs who are the cultural and commodity brokers, the innovators of new markets.

2

ETHNICIZED CONSUMPTION

'It's hip to be Asian': Asianizing markets

'Ethnically driven' consumer expressions are to be found across the socio-economic range in Britain. This is obvious from the many Asian consumer goods and food products sold in mainstream British shops. Food is perhaps the most conspicuous example of the Asianization of British consumer landscapes. Curry has ousted roast beef as the British national dish, at least in terms of frequency of consumption. The 'average British person' is reported to eat curry once a week (Zee *Euro News* 26 June 1996).[1] The Queen is reported to order two 'tikkaways' a week (*Daily Star* 26 March 1996), while Prince Charles had Indian food served for his forty-eighth birthday party in November 1996, accompanied by the music of famous sitar maestro Ravi Shankar (Zee *Euro News* 15 November 1996). It is estimated that 70 per cent of British people visit an Indian restaurant at least once a month (BBC *Good Food Show* survey reported in *India Abroad* 28 August 1998:36). The Indian restaurant is a familiar feature of every high street, with numbers nationally totalling more than 15,000. Even McDonald's have had to adapt their menu to include 'curry and spice'. Twice as much Indian food is sold in Britain as fish and chips (*The Economist* 7 August 1999). Indian frozen and fresh food is ubiquitous in all the mainstream supermarkets all over Britain. The British Asian food industry's annual turnover of more than £1.5 billion contributes more to the English economy than the coal, steel and shipbuilding industries put together (*Observer Newspaper, The Week* 6 November 1999:17).

Indian food's penetration of British food markets has led to the establishment of an academic research centre for Indian food at Thames Valley University, close to Southall, west London. Funded by a £285,000 UK government grant, the centre is designed to train new recruits into this growth industry to:

> ... update and extend their skills, not only in food preparation and service but also in business and management techniques ... The Centre will work in association with the Southall Regeneration Partnership that aims to promote and develop the restaurant and cafe sector in Southall as a major attraction.
>
> (*India Abroad* 28 August 1998:36)[2]

Southall, the Punjabi capital and 'the India of Britain' is a major centre for Indian food consumption. People go there to spend the day, shop for many ethnic commodities and also to eat. It is common to see whole families eating in Indian restaurants there.

Generally, the Indian restaurant scene is diversifying: a new trend in up-market Indian restaurants is being led by British Asians who are professionalizing this economy with their own design inputs, both in their interpretations of the decor and also menus, some of which have a fusion ethos. The restaurants, more spacious, more expensive, are designed to capture the markets of 'yuppified' Asians and a 'classier' clientele overall. New-style restaurants include, in London, Chutneys in Chelsea with a fusion Anglo-Indian menu, Cafe Spice Namaste in the City and Le Porte des Indes in the West End; nationally, the Shimla Pink chain owned by Kal Dhaliwal[3] has branches in Birmingham, Oxford, Manchester, Nottingham and London.

Most people in Britain are eating mixed foods on a daily basis at home. Pasta is now eaten regularly in British Asian homes and is also served as part of temple langars (the community kitchens) in a spiced Indian style, just as chicken tikka sandwiches are widely available in sandwich bars and supermarkets. Three out of four Britons now cook Indian food (India Abroad 28 August 1998:36). There is also a rapidly expanding market for a whole variety of cook-in Indian sauces added to and cooked with meats and vegetables – convenience food to create 'curried casseroles', for example. Homepride, major manufacturers in this field, ran a series of TV adverts in 2000 using British Asian actors with regional working-class accents from Glasgow, Liverpool and London. Madhur Jaffrey, the famous TV cook, promotes a similar range for Tilda, the ubiquitous basmati rice company. This culinary hybridity of food consumption is very much in concert with the hybridizing commercial agendas of the market generally.

For this hybridity is not limited to food alone. There are, in addition, mutually influential musics, dance and language styles. Such trends are not new. The consumption of 'orientalist' material culture was an integral part of the British Empire. Fabrics like Kashmiri Paisley shawls, Indian cottons, indigo cloth and dyes, as well as Chinese silks and porcelains, etc., have all been in fashion at some time or other, though the intensity of their influence is new (see, in particular, Adburgham 1975, James 1997 and Keay 1993). This is a consequence both of the changing cultural textures and demographic profiles of Britain through migration (in particular, the commercial agency of settled British Asians) and the growth of global markets which have facilitated the flow of goods produced in the subcontinent into European economies as never before.

Women are central interpreters of these cultural and consumer styles. These styles have moved beyond 'ethnic' boundaries to become part of the 'British mainstream' – a facet of the 'Asianization' of the 'West' and of 'occidentalizing' forces impacting on British Asians. All this is happening at many levels of cultural production, thus transcending class and 'ethnic' boundaries. What exactly this means for the story of the suit, I will make clear in the next section.

'Brown is the new black': recoding the suit in the mainstream

'Mumbai Designers' Outfits Feature in New Bond Film' reads the headline to a report about the salwaar-kameez that the actor, Sophie Marceau, wore in the 2000 James Bond film, *The World Is Not Enough*. The suit was designed by Abu Jani and Sandeep Khosla and bought by the film's producer in their London Knightsbridge store called Also (*India Abroad* 18 February 2000).

Mainstreaming suit trends were just beginning at the time I did my detailed ethnographic fieldwork in 1996. Now, I regularly see internationally distributed magazines with women in either a salwaar-kameez itself or in a style based on it. These suits are bought both from mainstream designers and from Asian boutiques in major cities all over the globe.

The suit's mainstreaming journey started with its appearance in newspapers and popular magazines such as *Hello!*, worn by international fashion icons and British royals like Lady Helen Windsor (daughter of the Queen's cousins, the Duke and Duchess of Kent) and the late Princess Diana[4] (see Figure 2.1). Others who were photographed wearing it included media stars such as Academy Award-winning actress, Emma Thompson, photographer and former girlfriend of Prince Andrew, Koo Stark, and the supremely wealthy and fashionable Jemima Goldsmith-Khan, daughter of one of the wealthiest men in Britain and wife of the famous Pakistani cricketer, Imran Khan. These helped women recode the salwaar-kameez suit from its stereotype of a dress-form of 'low-status immigrant women' to that of a high-fashion couture garment. Fashion megastars Princess Diana and Jemima Goldsmith-Khan's donning of the suit repositioned the suit in the mainstream in a way different from the recoding done by local British Asian women. The suit is no longer an 'immigrant thing'.[5]

In 1996, haute couture designers like Betty Jackson and street designer companies like Red or Dead demonstrated this at the London Fashion Week in September: 'Fashion Week Hails Capital's Many Cultures' (*The Guardian* 27 September). Red or Dead is the established mainstream, award-winning street fashion company of Wayne Hemingway: it received enormous media coverage in most mainstream British newspapers, including the ethnic press, and television news programmes, for its very 'salwaar-kameezed' interpretation in its Spring 1997 collection. For its London Fashion Show catwalk, the company used male and female Asian models picked from the streets of Southall in west London, alongside black and white models, all with Asian headdresses, who catwalked to the 'East–West' music of Kula Shaker's album, which was then at the top of the pop charts.[6]

The following week in Paris, Parisian designer Yves Saint Laurent's collection had salwaar-kameez-style lines in his interpretation of his 1997

Figure 2.1 Princess Diana in Catherine Walker suit with Jemima Khan (behind) and Imran Khan (right) during private visit to Pakistan in February 1996.

Source: Tim Graham/Corbis.

Spring/Summer fashion collections ('YSL Zeroes in on the shalwaar-kameez' in *Libas* 9.4:18, and *Hello!* November 1996). 'British fashion', epitomizing London's multiracial society, was captured in the much-touted notion of 'Brit-fash' – the buzzword and definitive theme of what was heralded as one the most successful London Fashion Weeks ever. 'Britfash' was seen as catapulting London back onto the fashion map after decades of losing ground to Paris and Milan because 'London is where it's at'.

These street-style interpretations of the suit can also be discerned amongst second- and third-generation diaspora Asian women who are beginning to market their own clothes companies. A new street designer label called Global Repercussions was a project that was being hatched during my fieldwork in 1996

28

by a British Asian team, a partnership between Sarb Basran, a young, second-generation British-born Sikh woman promoter and marketing agent, and the fashion designer I have already mentioned in the context of clubwear, Bashir Ahmed (personal communication, 4 December 1996). This label, says Sarb Basran, is about a clothing style which emphasizes:

> *It's not where you are from but where you are at in a global world.* It's a clothes label that attempts to unify cultures, races, and ideologies and attempts to harmonize the conflicts posed by a multicultural world. It reflects the choices you make in such a complex diverse setting amidst global changes [author's emphasis].

Princess Diana and Jemima Goldsmith-Khan both wore the British designer suits designed by Catherine Walker in the early stages. Both later bought suits from Ritu, at her upmarket shop in Mayfair, the story of which I will return to in Chapter 5. In May 1998, Jemima herself started her own shop A La Mode in Knightsbridge. The *Asian Age* newspaper's headline read, 'Jemima to turn kameez couture into world label' (2 March 1998). It reported that the profits would go to the Shaukat Khan Memorial Hospital in Lahore, started by her husband in memory of his mother. 'The designer line will take its inspiration from Eastern salwaar-kameez but will have modern influence, especially in the use of traditional embroidery' (ibid.). Jemima was working in consultation with UK-based Sheikh-Amer Hassan who suggested they should work together when they met after her marriage. Although made in the UK, each gown is hand-embroidered in Pakistan and costs £550–700.

Although Jemima Goldsmith-Khan was heralded by *Hello!* magazine as 'single-handedly [making] the shalwaar khameez fashionable in the West' (*Hello!* 23 May 1998:42), the dynamics of the popularity of the suit were, of course, much more complex. The actual groundwork of keeping salwaar-kameezes vibrant in Britain had been done by migrant women and their daughters. Jemima Goldsmith-Khan and Princess Diana were important fashion icons who catalyzed the mainstreaming functions, albeit in a secondary phase. (Lady Helen Windsor in fact wore the suit a couple of years before either of them.) Regardless of this, all these high profile women in fact represent a tiny moment in the ongoing suit story.

However, from a young British Asian point of view, the kinds of suit worn by Jemima are seen as passé 'old women's' clothes, as unfashionable salwaar-kameez suits which 'our mummies wear to kitty parties', as it was put by one of the short-skirted, leather-jacketed Asian babes in the hugely popular comedy BBC2 series, *Goodness Gracious Me*.[7] Jemima is not seen as 'with it' or in touch with the mores of young Asian women, many of whom are generating cutting-edge styles of their own. Jemima has been wearing clothes by Indian designers like Tarun Tahiliani and Ritu who are top-ranking in their own countries but do not capture the British trends.

British political women don the suit

Instead, these trends have been captured much more sharply by the suits worn by the British Prime Minister's wife Cherie Booth. Her suits are designed by the street-smart, locally raised British East African Asian woman, fashion entrepreneur Bubby Mahil, whom I shall write about in detail in Chapter 4. Cherie Booth wore a sari-suit first when she attended an evening reception of wealthy Indian businessmen and women in London in March 1998, an event captured by every major British newspaper alongside articles in leading fashion magazines. She subsequently wore a glamorous tunic of embroidered oyster silk, again designed by Bubby Mahil, to attend the Hindu Festival of Lights, Diwali, with her husband at London's Alexandra Palace in November 1999 (see Figure 2.2);

Figure 2.2 Cherie Booth wearing Bubby Mahil suit, together with her husband, Prime Minister Tony Blair, at Diwali Celebrations at Alexandra Palace, London, 3 November 1999.

Source: Graham Jepson. Distributed by Nunn Syndication.

and Bubby has gone on to design other clothes for her in the 'British Asian Bubby' style.

Other women in British political life have also adopted the style. Gaynor Regan, wife of Robin Cook (Foreign Secretary and then Leader of the House of Commons) stylishly wore a watered-down version a few weeks after Cherie Booth. Lady Judith Steel, wife of David Steel, Presiding Officer of the Scottish Parliament, wore the salwaar-kameez in August 1999. Patricia Hewitt, MP for Leicester West and now Secretary of State for Trade and Industry, arrived at the inauguration of the Sixth World Hindi Conference on 14 September 1999 'attired in the traditional Indian salwaar-kameez and made her opening remarks to the audience in Hindi' (India Abroad 24 September 1999). These political women are not aristocrats or daughters of wealthy men but professional women with their own flourishing careers. As J. Craik comments:

> The suit has been glamorized. It acts as a transitional item of clothing, spanning non-western and western fashion systems ... Both the sari and the kurta have been adapted for new conditions and endowed with new meanings.
>
> (Craik 1994:35)

Salwaar-kameezes are now worn by all kinds of women beyond those whose clothes are 'news'. Many white and black women on London streets have donned the salwaar-kameez, which is available in central London shops as well as in the Asian shops in Asian areas where they have been sold for more than a decade now. The same has been done by black and white women in Birmingham, UK, and San Francisco and New York in the US: in New York black Muslim women are wearing the suit regularly. Black women have tended to adopt the suit before white British women, especially in areas where they live amongst Asians, for example, in areas like Thornton Heath and Tooting in south London. Suit entrepreneurs and seamstresses in these areas sell and sew suits for them regularly. A suit-clad, London-based former beauty queen from Ghana in her mid-twenties told me she owned twenty of these outfits and loved wearing them. When I interviewed her in September 1996 at the Threads of Fantasy fashion show at Grosvenor House, she was wearing a pink net filigree-lined suit. She looked great, as did her peer group of Punjabi-suited Asian friends who were all from north London.

These trends were captured in the ethnic press through slogans like 'Brown the new black' (East newspaper 1 May 1998). Similarly, Glad Rags, an Indian lifestyle and fashion magazine, presented 'A report that proves brown is the new black' (September–October 1999:125) to describe the music created by second-generation British Asians. In another issue of East, the British Asian newspaper (13 June 1998), there was another headline, 'Asian Style of Ascot Season', with pictures of models in salwaar-kameezes with big elaborate hats. And so the suit stories continue.

In the following section, I move across the Atlantic to North America to describe these mushrooming consumer dynamics in American global domains. The national consumer processes that have been prominent in Britain, led by local settled Asian migrants, have in the late 1990s spread far beyond British borders. Many of these internationalizing consumer trends share British main-streaming features, whilst others have a new set of women entrepreneurs, the new cultural and commercial agents. 'Global stitching through local connections' is how I refer to the transnational commerce that goes on through tempo-rary sites, micro-markets of commerce with no physical bases, as well as through the conventional retail sites in major cities.

Crossing borders with suits: some American sites

Suits can be bought through many different channels and these have become much more extensive in the late 1990s. The 'designer' boutiques and more general suit shops that sell suits from £25–300 are just one market source, a con-ventional form of retailing. These retail outlets are now to be found in most major cities in Britain and North America where there are Asian women. They are a dominant feature in every ethnic shopping zone and also in a few spots in the high-prestige mainstream shopping areas. Los Angeles has 'a little India' in Artesia, an area that has developed fast since I first started visiting there in 1990. Then there were only a few sari shops with a tiny scattering of ready-made suits. By 1999, this whole area had developed, with big 22-carat-gold jewellery shops like Bindi Jewellers, household and electrical goods shops, restaurants, beauty parlours, bookshops selling Asian music and books, specialist suit boutiques like Chandni Collection, Meerasons, Yasmin Boutique, Sona-Chaandhi, and sari shops like Sari Palace that also stock a large number of suits. These boutiques have grown dramatically in the past five years, selling roughly the same kind of suits as those found in most of the major cities of the world. There is a great deal of standardization, with the same gradations of quality and price from $20–1,000. The Los Angeles suit shops do not negotiate sketches to produce a dialogically designed suit like the London diasporic fashion entre-preneurs I write about in Chapters 3 and 4. Some of the suit retailers say that they have their own factories that supply them directly. When I have been to Artesia in Los Angeles and in Gerrard Street, the Asian shopping strip in Toronto, and its equivalent in Vancouver, British Columbia, and to the Jackson Heights Indian shopping area in New York, I feel I am in a time warp. These shopping areas are like the London shopping areas of a decade ago. The London suit markets are, on the whole, much more cutting-edge and represent an older suit market. Generally, Britain has older Asian communities with developed second and third generations. The suit trend there has an older commercial and cultural history with earlier mainstreaming processes.

My local Massachusetts micro-markets for suits

Another aspect of the suit trade is the availability of suits in towns where there are no shops and no Asian shopping zones. Even though there are only a few stores in Boston that stock suits amongst the other items, suits are easily available through what I call portable travelling commerce, the 'table boutiques' which are micro-markets, temporary sites of commerce that are set up in motels; or in the leisure areas of big apartment residential complexes; or as part of festival celebrations like Diwali which are held in college halls; or at community-organized fashion shows which have side bazaars with products displayed on tables.

These little bazaar-cum-exhibitions take place all year around, at least six to eight times a year, for example, in a medium-sized city like Worcester, Massachusetts, where I live. These temporary commercial spaces are to be found in most cities where the Indian population is too small to support traditional Asian clothes retailers. People can also buy 22-carat-gold jewellery through these channels. For the past few years goldsmiths like Bindi, for example, the big Indian Los Angeles jewellers, sell in the Massachusetts area in grocery shops on pre-announced dates. Of the two local Indian grocery stores in Worcester, one has a clothes rack of suits amidst the lentils, rice and masalas, and the other has a regular gold jewellery day when the major jewellers display their wares for an afternoon or a whole day. Announcements for these sales are made through leaflets and small catalogues which are mailed to Asian residents in advance. This is also done by a woman goldsmith who sells gold jewellery in the same venues as the suits.

I have been to a number of these temporary mini-bazaars in the Worcester area. One took place in a large room in a big apartment complex. Some suits were hung on clothes rails while others were folded up and put on tables, with yet others displayed at full length, draped across chairs and tables. This is a common arrangement. There were two companies, a gold jewellery entrepreneur and a suit seller, who regularly organize bazaars in this venue and always together.

Another sale in the same venue by a different company, Choonri, had the same format, except the entrepreneur had everything packed into one room rather than the larger rooms booked by the gold and clothes entrepreneurial partnership. She also had Kashmiri chain-stitch cushions, shawls, scarves with the suits, and other Indian artefacts. Both these suit enterprises are led by women who have family connections with their suppliers. One has a sister in Calcutta who had travelled from India with her stock of suits, which she was selling in this venue with her locally based sister's help. The second suit entrepreneur has relatives in old Delhi who are in the suit business as wholesalers and retailers. The jeweller comes from a family business built up over generations, with uncles in both New York and India who are gold merchants with established enterprises. Both the Massachusetts-based entrepreneurs had established family enterprises which they benefited from. However, there are other women who do not have such commercial connections within their kinship networks to facilitate their commerce. Some have contacts with suppliers in India because they were raised in the subcontinent. Others have had to develop these connections as the ready-made and designer suit economy has taken off globally and they have wanted to participate in its commerce.

Most of these women who hold these one-day bazaars also sell from home. Suit customers ring them up and view the suit collection in the seller's home. This is much the same as the suit enterprises started in London by women who could not persuade the regular shops to accept their products. These male-owned stores were not interested in the women's wares, so the women had to start their own shops. Some started selling from home for a few years before they opened up their shops, having first developed a client base. I describe in Chapter 8 this home-to-shop commercial transition for Mala Rastogi who owns Creations boutique in Southall, west London. There are many women who still run their businesses from home and have no desire to open up shops in the established commercial zones in London. The Massachusetts suit-selling women do not have this choice of home versus shop because the Indian population is small and so there is no critical mass of suit-wearing consumers that they can service. Therefore, their temporary bazaars make eminent commercial sense. They can take their portable commodities and sell them, using equally portable equipment set up in temporary commercial spaces, thus generating marginal micro-markets.

Another example of these temporary micro-markets is one I saw in Los Angeles in April 1999. I was at the LA Conference Center for the 300 Khalsa celebration of the Sikhs. These tercentenary celebrations took place all over the world wherever Sikhs live. This was a major event organized by the Sikh Dharma group, the white 3HO (healthy, happy, holy) Sikhs led by Yogi Bhajan. Alongside the religious celebrations in the sacred temple space (created for the day), there was a bazaar outside selling all kind of religious paraphernalia from religious books, kirtan tapes and CDs, the steel symbols of the Sikhs, the gutkas (prayer books), pictures of the gurus and much more beside. Amidst this commerce of religious commodities were several table boutiques displaying suits on racks. One of them was Kaanchi whose publicity read as follows: 'Kaanchi, where image is everything. Visit us for our New Arrivals of stunning salwaar-kameezes, lenghas, lachaas and odhini suits'. The woman who owns this enterprise was herself selling the clothes, which she also sells through her shop in Northridge, outside Los Angeles. It was interesting to see this clothing commerce erupting in a religious commodities bazaar. The owner of Kaanchi had opened a portable boutique, a micro-market in an essentially religious space, although she had also recently opened a conventional 'fixed' shop: it was a reflection of the ubiquitous nature of the suit commerce which has spread across the globe in the most unusual spaces.

Pashmina shawls across the world

I now come to a new facet of the Asianized consumption which has emerged in the late 1990s but continues on from the early 1990s mainstreaming consumer dynamics whose agents are both white and Asian, both from elite locations. This is the rapidly mushrooming commerce in pashmina shawls which started in London but which had, by the middle of 1999, spread to the USA.

Pashmina shawls were and are the prized possessions of wealthy Indian women, who have passed them on to their daughters as heirlooms for genera-tions. These shawls, made out of the fine cashmere wool of Himalayan capra hircus goats, are soft and light yet supremely warm. Such shawls were commonly used as currency and given as rewards by the Mughal kings from the sixteenth to the eighteenth centuries and also by the Sikhs in the Sikh Kingdom in north India in the nineteenth century. They were used by all the wealthy north Indian groups as a means of exchange. Pashmina shawls have been part of Indian economies of fashion and design for centuries.

In the past couple of years pashminas have entered the global fashion realm. Even my American Lands End catalogue sells them, at around $250, the most reasonably priced ones I have seen. The shawls now have much more design input. Whereas in the past they were most often woven in the natural wool colours of light browns, beiges, and sometimes in black, they are now available in many more colours. In London and the USA, they come beaded, tasselled, blended with silks, and sell for £200–800. Others are finely embroidered, ver-sions that are also popular with Indian women. I have seen few Indian women in the full range of colours now available, as most more commonly wear the natural shades. *This Week* magazine (5 June 1999:31) reports that:

> Pashmina shawls are fast superseding the Prada handbag and the Gucci stiletto as the most wanted luxury fashion accessory … One of the main reasons for their popularity is that they complement any outfit, and indeed any age group. Draped across the shoulders they can be worn as a summer shawl, or alternatively knotted at the neck as a smart winter scarf.

The retailers are women like Bajra Camilla Ridley, Camilla Paul (reported in *This Week,* ibid.), Madeleine Trehearne and Harpal Brar (*Vogue* January 1998) and many others who are not well-known names but who retail through shops like Fenwicks, The Cross, The Cashmere Company (all London-based shops), and also through exhibitions held in private and public sites. The pashmina shawl entrepreneurs I know of are upper-class women, as is obvious from the revealingly upper-class coded names such as 'Camilla'.

A considerable amount of the pashmina shawl business is not conducted through established shops but through private, highly niched markets. This is a similar style of commerce to that used by home-based diasporic entrepreneurs, as I shall describe in Chapter 8. The shawl commerce has a parallel in the past in the demand for Paisley and Norwich shawls in the nineteenth century, largely based on local production in Scotland and Norwich and copying original Kashmir shawl designs. These shawls were imported from Kashmir by imperial British trading agents. Sky-blue bordered Paisley shawls feature in several portraits by John Singer Sargent, the Europe-based nineteenth-century American painter. There are also shawl-demanding women in Thackeray's *Vanity Fair* and Elizabeth Gaskell's *North and South*: either the characters have connections with travellers who bring the shawls from India or they purchase them in England from stock imported by the East India Company.

In the past, such commercial connections were created by male commercial agents. The big difference now is that the contemporary commercial agents are women who are themselves both plying and consuming the products in a trade that they have initiated. This commerce is almost entirely women-led and women-consumed (while the weavers and the embroiderers remain men). These are truly 'female aesthetic communities' to use Judith Goldstein's term (Goldstein 1995:310–29). In this respect they are similar to the design entrepreneurs who form the subject of the next section of this book, both the multiply-migrant London-based designers and the elite subcontinentals, even though there are fundamental class and race differences that govern their commerce.

Part II

DESIGN NARRATIVES

INTRODUCTION

In this section on design narratives, I describe the agendas of the design entrepreneurs who run the exclusive boutiques in the graded markets of the suits.
The emergence of the ready-made and designer retail economies represent
global commodity circuits that are dominated by women, who are using the
markets in different sites to create female aesthetic communities. Amongst
them are the professionalizing agents, whose design narratives I present and
who are design interventionists with clear agendas. There are elite subcontinental nationals who sell exclusive art and crafts clothes from their national sites
that encode their national heritage; but there are also locally raised British
Asian women, politicized and racialized people, who use a diasporic aesthetic of
improvisation to produce designs with the inputs of their local customers. My
descriptions of these women, their cases 'bring into life' these micro-interactions of globalized localized landscapes. I present this thick description to give
readers glimpses of the politics of identity, of being, the narratives of becoming
in an everyday way, and of developing a diaspora subjectivity.

From the mid-1980s, but especially in the early 1990s, the retailing economy
of boutiques mushroomed in all the major centres of British Asian settlement,
from Southall in west London, to Green Street in east London, Wembley in
north-west London and in all the major cities outside London – Birmingham,
Glasgow, Leicester, Manchester, etc. These retailing outlets of redistribution are
also to be found in many other major world cities, for example, Los Angeles and
New York in the USA, Sydney in Australia, Durban in South Africa, Nairobi
in Kenya, and Amman, Kuwait and Riyadh, among others, in the Middle East.
In terms of the graded markets, suits can be bought from market stalls for £20 or
less and for £300–8,000 in prestigious boutiques in central shopping areas.

The link between art clothes as crafted objects is the salient theme of three
of the shops, Ritu (Chapter 5), Libas and Yazz (Chapter 6), all of which were
run by members of the subcontinental elites. All three engaged in a discourse of
art and clothes. In the case of Libas, clothes are made under the design signature of artist Sehyr Saigol. Yazz was a boutique where, amid an artistically
inflected commercial space, the owner, Yasmin Hydari, recontextualized the
highly crafted clothes of various subcontinental designers. Ritu, the most

famous and successful of the subcontinental designers, the queen of revivalism, is an innovative contemporizing agent of the arts and crafts industries, as reflected in the 'classic chic' clothes that are sold in her shops in India and were sold in London. All these enterprises engaged in a form of cultural pedagogy through the market by performing the explicitly stated ambassadorial function of making a European public more aware of the ancient heritages and high-chic aesthetics of arts and crafts India and Pakistan.

First, however, I describe the stories of two British Asian entrepreneurs who are hybrid designers. Both locally raised, Geeta Sarin and Bubby Mahil's defiant diaspora styles and politicized voices are reflected in the hybrid clothes they design and sell. Their design discourses are not nationalistic ones of representing the heritages and ancient craft skills of the subcontinent but one of the diaspora context, as characterized by the fractures and ruptures caused by migration. In Bubby's case, her design strategy was reactive, responding to racist taunts which led her to a politics of identity and culture that blossomed into a hybrid style. This style created a new commercial space for her that has become influential and commercially successful. Neither of these British Asian women engage in nationalistic discourses nor do they represent themselves as ambassadors of their nations or their heritages. Both use the market not only as a mechanism of economic exchange but as a site for cultural battles that create new cultural and consumer spaces. These British Asian diasporics operate, like all the entrepreneurs described here, in marginal micro-markets. However, their niche markets are sited within their own local scene, which they know well, being local people. Their design process is characterized by co-construction and customization, the defining element of their diasporic aesthetics that are a product of multiple migrations and settlement in Britain. This way of working is also in synch with the current market moment, as characterized by the new capitalist processes that constitute the economic terrains of our time.

3

PIONEERING FASHION ENTREPRENEUR

Geeta Sarin

Geeta Sarin was amongst the first to open a boutique in London for British Asians. As a professionalizing agent, she has spearheaded the designer suit movement whilst also making ready-made Asian clothes more easily available in Britain. As well as her shop in Wembley in north-west London, she developed an alternative market – the first Asian mail-order catalogues of ready-made Indian clothes. She is a pioneer and a groundbreaker in this economy.

Rivaaz: Geeta's shops

Geeta Sarin, née Jasbir Kaur Gandhi, came to Britain as a teenager in 1961. She was born in Nairobi, Kenya. In her twenties she studied for a three-year fashion diploma, which included textile design, at the London School of Fashion. Geeta had always been interested in fashion and read fashion pages of magazines with great interest as a young girl. She was 'into clothes' because of her sewing background. Her mother:

> ... was an excellent seamstress and in Kenya, all the girls were supposed to know something about stitching or tailoring. My mother and other women in the joint household constantly emphasized that all the girls should know sewing, stitching and cooking, apart from anything else. That is how I learnt. Also, I had a little bit of talent and I always loved good clothes.
>
> (Geeta Sarin, interview with author, 1996)

Geeta represents the professional end of the sina-prona diasporic sewing cultures which I have outlined in Chapter 1. Later on, when she worked as a fashion journalist for *Image* magazine, she interviewed leading mainstream fashion designers such as Zandra Rhodes. At this stage, she also designed suits using her fashion school expertise to produce really cutting-edge designs. As a fashion-conscious woman from a sewing background, she noticed a deficiency in the market, as ready-made suits were just becoming available in Britain but were neither stylish nor of good quality. Shops selling fabrics and other general household goods like linens, haberdashery items, suitcases, etc., would have a few ready-made clothes hung up on racks. They were shoddily made, badly cut and made with no understanding of the British clothes codes of British Asian women in their different subcultural locations. Someone had simply gone to India and bought some suits and put them in the shop.

She identified a market niche from what she saw at the Indian social functions she attended:

> There were beautiful young Asian women who were wearing the ready-made salwaar-kameez but they were not the right cuts or the right colours . . . I could see that there was a definite need for the younger generation. Obviously they had no choice but to tell mum, 'alright fine, you are making me a salwaar-kameez, I will wear it because this particular function requires me to wear a salwaar-kameez or a ready-made Indian garment'. So I went straight into it but my cuts are very western.
>
> (Ibid.)

Geeta offers fusion elements in her clothes – this is what is attractive to diaspora markets and to the transnationally based Indians and Pakistanis who are also her clients.

A fashionable woman gave me a testimonial of why she shopped at Geeta's Wembley shop in the 1980s:

> It was such a delight to go to Geeta's shop because you could find something you liked and that suited you, even though she was always expensive. There really was not much around at the time, hardly anything available. In the early eighties there was such a lot of junk in the shops that was ready-made; you could not find anything that was subtle and interesting. Geeta knew about clothes and understood what was interesting. She also gave really good advice. She would tell you if something did not suit you, she would say outright, 'This is not good for you, it's not for you.'

Geeta says people interrogate her all the time, especially Asians who ask, 'What's the latest?' She says, 'The latest is what suits you.' A stylish informant of mine who has worn Geeta's clothes for many years told me that Geeta Sarin did not sell you clothes that were not good for you like the other shops who 'stuff things down your throat. For many years I bought her clothes and wore them a lot. You could go to her shop and find something that was stylish though it was never cheap.'

Geeta Sarin started her business in 1981 as a design consultancy in the offices of her husband: he ran his magazine *Image* and she had her studio. She had previously worked with some professional, big-name European designers but had had no control over her designs or a signature of her own, even when she had done the major design work on the clothes. She had felt exploited and wanted to be her own agent with her own design identity.

Geeta's first two shops in Wembley – she moved from smaller premises to the current larger ones in 1984 – established her in the market. The catalogue (with which I shall deal in more detail in the next part of the chapter) gave her commercial exposure in both national and international markets and further underlined her credentials with her customer base. She says, 'Wembley has been what you call the gold dust for me, that shop.'

Having established a customer base (about 80 per cent Asians and 20 per cent Europeans), and having been in Wembley for over a decade, Geeta wanted to move into mainstream markets. Her goal is, she says, 'to sell Indian clothes to the Europeans, period'. Of course, she has many Asian clients but she also has a tranformative commercial and cultural agenda of selling her style of Asian clothes to Europeans.

For seven years (from 1993 to 2000, when pushed out by an exorbitant rent hike) she had a shop in Beauchamp Place in Knightsbridge, *the* designer street in London. The shop was an undoubted success and now she continues to supply various boutiques in Beauchamp Place as well as large department stores such as Selfridges and Harrods. Her markets there and in Wembley overlap but also have significant differences in terms of the customer base:

> In Wembley, I always had 10 to 20 per cent European clientele but in central London the roles have reversed. We have got 20 per cent Asians coming in who are living in the south-west [of London] rather than in the north-west, and you get a lot more English clientele. Knightsbridge is the fashion capital of London and you attract not locals but a lot of international clientele, too.
>
> (Ibid.)

Geeta's customer base has shifted just as customer profiles have shifted for many boutique suit retailers. There are now public registers for these garments as never before. As I have shown in the previous chapter, these suits have become high-fashion clothes, positively coded in the popular imagination. Although British Asian women still constitute the predominant wearers of the suit, it is no longer exclusively coded as an 'immigrant' dress form.

One-to-one design dialogues

Geeta started Rivaaz not as a shop at first but as a clothes and design consultancy. People would visit her and she would design an outfit together with a client, then she would get it made up in India. She built up these workroom connections on various trips to the subcontinent. Her initial design consultancy emerged out of her fashion training and fashion journalism. This design concept then became a retail outlet as a result of the demand and interest from her clients. Her initial enterprise helped her discover a market niche and the processes to service this market. She says she always negotiated designs with her clients:

> ... always, the whole concept started from designing and it then became a retailing outlet because my clothes were so popular. I got the contact through demand. People desperately wanted suits. It was a demand and supply kind of situation where the demand started picking up and Rivaaz was the very first to start with and people got to know me and hence my mail order. Then I thought of the idea which was another nightmare of my life because I had a publishing background in magazines, I knew how to put any catalogue and a magazine together.
>
> (Ibid.)

Since she started her Wembley shop, the age range of Geeta's clientele has sta-bilized somewhere between eighteen and fifty years old, with most between eighteen and thirty-five. Weddings constitute 70 per cent of her business. She estimates that she makes fifteen to twenty outfits for each family per wedding just for the immediate family. She also makes bridal clothes, which often involves making twenty to thirty outfits for each bride. A bride's family give her an approximate budget which she uses as a guide to make the trousseau:

> For example, people come and give me a budget of £15,000 and say fine, just do whatever you think. I sit with them for two to three hours, these are the colours they want. I sit with the bride for two to three hours. I design pieces which she can wear.
>
> (Ibid.)

This co-constructing of wedding clothes has been ongoing for more than a decade. She now has an established record and works almost exclusively on referrals. Also, it is more straightforward now to create these individually nego-tiated bridal clothes because of the more rapid communications to India, the manufacturing site: design instructions can simply be faxed. Geeta states that people have become more aware of the fact that these garments are easily avail-able in London and that she can supply them according to clients' taste, indi-vidually tailored. Her modus operandi, even now, remains 'a guided dialogue' between herself and her clients. She is frank about what she thinks suits people and tells them directly what is right for them and what is not. She is there herself in the shops to deal with customers directly and is absolutely hands-on in her design enterprise. She negotiates patterns with customers all the time. She describes this as 'the engineering of an outfit'. She charges for this process if she co-constructs a number of outfits. It is part of the price for a garment which is individually designed but not every time. Her charge for a consultation is £35–75.

Although there are stylishly displayed clothes in both of Geeta's boutiques, and many people do buy off-the-peg, the major sector of her business is that of individually cut and tailored suits for both men and women. She says 80 per cent of her business is made-to-measure, 20 per cent of it is contracted and made according to her cuts and designs. She says:

> You pick a Lucknow kurta, a Lucknow kurta is a Lucknow kurta. It's a kurta with no shape. The same thing, if I was to define it, which I have done, and given my own style and idea, which is here [she showed me a kurta], it's a little bit more tapered. It has more shape and it's better cut. These are my designs from my paper-cuttings and fabrics and I contract it out to young designers to do it. The cut makes a lot of difference.

This emphasis on the 'cut' is what gives Rivaaz clothes the diasporic edge. This encodes their 'Western-ness'. The shape and the silhouette indicate their British Asian registers and the differences from the other boutiques, even though the clothes may look initially similar to those available in other exclusive designer boutiques.

So how is the potency of cut arrived at? I asked her about the process of negotiating the sketch, the design template of lines on paper that constitute the drawing, which is later faxed to India for production. The ideas within this design format often come from many sources, her inputs and her client's suggestions and desires, including ideas from fashion magazines. She is a mediator, both a design consultant and a guide who moulds these ideas through drawing and sketching. The sketch is a mechanism of design and social expression that is locally negotiated and transnationally executed. It is a tool of cultural production. The sketch is a powerful instrument of negotiation that allows her to be more democratic in her designs. She says, 'Ritu, Rohit Bal and other Indian designers sell you what they have made and designed. They do not make individually tailored clothes. Mine is very one-to-one. It's very individually done right from the beginning.'

The reason it is possible to get the British-conceived, India-manufactured suit in London within as short a period as four days is that Geeta has a manufacturing unit in India that can churn out these clothes. She has had this production unit for over fifteen years. It is now well primed for her design processes and instructions. She can expedite the manufacturing process in India by doubling the money she pays to the tailors and workers, who work overtime to complete urgent orders:

> The Hindujas[1] phoned me from Brussels giving me three days' notice, telling me that 'I want an Indian Tux made.' I said, 'Impossible timing.'

He said, 'No, you can do it.' I had a suit made in two days – forty-eight hours – menswear. Womenswear, ladieswear, it depends on how intricate the work is. Plain suits with no embroidery, I can churn out twenty a day. Minimum lead-time is three to four weeks. In the peak season I take six to eight weeks because the work load is so much and the intensity of the heat in India is so much, you can imagine people don't have the facilities to work.

(Ibid.)

The peak period used to be June to October but it is longer now as people are also getting married from April onwards and at other times of the year.

Geeta guarantees delivery times. In fact she has outfits ready ahead of time. She says, 'You tell me you want it on the 10th; your outfit will be ready by the 5th, a leeway.' Meeting the deadline given to a customer is a salient point of her marketing strategy. The convenience of ringing someone up in London and having the garment delivered to the customer within four days is an attractive feature of her business for busy wealthy people who are time-conscious and want interesting clothes without the hassles of shopping around. Geeta has the sizes and measurements of many transnationally based clients whom she can clothe with great ease and speed. It is also the case that London is a fashion capital and to wear clothes from a London shop has its own kudos. As well as the subcontinental Asians, her transnational customer base also includes people from the USA, Canada, Trinidad and Hong Kong. She keeps their measurements on her books. They just have to call and ask for an outfit to be made for them without setting foot in her shops, having once visited her in London. She can make adjustments to them if the body size has changed. People call her from all over the world and she can get their outfits made and sent to them using fast communication technologies. The considerations of time and space and the speed with which these garments are available in London are all aspects of market compression. Clothes that are made-to-measure and made through negotiated design act as conduits of transnational cultural production.

We talked about how fast this new phenomenon was, of getting clothes in London made in India in a few days. We talked not only about how rapid design flows are both from India to London, and vice versa, but also how the Indian fashion media – Asian cable TV channels like Zee and AsiaNet, and print – act as catalysts. This was not the case in earlier phases of migration or even a few years ago. All these dynamics are the result of a clothes market reaching maturity in a globally connected age. In East Africa, women used to eagerly watch neckline designs and embroideries (the galmas, as they were called) and examine the styles of women recently returned from India with new clothes made according to the 'latest rivaaj', the latest style. The design inputs that they were exposed to were necessarily much more restricted to the local economy than now. Although women did glean design ideas from European and Indian film magazines and from the Indian and Hollywood films which were watched in many households, these exposures were at nowhere near the same level of intensity as now, when not only are Indian fashion magazines available in ethnic markets but so are frequent programmes produced by India's fashion media and broadcast on the Asian cable channels. In addition, there are British-produced regular Asian programmes which have large amounts of fashion coverage on a regular basis. So, the media channels feeding the British diaspora fashion and design economies have grown dramatically. On top of this, clothes that are design-mediated in Britain and those that are designed and produced in India are very easily available in the British markets and with great speed. All these fashion entrepreneurs make frequent and regular trips to India. So the movement of fashion entrepreneurs and retailing personnel and their commodities has increased rapidly in recent years.

The market is used not just as a straightforward mechanism of exchange but also as a means of negotiating a diasporic material form which expresses cultural pride. Geeta, as a fashion entrepreneur, is using the market to create a new commercial space in London. Indian design, tailoring, embroidery and craft expertise are an intrinsic part of the clothes economy Geeta has generated in a diaspora context, but through her own redesigning and marketing functions. She creates diasporically inspired, professionalized style manipulations into which she makes both minimal and also radical design interventions. It is this hybridized design that she sells in her shops. It is a new material form and cultural and commercial space that is created in London, which one might call an oppositional, subversive place. This consumer material culture is a product of many design journeys, movements, displacements and ruptures. These production and reproduction processes encode the expertise of both diasporic inputs and of local design markets of India, thus producing goods sold in London markets to another set of transnationalized and local populations.

Before moving on to the story of the Rivaaz catalogue, I want to emphasize here both the movements of commodities and design vocabularies to produce a new cultural and consumer syntax. The very potent sketches that Geeta and her clients negotiate are the product of a diasporic dialogue. She guides clients through the sketching, moulding the ideas they come with. Hence, the sketch, the conversation around the lines on the paper, and the talk around the design create a dialogic interaction. So emerges a new entity, mediated by an agent of the diasporic sina-prona culture background and the forces of local, national and transnational market dynamics. These dialogic design vocabularies are created by a multiple-migrant fashion entrepreneur who manipulates design markets to create new products for European markets. These commodities are then bought by local British whites and Asians and other clients from the USA, the Middle East, South East Asia, Canada, etc., who take them on further diasporic voyages.

Rivaaz catalogues: recontextualizing and classifying designs

As well as having a pioneering role as professionalizer of the suit economy through her design consultancy and her early shops, Geeta also developed a distinctive way of marketing her clothes through her influential Asian clothes catalogues. The catalogue established her as a professional retailer and acted as a design dictionary and template locally and globally.

The catalogue emerged at a time when the clothes market was being professionalized in India and ready-made clothes were becoming available there. What Geeta did was to make ready-made apparel available in the British market. It was a good piece of marketing that made an impact on many retail and domestic sewing domains beyond the immediate area of influence of her shop. The catalogue was sold by newsagents and other retailers all over Britain. Excerpts from the catalogue were also put into Indian home-view videos of Bollywood films which could be rented easily and cheaply from the same Indian shops. These catalogues sold Indian ready-made clothes selected by Geeta, many of which had her design input and also design signature.

The capital base to start the catalogue came from Geeta's savings and, she says,

> ... from borrowing money left right and centre. Whatever little saving I had from what I used to do, I ploughed it back into it. Like they say you have got to spend money to make money; if you do not spend money, you are not going to make money. And that is what I did.

For the initial picture shoot, she went to India, using Indian personnel and expertise, a local photographer and models; the editing, collating, and printing were all done in London. The clothes in the catalogue were produced by manufacturers she was already familiar with from running her Wembley shop. Thus the catalogue was a recontextualizing and classifying activity, where she was marketing and presenting Indian-made clothes with her design input in a new commercial domain.

Having printed 50,000 copies of the first catalogue she went through an anxious period when the newsagents and retailers who stocked the catalogues told her that they were too highly priced and that they would not be able to sell them, hence the decision to pay for putting excerpts of the catalogue into the Indian home-view videos which were very popular amongst British Asians. After that, the catalogue sold out rapidly. It was like:

> ... sliced bread for Asians living here away from the subcontinent. Everything else was accessible, looking at Littlewoods and all these other catalogues you have, Freemans, whatever. But Asians did not have any kind of clothing and garments they could identify with. I had

in my very first catalogue all categories of clothes including bridal gowns. I also had children's wear, shoes and bags and accessories. It was such a thrill. Every catalogue was sold.

(Ibid.)

The success of the catalogue opened many more avenues for her. In particular, the subcontinental commercial fashion producers, who had not taken her seriously before, now offered her their services and goods more readily. She was the first in the market and

... set the ground for everybody. Nobody knew about ready-mades. Nobody knew about catalogues. Look at Sheetal [a famous Bombay Department store], look at everybody else who followed the first Asian mail order. Burlingtons in Bombay started it after they saw Rivaaz.

There is no doubt that she was an innovator, creating a new entrepreneurial space through a commercial text. British Asian and Indian catalogues that have appeared subsequently include Bombay Connections, Sheba, Creations (all from London shops); and subcontinental Indian catalogues like Bandej, along with (much later) in-house publications produced by famous Indian department stores. Catalogue marketing was a new thing in India also at that time.

The catalogue had other consequences and impacts. It acted as a design template for both commercial manufacturers and retailers of fabrics and clothes in the subcontinent and among domestic seamstresses in Britain. They used it to replicate suits and also originate new designs for themselves and their customers. For the domestic seamstresses, in particular, the catalogue was a design tool to negotiate new patterns for customers and to combine styles and ideas. The commercial producers tended to do straightforward copying from the catalogue, to increase their own markets. These manufacturers' rationale, sometimes explicitly stated, was that they could produce similar clothes to the ones displayed in Rivaaz, a London-based catalogue, products of a high prestige fashion centre of the world.

Of course, it could be that there were manufacturers who already made and currently make the kind of clothes Rivaaz sells and that the catalogue gave their existing markets a boost. It could also be the case that the catalogue as a recontextualizing exercise was categorizing and marketing clothes and commodities already in the market to new commercial zones. The innovation here, then, lay not in the new designs but in their marketing and presentation.

Multiple design flows: local and international impacts of the catalogue

In the following, I describe three incidents that illustrate the multiple impacts of the catalogue. I describe how in London raw silks sold rapidly in a cloth shop in Southall called Sethis, as Asian women translated design ideas they borrowed from Geeta's catalogue to make their own clothes; I refer to my own use of it before I came to know of Geeta's shops and to meet her personally; and how a Pakistan-based clothes manufacturer appropriated her catalogue designs. These incidents are illustrative of the ways in which Geeta's catalogue and also the suit markets are simultaneously transnationalized and localized. They encompass complex flows of information across multiple sites through the copying and the transference of designs both within national markets and across the world. They also tell us about the impacts of the London suit market and legitimizing status of London on subcontinental clothes economies.

Geeta told me that:

> I did a lot of justice to a lot of retail outlets. Just to name one, in fact Sethi Silk House in Southall Broadway. He phoned me and said, 'Geetaji, you have done a wonderful thing. The reason for that is the raw silks that you have used here, people did not really know what to make of them, and today we have completely sold out.'
>
> (Ibid.)

Mr Sethi is someone Geeta's family had known in Nairobi, along with many other Kenyan families. I remember, as a child, visiting his shop often with my mother. Mr Sethi told her that many of his raw silks that had, until then, constituted dead or slow-moving stock, sold rapidly after the catalogue came out because of the innovative designs she had illustrated using these fabrics. The catalogue helped women devise new designs and novel ways of sewing existing fabrics that they could previously use only in restricted ways on fairly standardized styles. In the catalogue, raw silk is used for the tops with crêpe trousers, thus mixing both styles and fabrics. There are also many combinations of clothes and fabrics using this 'traditional' fabric in fusion-inspired clothes (see Figure 3.1).

A further interesting aspect of the Sethi Silk House story is that the owner has a well-established diaspora fabric shop which is itself a migrated and re-settled shop; many East African Asians who went to the Sethi Silk House, Nairobi, for many years, now continue to frequent it in London. Mr Sethi knows his old clients well, their progeny of different ages, their extended families and family histories over generations. He also remembers the different weddings and family life cycle ceremonies over the years in multiple locations, having serviced their fabric needs for years. He remembers the Nairobi families especially well, ones he knew before migration to the UK in the 1960s.

The impact of the catalogue on Mr Sethi's sales of raw silk is interesting in the sense that the catalogue extended women's design ideas. However, this design input was through a professionalizing agent who had access to sub-continental Indian and Pakistani markets where the clothes in the catalogue had been made and where local Indian manufacturers had also made their design

Figure 3.1 Fusion-inspired raw silk high-neck kameez worn with low square-neck beadwork jacket, typical of Geeta Sarin's hybridized cut and innovative mix of
fabrics.

Source: Geeta Sarin.

interventions in making these clothes. Geeta had recontextualized these clothes with her own marketing functions, facilitating diasporic dialogues through a print medium. She had increased British Asian women's access to suit designs as much as the suits themselves, thus extending the stitching vocabularies of British-based seamstresses. So in this case a diasporic British Asian commercial/retail and sewing economy is catalysed by India-produced, diasporically inspired clothes. A local British clothes economy is renegotiated and extended through the transferral agency of the catalogue, itself the product of a diaspora agent.

I, myself, used the catalogue for ideas for suits I have made and have had made. On a trip to India in 1988, I had an outfit made in Chandigarh similar to one in the second catalogue. A seamstress in London showed me the Rivaaz catalogue that she shows to her customers so they can look through for design ideas for the outfits she stitches for them. She often replicates suits shown in the catalogues. She said that her sewing enterprise benefits both from Geeta's catalogues and also the clothes in her shop. She says, 'my work moves along riding in [the wake of] the designs from the catalogue'. So the designs and information about combining fabrics in the catalogue are continuously circulated, both within local British sewing circuits (even now) and within transnational ones.

In subcontinental markets the catalogue allowed Geeta to be perceived as more established than she really was. Geeta told me that a Rivaaz catalogue was taken to Lahore by an American woman who had picked it up in London en route from the USA. This American woman gave it to a Lahore suit manufacturer for him to copy the designs presented in the catalogue for some suits she wanted stitched for herself. Sometime later, Geeta also happened to be in Lahore and went to see this same manufacturer because she liked his clothes and wanted to find out more about them. When she visited his showroom, he showed her her own catalogue and told her, 'You have a person in London who has made a really good catalogue, look at the designs, they are first class.' He had assumed that Rivaaz was a big London-based company. It soon dawned on him, much to his embarrassment, that he was talking to Geeta Sarin, the owner of Rivaaz. But later he was happy to show her the clothes he copied, which were well made. A local clothes merchant boasted to her, also not realizing who she was, that he had excellent connections with 'a big company, Rivaaz, in London' and that he exported his clothes to them. The catalogue alone had projected the image of Rivaaz as a substantial, London-based clothes company. The London-based catalogue had made design interventions on subcontinental clothes, a reversal of the usual flow of influence.

The merchant was using the catalogue not only to copy the outfits presented in the catalogue, but also to legitimize the sales of his commodities to locally based retailers and to develop his connections with transnational vendors. He was using the kudos that goes with copying a London-based fashion enterprise. The outfits that he copied were those originated by a London-based fashion entrepreneur even though they were manufactured using India-based design and embroidery expertise. Geeta's designs encoded the aesthetics acquired from her multiple movements from Africa and Britain. These clothes sold through her catalogue and her shop in British ethnic markets; the ideas were then transported back to Pakistan by an American woman who took the catalogue to Lahore. In Pakistan, the British Asian designs are absorbed by the Pakistani clothes manufacturing sectors, which further re-export them to Britain and America. In turn, suit designs are brought over from the subcontinent, stitched according to British Asian design sensibilities, and are then copied by Indian and Pakistani clothes manufacturers. These are cross-cutting local and transnational flows, suit designs brought over from the subcontinent which are stitched according to British Asian design sensibilities, are then copied by Indian and Pakistani clothes manufacturers. These conduits that reproduce clothes designs from multiple sites in multifarious ways represent the nitty gritty of global and local markets. These continuously mingling and flowing textures, the deeply multiperspectival planes that Arjun Appadurai refers to in describing transnational landscapes, constitute these design economies (Appadurai 1996).

A point which emerges from the story of Komal Ravel and the Bombay Connections catalogue (which I tell in Chapter 8) is also relevant here to the experience of Geeta Sarin. The text created a distance between her, not just as a designer but also as a woman, and the men she had to do business with. The catalogue was a source of power, a prop that she and other dynamic women entrepreneurs could use to blur their gender. The polished, depersonalized print form of the catalogue (depersonalized of the personality of a female designer, at least) enabled a new gender dynamic to be established. The distancing effect of the catalogue either neutralized its creator's gender or perhaps even re-gendered the designer as an active agent no longer defined by the passivity traditionally ascribed to womankind by male suppliers and buyers.

Although the catalogue was very successful in establishing Geeta and her enterprise, extending her markets and legitimizing her credentials, there were problems. These were partly to do with the unlicensed copying of designs but also with the sales and the customer base that used the catalogues. (Some people returned the clothes, having worn them, and their money had to be refunded if it was within the time legally allowed for returns.) However, the mail-order aspect of her business persists for clients she already knows but not via the catalogue.

Cultural pride design sensibilities

Geeta emphasizes the importance of her cultural background to her design aesthetics. She makes the point that when the British ruled India, they took away with them the finest Indian crafts and attacked the finest craftsmen and their skills:

> We still let them keep doing it to us here and in India. Why are we ashamed of our culture? My inspiration is cultural. Absolutely. Most Indians from India living abroad were ashamed of their background.

I have seen that wealthy Indian elites would wear only [European] designer clothes and shoes like Louis Vuitton, Versace, Cardin, a whole bunch of other designer names. Now there are people who can afford to buy designer clothes but also wear the salwaar-kameez and with confidence and pride. They can afford both European designer clothes and also wear our own clothes.

(Geeta Sarin, interview with the author, 1996)

Geeta is emphatic in her assertion that she has:

... stuck to my roots. I stuck to my cultural heritage, I have never been ashamed of it. I have not moved away from my cultural background. People like us are making their mark now. People don't bother with all these others who were ashamed of their cultures. These are the people who are behind. Nobody is interested in them, they have just been left behind. They were culturally ashamed and never spoke their language to their children, who were so confused, they didn't know where they were coming from and where they were going.

(Ibid.)

She also says that she never imagined when she started that suits would be worn by leading fashion icons. She had wanted to provide well-designed clothes for Asians like herself, who were into clothes and wanted to dress well:

It was never the aim that somebody as famous as Diana would be seen wearing this. It was such a futuristic idea as such. What it actually was, on a lot of catwalks and ramps around Milan and Paris, you could see a lot of inspiration from India. I saw Benarasi saris converted into ball-gowns, I could see those. I said, 'Look when these people can do it, what is wrong with us?' We Indians let them steal all the ideas from our countries, in fact, forgive me for saying this, it's like raping. You let them rape your country once, why do you want to let them do it again? What is wrong with us Indians? We are always so cynical about our own culture and things like that, why not be proud of it and bring it forward? Today, I am wearing this [she was wearing a black skirt and a striped sweater-like top], I am always in a salwaar-kameez or in a sari. The thing is to bring in the culture which is yours, you are Indian and this is your Indian collection. That is what I want to do, *I want Indian fashion to be global.*

(Ibid.)

Geeta talked about the derogatory ways the salwaar-kameez suit was viewed in England as a 'Paki' dress. However, her strategy in developing her style was to negate this racism and to emphasize cultural pride in the face of the destructive effects of British imperialism:

The salwaar-kameez used to be a Paki dress. We were told that all the time. Today, every high street store has outfits that are and look like a long kameez with kaajs on the side and trousers, sometimes straight-cut ones. The salwaar-kameez has come a long way. There was a lot of racism. Gone are the days when people used to say 'you smell of curry'. They are eating curry all the time. Every time I go to the supermarket, I see chicken tikka masala, or some onion bhaji or some curry something or the other in their trolleys.

(Ibid.)[2]

Geeta Sarin's articulation of how and why she has defined her own style comes from her ability to sustain herself on the strengths of her diaspora roots and cultural heritage, all the more powerfully ingrained through the East African experience in Kenya. She has developed an anti-imperialist and anti-racist discourse around clothes. It is her cultural background that she emphasizes, her roots and cultural heritage which, she says, a lot of people – especially upper-class Indians from India – often denigrated. Her interpretation of her clothes and her enterprise is explicitly couched in terms of cultural pride and its maintenance despite negative comments from both local whites and upper-class Indians who often express disdain for Asian immigrants and second-generation British Asians' taste in clothes. Geeta's commercial projects and cultural statements are political acts of projecting her own hybrid style. Her recoded designs of Indian clothes are inserted into the European and international markets to create new commercially and culturally subversive spaces.

4

SECOND-GENERATION DESIGN GLOBALIZER

Bubby Mahil

Like Geeta Sarin, Bubby epitomizes what I want to say in this book particularly well because she is a fashion entrepreneur from the diaspora, who has developed the diaspora sewing culture to literally stitch and tailor an identity for herself that is absolutely reflective of her context and biography.

Younger than Geeta Sarin, Bubby reworks traditional designs more radically, involving a greater fusion of different elements. The salwaar-kameez features, but is not central. Like Geeta, Bubby is also a pioneer in the fashion field.

Bubby's story

Bubby came to Britain when she was three years old. Her parents both come from Kenya and were born and raised there. Her father was a teacher in Kenya and is a deputy head in a primary school in east London. Her mother is a full-time homemaker. Bubby's sister, Nina, who runs her shops with her, was born in Britain.

Bubby went to school in east London and went on to do A levels in accounts, economics and English. She started a B.Tech. Diploma in Fashion but left after a year and half because she was already knowledgeable about fashion and good at sewing, having learnt to sew at home from a young age.

She was already making clothes for her own friends so she decided to leave college and set up her own business. For the first three years, she did all the stitching herself. She would buy the fabrics, make the outfits and sell them at suits parties she organized in people's houses. She used to make between fifteen and twenty suits for these parties, all products of her own sewing labour. She got a really good response. People used to see her clothes and like them and then place orders. She was supremely successful and got busy so fast that she decided to open up a shop. She was helped in this by her Punjabi Sikh husband, Michael Singh Mahil, whose family has local businesses in east London. She had gone to school with him and married him in 1990 despite some opposition from his family because Bubby was from a different caste.

Chiffons: Bubby's shops

Bubby's commercial success continued. Her first boutique opened in 1989 on East Ham High Street in east London, close to her current shop in Green Street. She opened her second one in Birmingham in July 1996 and a childrenswear section in the basement of her London shop in 1997. She has further plans to open a shop in Toronto and wants ultimately to have a clothes label of her own, like well-known mainstream white designers. Her shops, all of them called Chiffons, are 'upmarket and slightly expensive'. She says, 'We always felt we were a little expensive.' Being expensive is often recommended for designer boutiques because it also gives them the cachet of being exclusive. She estimates that 40 per cent of her customer base is non-Asian.

Her shops are elegant boutiques with smart wood-lined interiors. The clothes are displayed on wooden racks and in glass display cabinets. At the time of my fieldwork, lime was the dominant fashion colour and her window displays included outfits in different shades of lime and lime-yellow. Generally, most of her clothes are made in light shades of beige, gray, tan and creamy brown. She is supremely conscious of the presentation of the shop space and takes pains to display her clothes to create the appropriate shopping experience.

Bubby's clothes are made up in India. She started going to India during the time she had her first shop. However, even though she found people who could manufacture her clothes, it took her a long time to establish a viable relationship. It proved difficult to get to the stage that she is at now, when she faxes a design, specifying fabric colours chosen from a fabric chart and embroidery details, and the manufacturers actually get it right. Bubby has three production bases in India. Two are in Delhi and one is in Agra. She says one factory works exclusively for her; the others do work for the local market as well, although they are not allowed to sell clothes made to her designs. She does not in any case think that there is demand for her 'type of clothes over there'. There are some clothes that only sell well in the British market and have a 'Britishness' that is specific to them. These include the lungis (wraparound skirts) and short tops, which were very popular at the time of my fieldwork; and the maxi, which is made of silk and crêpe de chine fabrics with beadwork and other embroideries that make it 'Brit-Asian'. She says, 'A lot of the things in this shop you would not find in India because the local market is so different from ours.' I have been told this often by people who have gone to India to buy clothes and come back not having found what they wanted to buy. Bubby confirms this. Customers come to her shop sometimes before going to India to get their suits made but they do not find what they like there and 'they have always, always, ended back in my shop. They have been to India and have not found what they see over here, over there.' she says.

In the shop, Bubby and her younger sister Nina serve customers themselves and are helped sometimes by assistants (all in their age group) who tend also to be their close friends. Bubby does not wear salwaar-kameez suits in the shop and favours the up-to-date 'Western clothes' worn by the most trendy young women of her peer group – in 1996, designer track suits like Versace and DKNY, together with fashionable sports shoes. Bubby says:

> Several people ask me why I do not wear a salwaar-kameez in the shop. I think that I sell salwaar-kameezes but a traditional salwaar-kameez isn't me. A lot of youngsters come into the shop because they see me. They can relate to me a lot more than with other boutique owners.
>
> (Bubby Mahil, interview with the author, 1996)

This process is similar to the one described by Angela McRobbie (1989) for second-hand clothes stalls run by young people who have a second-hand style and sell to customers who are like themselves. The consumers and entrepreneurs share a common subculture and bricolage (i.e. using whatever comes to hand) clothes style.

Bubby's appeal to the young, she explains, was demonstrated by the overwhelming response she and her husband Michael got at a fashion show held in the mid-1990s, at a nightclub, Equinox, in London's Leicester Square, where some of the other fashion houses also presented. After every fashion house showed their garments, the designer came on stage:

> Me and Michael went on stage. We got so much attention. I had so much feedback and it paid off because it was in a nightclub and obviously that attracts a lot of young people anyway. And after seeing the clothes they liked them a lot. Plus people really appreciated us. We were younger than everyone else and those people have become my customers.
>
> (Ibid.)

She attracts the youth market particularly well because, as a young woman, she is in tune with their fashion styles. She knows the venues they frequent and, a trendy dresser herself, she wears the styles that young people wear and transfers these to the suits she designs. The youth market is also a profitable one for her, as young women have a great deal of expendable cash that goes on fine clothes. Bubby told me that:

> Every time we do a show, I make sure it is in a nightclub or a trendy place that captures that crowd. It's the young working girls who can really afford to spend the money, obviously young unmarried and newly married girls. It's the eighteen to thirty group but I do have older customers and that is why I have the traditional salwaar-kameez otherwise, if I had my way, I wouldn't have them.
>
> (Ibid.)

But she is happy and good at catering for the more 'traditional market' as she has many fashion-conscious older customers who also like her clothes and style.

Opening up the childrenswear section in her Green Street shop is part of her strategy to develop the younger market. She also targets the graduation market for college students and the Christmas parties and annual dinner-and-dance events of white and Asian customers who do not want to wear traditional ball gowns. They would rather wear, she says, 'Something that is Asian and a little bit Western as well. At least with an Indian outfit, they will wear it more often than just for that function. It's more wearable than a ball gown.' So, with fusion clothes, customers can get more out their clothes and can wear them at more occasions. They are multiple functional because they are combining different elements.

The 'mix': a cultural battle becomes a commercial space

Bubby's genius is that she has developed a fusion style that is reflective of her context and which also captures the youth consumer styles of her time. She is not 'just bringing India to Britain', as she says, but is developing new styles which reflect her hybrid context. She achieves a voice through the clothes and asserts her own version of her ethnicity and culture. Her fusion style is the product of her own experience of growing up in an often hostile, racist environment. She was politicized by her friends' racist comments and decided to respond to them defiantly. She says:

> I know it sounds really stupid, but in those days, I mean, if you were walking down the road, I didn't have any Indian friends, all my friends were English, if you were walking down the road going down somewhere and you would see an Indian girl wearing the salwaar-kameez, my friends would automatically say 'Paki', just because they were wearing a salwaar-kameez. That is when it offended me and I thought … 'Why am I ashamed of wearing what we do? That is our culture, that I have got to do it in such a way that they accept it as well.'
>
> (Ibid.)

This was the backdrop to Bubby's desire to make suits that combined different elements to create new silhouettes and designs and also define a style for herself. Her reaction to the racist anti-salwaar-suit domain she found herself in catalysed her to channel her cultural anger into developing a new fashion style that reflected her cultural politics and created a distinct commercial space. She remembers two designs as crucial in the development of her style. The first was a wedding dress for a white girl friend. She was eighteen or nineteen years old then. Bubby says:

> It was something that was very Eastern and Western as well. It was a really good mix. It was only when I made it for her that I realized it can

be accepted. She loved it, she really did. And I realized how much the Western market appreciates our embroideries and our fabrics, although the designs and shapes they do not really go for.

(Ibid.)

She got the embroidery done in India because she had gone there for a trip and because she could not find anyone to do it in London. She made what looked like a lengha, an ankle-length skirt cut on the bias, with a hip-length top. It was a mix between a European white wedding dress, a lengha and a chuni, the long scarf. She refers to this as the 'mix', hybrid forms that characterize much cultural production in diaspora settings.

Her second breakthrough design was a dress she made for herself: a ruched, chiffon-lined, high-waisted frock with choost-pyjama, long parallel trousers which form folds at the ankle. She made this outfit in the late 1970s, when she had to attend a cousin's wedding. She had been out with her sister 'hunting for suits to wear' everywhere but could not find anything. In the end she made 'something':

What I made was churi-dhar pyjama and, you know, the frock-style you get with a bodice. I bought chiffon and put the chiffon over the top and ruched it all up and it just looked so nice. Now it sounds awful but at the time it really did look lovely. It was all one colour.

(Ibid.)

Her sewing skills helped her negotiate a style for herself that reflected her subcultural context and asserted her design sensibilities. Her confidence soared as she created more of the combinational styles from her design imaginations. She created a style that suited her design agendas: from this emerged a market, a commercial space from a grounded aesthetic.

Bubby says she is not 'traditional'. I think what she means by this is that she is not just plucking India and replanting it in Britain. Her recontextualizing is much more creative, transformed as it is through her 'Brit-Asian' input. There is a transformative design intervention that emanates from her knowledge and command of specific subcultures and subclasses of British Asian markets. Her biographical experiences, especially as a teenager in a racist subculture, and as a participant in the youth market from which she now draws her customer base, are reflected in the design of her clothes and the codes that are inserted into their patterns and silhouettes. Her hybrid style contests what it means to be British, a theme to which I shall return later in this chapter. Her reaction to Indian designers and retailers as 'conservative and traditional' is a negative coding on her part. For her, the classic chic of famous Indian revivalist designer Ritu, for example, whose work I describe in the next chapter, cannot represent her own specific location.

Bubby is determined to adhere to her own style and she emphasizes this vehemently:

60

Because of things I experienced when I was young, which I was ashamed of, I do not want to lose it now. Wearing salwaar-kameez and the way everybody always used to look at us and our dress, you know, I just do not want to lose that.

(Ibid.)

Micro-design through dialogic sketching

Bubby's innovative working style contributes to the vitality of the finished garments. A design is negotiated with the customer, later elaborated by Bubby, and faxed to India where the outfit is made and then sent back to Britain within three weeks. This is why Bubby is on the phone to her Indian manufacturers constantly whilst in the shop and after shop hours, checking on deadlines, getting the latest on the manufacturing status of various garments and giving instructions. At all times of the day, regular couriers arrive bringing packages and assistants scurry off to collect packages from customs clearance at airports. The courier services and their drivers are a very visible part of the action in Chiffons and similar shops. I met Bubby once at Creations, Mala Rastogi's shop in Southall, because they had had their packages mixed up. Apparently this happens now and then. So there is a network of women suit entrepreneurs who know each other through helping each other out over their package mix-ups as well as through common fashion activities. Of course, all of them are also competitors in a market that is being saturated rapidly, with more and more boutiques opening up, selling suits at very competitive prices.

The intensity of these phone calls, the frequent faxing and extensive use of courier services really brings home to the observer the use of technology to compress markets. Bubby's own diasporic connections with India are also crucial:

[It] makes us different from them [white British entrepreneurs]. We can use India and we can use the influence of people over there and get something different which no one else can do.

(Ibid.)

But the pencil sketch is the first stage in this sophisticated global process of production. It is through the sketch that she negotiates designs with her customer. She says she has always done this, right from the beginning. I witnessed this dialogue of co-construction and found it absolutely fascinating. As I pointed out in my introduction, it captured so many of the processes of globalization and time-space compression. These design dialogues, micro-interactions in micro-markets led by women for women, represented the high points of my fieldwork. All the hard work and missed appointments and disappointments because informants are super-busy in major commercial cities like London, were worth these key, revealing moments.

61

Bubby and I examined her order books. She described an outfit that a Muslim woman chose after seeing it at a fashion show she (Bubby) had participated in. They jointly came up with the design concept in which she changed the skirt from the one in the show to how the client wanted it and then modified the top to complement it. So a design was negotiated with a client. Bubby can *never imagine* not negotiating a design, she says, even ten years down the road when she might be better established.

The process of the design dialogue and sketch was clearly demonstrated again by the incident of a tall, plump woman who came into the shop. This woman knew Bubby socially and also bought from her regularly – definitely a good customer. She was suggesting to Bubby that she should stock large sizes. The daughter of a businessman in East Africa and married to a local Indian businessman, she visited India regularly with her husband. Although she therefore had access to Indian markets, she still preferred to buy from Bubby most of the time. I watched Bubby draw a simple sketch with her as the client described the type of neckline she wanted, the shape and the collar, the embroidery and the extent of it, using some of the styles already in the shop. She decided on a lungi suit with a short, just-below-the-hips kameez. Bubby convinced her that a lungi, a straight, ankle-length skirt rather like a sarong, would be flattering for a plump person, giving her height, especially with a shorter top. A rough sketch was drawn by Bubby as they discussed the various possibilities and finalized the style, fabric and embroidery. At this stage, the woman left.

Bubby later elaborated the sketch (see Figure 4.1), now number 153 in her order book, into a fully fledged drawing with the instructions for all the various details (see Figures 4.2a and b), elaborating on the conversation with the outline sketch. She faxed the drawing to India that day. She also talked the sketch through on the phone to India, to clarify the instructions, and made several subsequent calls to check on the progress of the outfit as it went though the various stages of being made. The outfit was ready for the customer in the shop within three weeks at a price of £225.

I observed all this riveting interaction and dialogue of discussing and drawing this outfit. They came up with a new design, dialogically produced; two British Asian women co-designing a product to be faxed to India for production for it to be back on the London scene within three weeks.

She had at that same time made the same woman another outfit for £240. If the outfit is more elaborate, for example, a wedding lengha with heavy embroidery, getting it back to London takes four to six weeks, longer during the summer wedding season. A simple suit with little or no embroidery can be made and sent to London within five days. On a few occasions, semi-ready outfits are cut and embroidered in India and stitched in Britain by the seamstresses Bubby employs in London. However, the majority of outfits are made up and finished in India. The cost of sewing in London puts the price of the outfit up by £25–40.

Bubby does not charge any extra money for her consultations and dis-

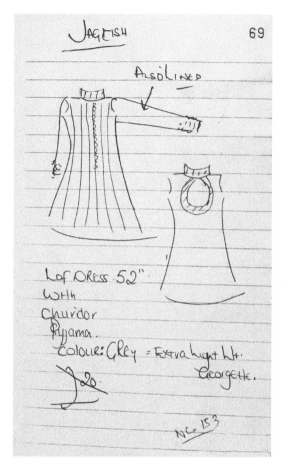

Figure 4.1 Simple sketch of kameez made by Bubby Mahil with the customer in the shop.

Source: Bubby Mahil.

cussions. The price for the outfit remains the same whether it is bought straight 'off the peg' or dialogically negotiated. She says she cannot imagine charging customers more for these individually designed, co-constructed outfits because:

> You have to make them feel that it's a homely atmosphere. You have got to make them feel relaxed. I would be put off if I had to pay for a consultation. I would feel uncomfortable. So ten years down the line I don't think I would do it. Everybody is busy – you still have to make time for your customers.
>
> (Ibid.)

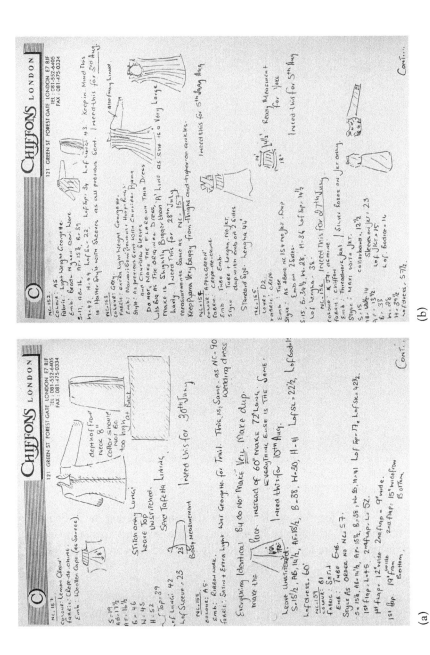

(a)

(b)

Figure 4.2 Elaborated sketch – front (a) and back (b) as subsequently faxed to the factory in India.

Source: Bubby Mahil.

Bubby does not feel co-construction should involve extra charges as it is her distinctive way of working, a facet of her diasporic aesthetic, inherited directly from the East African Asian sewing culture within which she grew up. Like those of her East African Asian forbears both in East Africa and in Britain, Bubby's design dialogues also bring together disparate elements to create a new design. In this case, the design is locally produced in Britain to be made at an Indian production site and then reinserted into the British market. But the initial process of dialogue and sketch is not so different from the local seamstressing processes which took place in East Africa and that take place in the same transplanted sewing economies in Britain I describe in detail in Chapter 10. Bubby, of course, started off by sewing her clothes herself and says, 'It's only been about three years that I have stopped stitching myself. Even in this shop, when my seamstress is really overworked, I help her. We have three machines at the back and one of them is mine.'

Bubby uses her diaspora sewing background to craft a style that is reflective of her context. She uses technical skill pools of cultural reproduction developed elsewhere in her family's earlier phases of migration to create a style that represents her hybrid experiences. She has kept alive the skills she started off with, using that experience to negotiate designs with customers. She combines different elements to produce something that makes sense to her and to the young Asians who buy from her; their context and subcultural tastes and norms she shares, represents and incorporates in her clothes. Her diaspora skills, in particular these innovative recontextualizing processes, have enabled her to develop a style of which she is no longer ashamed. These processes reflect precisely the ways diaspora cultural forms are created through constant negotiation and transformation in new spaces. Displacement and rupture are sutured through recontextualization.

New design lexicons are thus negotiated in transnationalized localized spaces. These connections and transformations are what makes Bubby commercially successful in diaspora markets, the customer bases that she serves and of which she is a central part. She is rooted in the arenas in which she sells: she is commercially savvy at the same time as being a politicized and racialized cultural agent.

Cultural defiance through commerce

When the new design is negotiated with a customer, the sketch encodes the different influences, borrowing many bits of Indianness, bits of Britishness, bits from the mass media and general fashion trends, etc. This much is already clear from the examples I have described. However, this process is also subversive. Bubby subverts what a white British bride wears and also what is considered to be traditional Indian design. At the same time, in co-designing with her customer, Bubby allows them to act as an agent in creating a new design; the design dialogue is a dynamic, democratic process. By working in this way, she is subverting existing designs by saying 'you do not have to buy what is here, we can make it together'.

Bubby negotiates an identity both for herself and her customers through her designs that have their roots in her diaspora cultural background through multiple movements and the racist landscapes in which she grew up. Bubby has developed an almost subaltern voice through style, expressed in the fusion clothes she designs. She has created this style because of the racist remarks of her friends and the negative views of the clothes of immigrants. The suits previously had no positive public registers, especially as worn by immigrant women. In the late 1990s, however, the subversive voice that speaks through Bubby's clothes has acquired new, positive registers in a mainstream public domain. Bubby has thus used the market not just as a mechanism of exchange but also as a way of negotiating a new identity, and, at the same time, of shifting the consumer landscapes of Britain. For this identity is given further, new inflections when Bubby's clothes are worn by members of the white British elite, such as Cherie Booth.[1]

As a result, Bubby's commercial space has influenced the sartorial style of the powerful elite in Britain. This is the dynamic, I have suggested, that dressed Princess Diana in a salwaar-kameez, the critical influential presence of diaspora Asian fashion entrepreneurs and style innovators who are transforming the cultural and consumer landscapes in Britain of which Princess Diana was a part. As I have stated earlier, although the princess was a high-profile catalyzing agent who gave the suit wider markets and exposures than it might have had otherwise, she represented only a recent and short moment within the overall narratives of the suit. I am suggesting that, above all, it is the presence of Asian women's commercially successful diasporic style that is transforming this fashion economy and, in turn, what it means to be British. Entrepreneurs like Bubby have opened commercial spaces which are now part of the common landscapes of white and black and all British women.

Bubby's design significances

As I have shown, Bubby moves in the commercial world along routes which derive fundamentally from her roots within the highly elaborate domesticity of the diaspora. Her domestic skills have become the commodity of the commercial market. She has converted these skills into a commodity context, making them commercially viable, a defiance against the derogatory comments of her white racist detractors. Her battle is resolved through style, a diaspora voice expressed through fashion that encodes the multiply-migrant communities' cultural forms and transplanted skill pools. These dynamics are further developed by her dialogic design activities by which globalized spaces are generated in her shop, through the faxing of designs, constant phoning and the endless courier activities and negotiations with customers in different parts of the world. The market is transnationalized and time and space are compressed, a process made possible only by advances in global communications technology.

Bubby's design process, like that of Geeta Sarin, is at once local and global. Bubby is using global communications technology to create a British Asian mediated transnational space through localized design dialogues to create new markets. These British Asian design inputs go into the Indian scene where the garment is made and are then later inserted into British, Canadian and American markets.

She has used communications technology and multi-sited markets, thus collapsing time and space in her economic activities. This, combined with her consciousness of her Britishness, is encoded in her design innovations. Such new material cultures, produced through diasporic mediations emerging out of the multiple movements and displacement of her community, create her relocated forms. At the same time, the market is the politicized site of important cultural battles that alter mainstream sartorial consumer and cultural economies, whilst colluding with capitalist processes.

These syncretic clothes forms are far more complex in content than, as she says, 'just picking up India and bringing it to Britain'. The cultural politics and histories of displacement and movement that are encoded in these clothes are not easily decoded if the context from which they emerge are not understood. They represent much more than 'gypsy cultures of confused immigrants', as one Indian elite designer summarized them for me (see Ritu Kumar's comments in Chapter 5). But Bubby's clothes are quintessentially the product of her lived experience and very much the result of clear thinking rather than haphazard confusion. So Bubby's suit parties were presenting hybrid clothes that she stitched herself. Since she knows how suits are constructed, she is also willing to dialogically negotiate designs. She says she always worked on designs with her customers and plans to do so always. Her ambitions are to have a label in her own right like all the mainstream designers. This is the background that makes her react to the 'traditional clothes' sold by many other shops because she is not just transplanting India into the British markets.

Diaspora fashion entrepreneurs have different origins, visions and intentions. I am looking at these diasporic spaces, as Avtar Brah puts it so well, from a transnational perspective (Brah 1996).[2] These are different configurations of the global, from the perspectives of localized diasporic subjects who do important work of cultural politicking with many commercial implications. Bubby Mahil and Geeta Sarin navigate global spaces from their localized politics of a racially constituted political base, as opposed to the subcontinental fashion designers and retail professionals who, looking for new markets in Britain, form the focus of my next two chapters.

5

SELLING THE NATION

Revivalist Indian designer Ritu Kumar

The clothes shop Ritu was opened in London's North Audley Street, Mayfair, in May 1996 by the famous 'revivalist' designer of beautifully embroidered and crafted clothes from India, Ritu Kumar. Thus she extended to twelve her chain of shops already well-established in major cities and India.

Ritu Kumar has innovatively revived many languishing embroidery and craft traditions. She designs for famous celebrities in India where she is a very big name. Her publicity states that she is 'Couturier to the Stars'. These include former beauty queens like Miss Universe and Miss World (the latter title being won a number of times by Indian women in the 1990s), Sonia Gandhi (the Italian widow of former Prime Minister Rajiv Gandhi), leading film stars, Indian aristocrats and fashion icons like Princess Diana and Jemima Goldsmith-Khan, as well as television cook and actress Madhur Jaffrey in London. A designer now for over thirty years, she is considered 'a national icon' in India. She is an executive member of the Delhi Crafts Council. On top of her design work, her book, *Costumes and Textiles of Royal India* was launched at Christie's in London in 1999. She is currently working on another book, *Indian Costumes in the Collection of the Calico Museum of Textiles dated Eighteenth to Mid-twentieth Century*. She talks like a supremely articulate, commercially savvy profesor of cultural studies, as can be seen from her many television interviews. She trained in museology (museum organization and management) in the United States before embarking on her career of reviving traditional arts and crafts in India.

Ritu Kumar had already been commercially successful and renowned in Indian markets, described as the 'grand lady of revivalist ethnic fashion' and as the 'high priestess of traditional zardozi'[1] (*Galazee* May–June 1996) but was new to the London scene. Her estimated annual turnover from her Indian domestic enterprises alone is 10 billion (crore) rupees, higher than any other Indian designer (*Outlook* 20 April 1998:63). Her London shop, however, closed just three years after opening.

Clothes and art: Ritu – the London shop

The day I went to Ritu's, I met the artist Gogi Saroj Pal whose paintings were on display in her exhibition *Icons of Womanhood* which inaugurated the ARKS Gallery of Contemporary Art, which was on a floor below the shop itself. On an interview on BBC Radio Four that week, Ritu spoke about this as a significant part of her extensive enterprise which involves women in research and design as central members of her design teams. Ritu said in an earlier Zee TV interview in May 1996:

> In our organization, we have almost 100 per cent women both in research and design and organization ... this is a reflection of contemporary India. The norm today is that the Indian woman is a corporate person, she has a career, she has children, she has homes. In some ways it's not only a reflection of India but also a reflection of the new contemporary lifestyles that are in India.
>
> (Interview, Zee TV, May 1996)

ARKS is an acronym of Anwar, Ritu, Kiki and Sashi, the four main people behind the gallery enterprise. Kiki Siddique, Ritu's London partner, told me that they kept this name because they wanted a new name distinct from India–Sanskritic specificity. Their agenda for the art gallery, as stated in their press release, was that of 'a bold new project to present the best of contemporary Indian art to collectors in Britain'. This exhibiting and selling of art objects in a contemporary art gallery, combined with high craft art clothes in an essentially commercial landscape, represented their joint interests. The art narrative was further elaborated by Kiki Siddique whose husband, Anwar, was the curator and person responsible for the gallery. Anwar has been a collector of Indian paintings, as well as encouraging others to buy Indian art. His goal in setting up the gallery was an educative one for the British public. Kiki talked about the nurturing role of the gallery 'in educating the local Indian and British population about these contemporary Indian art works'. Their publicity stated that:

> The contemporary art scene in India is charged with vitality, but little is known abroad, apart from fleeting glimpses at public exhibition spaces and auction rooms. The British public is familiar with the ancient artistic heritage of India, as seen in the collections of the British Museum, the V and A [Victoria and Albert] and other museums, acquired at the height of the Raj, but remain unaware of the range and quality of contemporary Indian art ... Indian artists are painting with confidence, evolving a language all of their own, and making bold statements about their contemporary reality ... ARKS Gallery will introduce something of the diversity and vitality of contemporary Indian art, in the hope of confronting and challenging people's expectations and perceptions.
>
> (Press release *East Meets West in the Heart of Mayfair* 14 May 1996)

The point that I want to emphasize here is the congruency between Ritu's merchandise and the agenda of the gallery, which is to change perceptions of India, to present a picture of the East, in the form of a contemporized dynamic Indian aesthetic in art and design. It showcases contemporary India in crafted art clothes and lifestyle products through to contemporary Indian art. This commercial art space is thus intended to have an educational role, as much as being an arena of economic exchange. The contemporary art gallery reminds people that the space is an art space, hence the commodities sold within the perimeters of this space are also reflective of that art. Ritu clothes are highly crafted art clothes, art suits that have a defined design aesthetic which is strongly controlled through Ritu's definitive design signature. I was told a number of times by discriminating consumers of such creations that they can recognize a Ritu immediately. Her clothes are distinctive and instantly recognizable as Ritu clothes.

Representing India: 'a window to the East'

Before Ritu opened up her own exclusive London shop, she already had an international presence. She had a shop within a shop at the Galeries La Fayette, Paris. Kiki, her partner in London, told me that Liberty's, the famous London store that has sold 'orientalist wares' since the nineteenth century, had wanted Ritu to open an outlet within their store but she had not been interested, preferring her own shop with her own defined identity. Besides her commercial activities, she has participated in many prestigious exhibitions connected with the Festival of India in China and in the USA, and had her own exclusive exhibits in regional and central government-sponsored craft councils and handicraft corporations, both in India and in Britain in places like the Commonwealth Institute in London and Cartwright Hall, Bradford. She has also had a presence in South East Asia, having participated in *The Hong Kong Asia Trust Presentation on Traditions and Adaptations in Textiles and Fashion from Hong Kong, India, Pakistan and Bangladesh.*

Ritu considered that her London shop was:

> ... very much a window to the East, and in particular a window to India. What I always thought was there was reflection of India in various ways, one was from the Indian film industry, which was very strong, the reflection of India from that side. The second is you would get some merchandise that is available already in different shops, even in Mayfair. But there was a certain thing missing there. There wasn't one *defined design identity* that was coming in with the merchandise. It was assorted merchandise. Accompanying it, what I wanted to do very much was have a reflection of contemporary Indian art.

> (Interview with Zee TV, May 1996)

Her idea is that she is selling contemporary 'top of the range' India, an India that is to do with 'ancient traditions of Indian craftsmanship' and not kitsch India. Her commerce in highly crafted clothes representing sophisticated Indian products is designed for elite Indian markets. These chic products are further transferred, primarily for a market of white elites in Britain (preferably the upper classes), and secondarily to wealthy, locally resident Indians. Ritu emphasized that in presenting a window on the East she wants to stress India's dynamic modernity as played out through a revived 'contemporaryness' and its location in an international arena. Both the gallery owners, Kiki and Anwar, and Ritu, the designer of classic chic, present their position as representing 'India to the world', through contemporary high Indian aesthetics which are, as Ritu states, 'not folklorish India, it's not ethnic India, it's contemporary India'. Their discourses are about representing India as a country that has been and is evolving a contemporary handwriting that 'Western audiences' are not familiar with since Bollywood images have dominated India's representation abroad. The press release for Ritu at the opening of the shop stated that:

> Ritu Kumar is one of India's foremost designers who has developed a unique style of her own reflecting the ancient traditions of Indian craftsmanship in a contemporary vocabulary ... Ritu London will feature a multi-faceted showcase encompassing the very best of Indian design with a specially produced range of western apparel using silks, leathers and cottons ... For the first time in the UK, the discerning Eastern or Western audience will have the opportunity to choose from the very finest quality fashion or from the special hand-crafted range of merchandise, whatever the occasion.
>
> (Press release 14 May 1996)

Dev Sagoo, the Zee TV interviewer, asked Ritu if India had not been 'rightly represented' in the past. Ritu replied:

> No, it has been represented in different forms. You have an art gallery, you have places where garments are available and you have places where lifestyle products are available. But, as a total entity, where one person is designing ... and may be editing and curating an art show, and bringing it in ... [that has not happened]. In India, art and crafts and textiles are not diverse. They are very interrelated. The concept of going to a gallery to see art is non-existent. It's all interrelated, the mechanized world really in some ways has not touched that way of life in India.
>
> (Interview, Zee TV, May 1996)

Ritu wanted a defined design identity (which she saw as missing from the British scene), which would be designed to educate exclusive 'Western' markets about classic chic India with its sophisticated contemporary design economies, regulated by influential design professionals like herself.

I asked her how she understood her market and customer profile in London and whether there were differences between what she was selling in India and in London. She said:

> We haven't changed. We are coming with our own identity. More than perceiving our markets, I think there is an education process that there is an alternative. We are not slotting ourselves into what the market needs. Here is a question which will be a hard struggle. We are saying this is what we are, this is what India is, we will not change. How we are perceived in the market we do not know.
>
> (Ritu Kumar, interview with the author, 1996)

I asked her who she thought would buy her clothes. She said, 'I have no idea. It will take time and the second generation is beginning to understand the change here. The first generation was looking at Bombay movies. But I really don't know. We will learn.'

Her posture of commercial disinterest[2] in the market occurs despite her huge commercial success in the Indian market. As I have indicated earlier, she is a famous and successful market leader, and commercially more successful than any of the other competing Indian designers who barely reach half her annual turnover. She centrally uses the market for both commercial and cultural exchange, even though the explicit agenda of her joint enterprise with the ARKS gallery owner has the subtext of educating the 'West' about the sophisticated high chic and art and craft aesthetics of India. Both Ritu and Kiki explicitly presented themselves as pedagogues wanting to inform 'Western audience's about 'the Indias' that are not represented by the familiar images of the Bollywood film industry. They also wanted to present a coherent, defined and edited, singular design identity in the presence of the haphazardly presented Indian products and merchandise already available in Britain. Ritu's design identity, encoded in her strongly edited merchandise, is the central core of her commercial enterprise, 'because that is the one niche that has to be portrayed right. The product line is sent down. They [the shop managers] just do the running of the shop,' she says. Kiki explained that Ritu's production processes involve all the stages of bringing the garment to the shops, starting from buying (and often also weaving) the cloth. Ritu takes the plain cloth through all the processes of painting, dyeing, printing, embroidering, sewing in her industrial units and then the finished clothes go to her shops. She and her design teams have central control over manufacturing and design, all the production and the retail commercial processes. This control of all the presentation, production, and design processes is not something most India-based designers are able to manage. Ritu is therefore in an extremely powerful design location.

Ritu's design agenda is couched in a nationalist and anti-imperialist discourse about revival of tradition. It is very much a culturally mediated commercial narrative. The statements about high arts and crafts do hide market interests, which this supremely class-conscious commercial sphere caters for. The implicit agenda is of selling to the 'West', which is, from the perspective of Ritu and others like her, populated by wealthy elite whites and transnationally located South Asian elites, not locally based Indian immigrants living in and produced by racialized contexts.

Ritu stated in my interview with her:

> But what comes out of the country and what represents India to a lot of people who live abroad, especially to the Indian who has kind of lost touch with India and others due to shortage of time, do not feel the nuances of what is or meet far too few people to understand these nuances. For them, unfortunately, it's still a limited gypsy clothing culture. And I think they are looking for something to identify with and there's a great deal of confusion there outside the country as to who people are; particularly, I see it through the clothing.
>
> (Ibid.)

Having been very successful back in India, she clearly wanted to go 'global' and become more of an international designer. Her CV indicates that she already had international commercial connections. She had designed for other entrepreneurs and also had sold her own brand merchandise but not through her own signatured retail space.

Revivalist designer of classic chic

Ritu explains her revivalist work thus:

> I was a museology student in America and when I got back to India, I realized how little I knew about my culture. That came as a great shock. I just felt that there was great need for the revival of crafts as well as an awareness of what the richness is in our own country. And, to locate that, I had to do a lot of research, and through the research, one thing led to another and I got into revival of textiles. And the next thing was to make them into a useable commodity. It happened by accident rather than design that I have to do this.
>
> (Interview, Zee TV, May 1996)

She talked about her revival of zardozi which is:

> ... one of most glamorous embroideries in the country. It was one great art form that belonged to the courts of India, to the royalty of India. Then there was patronage for this art. It was done with pure silver

plated with gold, and the gold thread was used for embroidery for royal costumes and there was a feeling of grandeur and so on. All of that has disappeared because the gold thread itself has gone. It was substituted with lurex. Lurex is a little cheaper looking. The aesthetics are not the same. So . . . that took me . . . to the Victoria and Albert Museum here because [it has] the best examples of Indian textiles you find here because they are preserved better. The climate was more conducive to them being available here. And actually, it was very lovely, they gave me all the help that I needed. Then I took back a design vocabulary and reintroduced it into the craft areas and zardozi was one of them. And then we put together a collection which reflected the royalty of the Mughal times which was called *Tree of life*.[3]

(Ibid.)

Another significant aspect of this revival narrative is that Ritu represents the second generation in the art and crafts movement started by an earlier wave of pioneering women who were involved in the Indian nationalist struggles, the freedom movement. They spearheaded the arts and crafts movement, in particular, the revival of the handloom movement.[4] They did the groundwork that Ritu benefited from. Implicit in her narrative are the tensions between the two generations as she struggled to find and develop her own contemporary styles amid the existing agendas of the older women, 'cultural czarinas', as she calls them. These 'remarkable' women included Kamaladevi Chattopadhyaya and Pupul Jayankar, who were leaders in the post-independence revival movement. They were amongst the initiators of the official, state-sanctioned institutions of the handloom and other craft industries and the government boards in the early 1950s that monitored and sponsored these then nascent industries. These included the All India Handicraft Board and later the government emporia that dealt with the commercial aspects and where these craft products were retailed to the public. All this was backed by the Nehru family, in particular Mrs Gandhi.

Ritu told me that she acted as a calalyst for the modern revival although:

> . . . it was spearheaded by Kamaladevi and Pupul Jayankar, what they did was really the revival. What I tried to do was take it to step two from there. They had laid the ground, people were available, the addresses were there, you knew where to go, you knew which part of the country and what was done. At least that vocabulary was there. Then I went one step further and made that vocabulary possible to be put into a more modern medium.
>
> (Rita Kumar, interview with the author, 1996)

Ritu created a second-generation design directory, by recontextualizing these designs into a contemporary frame. She developed a new design syntax which she took to new design and commercial heights. This was the crux of her revivalist agenda. Her story is both a revival story and a commercial story of these contemporized revived crafts and crafted art clothes. It is also a story of commercially inflected nationalism, as reflected in her design-signatured merchandise, which represents India and the ancient heritage of her country in contemporized form. She says:

It was like in most of these areas there had been three hundred years of discouraging that particular craft processes because of the Industrial Revolution. It did not suit them [the British rulers] to continue buying Indian goods. So they were more interested in sending goods to India for Indian consumption. So that dealt a death blow to the craft areas and they were literally wilting or were on their deathbed because in the traditional areas, there were one or two people left who could still do the craft. When you went there the first job was to revive what used to be. That was not an easy task because you had to source things that were 300 years old to bring back an old aesthetic into that area. Once that revival was done, I think we are now in the process in India to go through a contemporization and an evolution within that particular craft form. Some of it good, bad, and indifferent, but it is happening.

(Ibid.)

Ritu says she was forced into retailing by her desire to develop her own design identity that reflected her youthful contexts of the mid-1960s. She says:

I had to go into retailing. I had no desire to as a matter of fact. Running shops was not my real joy or anything ... I did need one little shop to stick this in where I didn't have to ask somebody. Like Mrs Jayankar [one of the cultural czarinas] would say, 'No this doesn't fit the standards of the board' and whatever. I wanted to wear a tight pair of jeans with a handprinted blouse. She would say, 'It's cute but why aren't you wearing a sari?'

(Ibid.)

So Ritu's contemporizing design interventions were in part a reaction to some conservative elements of an earlier pioneering generation which had established the initial design trajectories. However, in another arena in late 1990s London, young British Asian women found her styles too conservative for their tastes and context – perhaps Ritu herself is now becoming an Indian design czarina.

Ritu was inspired to develop a contemporary framework and generate a modernizing force into these dying traditions, galvanized by her education in the USA, which made her realize how little she knew about her own culture. Her exposure to 'Western' educational institutions educated her into her lack of

consciousness of her own cultural scene and this, in turn, led her into her subsequent, very successful role as a second-generation revivalist. In some ways this
process is similar to the border experiences of 'discovering ethnicity' that characterize immigrants' heightened consciousness of their racial and cultural backgrounds when placed into a minority/majority context. Their marginality and
the questioning of their ethnicities forces them to construct themselves and
position themselves vis-à-vis their cultural background. Similarly, Ritu's experiences in America also gave her a renewed respect for India's arts and craft traditions and a desire to be more knowledgeable about this background.

Her education and her ability to translate old craft traditions into an innovative modern format resulted in a contemporized design vocabulary, whose
syntax created for her the supremely successful commercial markets of art and
craft commodities. She was and remains a central agent in generating these
markets. As I have said earlier, despite her disavowal of the economics of her
enterprise and apparent disinterest in the market, she strikes me as being a commercially astute design entrepreneur. Her twelve outlets in India are testimony
to her understanding of the market and, of course, to the high-quality innovative commodities that she manufactures.

Another reason for the urgency to contemporize was that a whole gamut of
craft industries was destroyed by British imperialists, when craft vocabularies
were raided and looted and transferred to other sites for use by white craftsmen.
She says:

> India is the one country with a live tradition of textiles which are not
> museum pieces, and we have to preserve this identity ... a whole direc-
> tory of design is missing from India, our aesthetics have gone into
> someone else's library, the ambi has become a Paisley.
> (*Galazee International*, May–June 1996:15).

Taken out of the country at the height of foreign rule, these collections are to
be found in British museums such as the Ashmolean in Oxford and London's
Victoria and Albert. Ritu spent months at both, taking notes and photographs.
Some of the textiles and skills could not be revived, for example, the Kashmiri
Paisley shawl industry, because of the systematic destruction and appropriations
by British shawl manufacturers. Ritu explained in a telling narrative that:

> The last weaver who could do this died in 1927. The British realized
> the immense popularity of this expensive material which they
> imported in large quantities. Then they banned the import. They
> managed to reproduce it on the loom in Manchester. The design
> remained but the craft in itself was changed. They couldn't do what
> the Kashmiri weavers could do, neither were they trying. Unfortu-
> nately this is one craft that has not been revived. It's a tragedy ... as
> anybody in textiles will tell you. One of the things that really upset me

was when fashions changed, they had no use for this craft. And that's
when I became a revivalist ... Why follow cyclic fashion ... ? We
wouldn't want to do this in the arts and crafts.

(Ritu Kumar, interview with the author, 1996)

This desire not to respond to cyclical fashions and to avoid their transitory
nature is very much in tune with her revivalist agenda.

Subversions through local and global markets

Ritu initiated a fascinating circular process. The conduit Ritu initiated through
her revived designs recontextualized elements from her research in the Victoria
and Albert Museum and then inserted them into London markets via commodities made in India: a circle was thus completed. These design inputs were
borrowed from a premier British institution of arts and crafts instituted at the
height of British colonial rule; they represent a design economy which was
usurped by British colonizers in the past; in our own times they are further
appropriated by an Indian commercial and cultural producer of arts and crafts
texts, an agent of that once-colonized though now independent state. These
processes are also about subverting established versions of Britishness, through
design vocabularies and sartorial commerce spearheaded by diaspora British
Asian fashion entrepreneurs, and subsequently engaged in by Indian and Pakistani designers from the subcontinent. These new commercial and cultural
entrepreneurs are innovating new markets which are getting British women
into 'Indian clothes'. These are acts of subversion. Princess Diana in Ritu suits,
Lady Helen Windsor in Egg clothes, and Cherie Booth in Bubby's clothes – all
these represent striking testimony to these complex local and global dynamics.

Of course, some of these consumer processes are similar to the earlier desire
of upper-class British women to consume orientalist material culture in the form
of calicoes, Kashmir shawls, the mul-mul cottons, the Indian brocades and
many other Indian commodities. These Victorian and Edwardian upper-class
white women's acts of consumption were themselves politicized acts, going
against the grain of masculine, nationalized consumption. There are, however,
some differences from the colonial period, crucially, that the traffic of these new
commodities is controlled by Asian women entrepreneurs, both locally raised
British Asian daughters of immigrants and also India-based elite Indians.

Ritu is also representing her country's heritage through her merchandise. In
the past, the revival work that she has done successfully for commercial
domains had originated in the arts and crafts domains, the revival of which was
initiated by people involved in nationalist freedom struggles and then becoming
government-sponsored. In the 1990s (and still now) there is still government
sponsorship for the development of these 'apparel sectors' of the Indian
economy. For example, the Indian government, through the Apparel Export
Promotion Council, sponsors fashion shows featuring leading Indian designers,

like the Oorja-Indian Fashion Show in New York in July 1998, where Ritu was among the exhibitors.

For India-based fashion personnel, this government sponsorship continues and there is state backing for attempts to develop new international markets. At the same time, the Indian government has initiated fashion and design schools like the NIFT, (National Institute of Fashion Technology) to professionalize design education for upcoming designers and those already fully fledged. This is a position of privilege in comparison to diaspora designers, who have had to develop their own markets and commerce without any state or institutional help. Diaspora designers from marginal immigrant backgrounds do not represent a national codified aesthetic in their clothes merchandise. They interpret an individual experience, an experience of migration that is about displacement and replacement. They also bring a diaspora expertise developed in previous sites to negotiate a new Britain, new national identities, and novel consumer and cultural landscape.

Indian fashion entrepreneurs are very differently located, in terms of class, experiences of the nation and their design intentions in the marketplace. Whilst diaspora design dialogues highlight cultural pride discourses articulated through reactions to racism, elite Indian designers are about national pride and craft industries, ancient heritages destroyed and usurped by colonial oppressors of the past and by mass production through industrialization.

Perceptions of Ritu's shop

In the following I want to refer to some of the perceptions of Ritu clothes and the shop in London amongst British Asian women. Their perceptions give some clues about why Ritu, the shop, closed within three years of opening in London. I do not know the actual business decisions, the financial details and the specific processes that led to the closure of her enterprise. I am sure that there are complex issues that I am not party to. But, perhaps, some of the reasons for the closure of her enterprise might be gleaned from the comments which follow. I present both some reactions of London fashion entrepreneurs as well as those of a Ritu fan and others familiar with her shop. I, personally, liked Ritu's clothes enormously although I do not own any. They are beautifully crafted and pleasurable objects of art for the body, with intricate work, delicate embroideries and embellishments (see Figure 5.1). They are wonderful creations.

I first became conscious of a critique of her clothes during my interviews with the locally raised fashion entrepreneurs whose work I have discussed in the previous two chapters. Both Geeta Sarin and Bubby Mahil knew Ritu clothes well but said their young customers raised in Britain would not be able to find anything in Ritu's shop. They found her clothes 'too traditional and conservative'. One of them said, 'People say that India is forward but I do not see it. Every time I go to there and look at the local market, I can rarely see anything I like, very rarely ... It's very traditional. There is a gap between us and them.' This echoes

Figure 5.1 Classic chic – a Ritu Kumar-designed salwaar-kameez embellished with fine zardozi embroidery in the traditional gold thread. With thanks to Ritu Kumar. Model: Dirya Chauhan

the BBC2 comedy show *Goodness Gracious Me* satire of Jemima Goldsmith-Khan's salwaar-kameez as 'mummies' clothes', which I referred to in Chapter 1.

Another common view of Ritu's clothes was represented by a trendy British Asian woman raised in London, a fashion-conscious metropolitan Londoner who initially liked Ritu's clothes but who subsequently changed her mind. She felt that these clothes designed and produced in India did not represent the local London contexts and the dynamic local cultural scene since Ritu was not of this scene and not attuned to its changing cultural and political nuances. She explained that:

> Ritu is jumping on the bandwagon. They come along here when Asian kids who grow up here are making these clothes available here and can cater for what their local peers and markets need. They can capture the markets of the people who live here. The Ritu type of fashion has nothing to do with people here. It does not represent them. It's nothing new. If you went to the shop after a year or so, it was the same stuff over and over. Clothes have to show what is happening here in this country.

A view often cited is that some of the Indian designers who want to capture markets in Britain might be successful in India but lack the local knowledge of the street styles to which young Asians are socialized. They cannot speak the local language because they are not local products. One trendy informant explained, using a famous British white designer as an example:

> Vivienne Westwood succeeded because she could understand what was wanted here. She was from the local scene. Ritu thinks that because she is big in India and has big customers in India that ... she will be big here, because she thinks we do not know, but we know a lot more than she thinks we do. She does not realize that. She also does not realize that whites know more of what is here. Whites go to the same streets like Green Street and the Broadway in Southall and Ealing Road in Wembley. They like the East/West mix that young designers from the East End produce that parallels what happens in 'Western' fashion. Brit Asians are challenging these local fashion markets and they want to challenge them in return. What Ritu does is boring for people here.
>
> (Interview with the author, 1996)

She also criticized the attitude of the assistants in the shop:

> Also Ritu and her shop people are arrogant ... [mimicking] 'We have come here to educate the people here, that is our role, we can teach them.' Well, we guys do not need any teaching!! Ritu lacks the excitement that is here. It's exciting to wear what is happening here, a mixture. Ritu and her partners cannot capture that.
>
> (Ibid.)

However, Ritu had many fans whilst her shop was still around, for example women who liked the classic, classy and beautifully crafted clothes. One such case was that of A, a very classically trendy beautiful older woman of about fifty, who loves Ritu clothes and was delighted that the shop was in London because Ritu-type clothes were ones that she had always wanted from India and could not get in London. She does not go to India, having only been once as a child in the early 1950s. A liked Ritu clothes because they are classic pieces which she will wear for many years and that her daughters will be able to wear, as they are timeless clothes to be passed on. She liked 'the complexity of the work on clothes which is rich and subtle. Her suits are like wearing traditional Indian art. I do not like anything loud. Although her suits have a lot going on them, they do not look gaudy. There is richness to them and they have intricate embroidery and work on them.' However, even though she likes Ritu clothes enormously, she too commented on the attitude of the shop assistants towards their British Asian clients, to whom they were, she felt, quite rude, 'whilst bending over backwards to treat their white European clients really well'. This 'pandering to whites' (which I heard of very often from other sources) she characterized as wanting to sell to 'classless whites rather than classy Asians'. The first time she went into the shop, the fitting rooms were busy and priority was given to a white woman, whom the assistants were flitting around, whilst she was asked if she would like to change in the toilets! This was, apparently, only one of many such incidents.

As I thought about this enterprise and re-read my field notes of my interview, I was struck by the comments of a local British Asian intellectual, who suggested that:

> These Indian, India-based enterprises, when they open up in international European cities, have similar intentions but different outcomes and different reasons for entering these clothes markets. They are responding to different dynamics in their contexts. In all these various levels, it's all highly political and the political subtexts and responses are very interesting. In relation to Ritu and her ilk, especially as you say [referring to me] their negation of market and commercial interests, what is interesting to me is that even in their nationalism, and their involvement with the Quit India movement and its agenda of freedom for India, they are colonized. They are very elitist and conflicted and show signs of colonization in the way they approach these issues. In responding to colonization, their neocolonial response is very colonial, especially their pandering to whites.
>
> (Interview with the author, 1996)

These attitudes are a product of elite Indians' negative interpretation of British Asian society. Those Indians who occupy an elite class position in India do not want to forgo their privileged placement as Indians, as it accords them enormous local advantage. If they were to identify themselves as British Indians, they would have to assume a whole different class and race location, and relinquish the hierarchies of their country of origin in which they have positions of power. Therefore they refuse to acknowledge the local Asian scene. This British Asian intellectual also suggested that:

> They do not want to be seen as people of colour and are not going to be denigrated immigrants, as British Asians. There is a very racialized consciousness among South Asians from India. They do not want to be identified as people of colour, racialized subjects in very racialized countries. So by keeping to their India label and being transnational, psychologically and otherwise, they do not have to fall into racialized hierarchies.
>
> (Ibid.)

It seems to me that what is being suggested is that Ritu and her milieux are transnational, cosmopolitan, urban Indian national elites whose comprehension of the British Asian scene and lack of understanding of diaspora aesthetics emerge from their very class-laden perceptions. Ritu is a member of a trans-national elite and Bubby is an immigrant diasporic. There is a tremendous difference. People are just beginning to sort these issues out because the discourses of globalization are under-developed. A transnational is an Indian and identifies herself in that way and in fact capitalizes on this national identity, both culturally and commercially. The difference between a transnational and a diasporic is neither well understood by academics nor conceptualized well culturally.

These perceptions and testimonials present some clues about why Ritu the shop did not succeed on the British market. As I have stated earlier and I reiterate, enterprises close for a complex range of reasons.

6

SELLING ART CLOTHES IN CLASSED MARKETS

In this chapter, I describe enterprises led by two Pakistani women who sold combinations of art, antiquities and classic embroideries brought together in clothes designed for the classed markets of wealthy local and transnational elites. Their design agendas echo Ritu's design styles, though Ritu is a pioneer and in a mega-star league, as a commercially successful and powerful revivalist designer in Indian markets. However, there are some resonances of design aesthetics and sensibilities that I have described in the previous chapter which also apply to the enterprises I describe below. The first of these is Libas, which opened in 1988, and the second, Yazz, opened in 1995. Like Ritu's enterprise, Yazz and Libas are also now closed. My discussion of the differences between British Asian diasporics and national design elites, many of whom are also transnationally located, also applies to the cases I detail below.

Libas: a Pakistani revivalist design agenda

Libas, the shop, was at 10 Berkeley Street, Mayfair, London, from 1988 to 1999. The quarterly magazine, *Libas International: Exotic Fashion and Lifestyle Magazine*, was also launched in 1988, distributed through newsagents and (international) subscription. Libas's beautiful clothes, with supremely well-crafted embroideries and embellishments, are explicitly designed for sale outside Pakistan in, for example, New York, Nairobi (in Kenya) and in various boutiques in Britain. In Pakistan the suits, originally and innovatively designed, are too easily copied by local clothes manufacturers and sold at lower prices, so undercutting Libas markets.

Libas magazine, referred to as the 'Asian *Vogue*', presents the latest Libas clothes, together with fashion articles with a subcontinental slant; as well as covering the South Asian social calendar in Pakistan, India and Britain, including fashion shows, charity functions, etc.

> It caters for a new generation of wealthy Asians who are interested in being educated and adopting the exotic lifestyle explored by the magazine ... *Libas* intends to be Asian in content, yet deliberately Western in layout.
>
> (Jalan 1997:95)

Libas also carries advertisements for suit shops in the subcontinent and in Britain, including those I write about in this book. Readers would order clothes from the central London Libas shop, based on what they saw in the magazine.

The magazine's own publicity presented it as meeting 'the growing needs of the cosmopolitan reader who for generations has become part of his or her adopted country'. The magazine 'would unite them with their inherent traditions, arts, food and fashions and at the same time act as a window on two cultures, enabling the East and West an appreciation of each other' (publicity material given to author in 1996).

There is also another agenda at play here. This is the agenda of Pakistani and Indian designers who want to 'make it in the West' and with a transnational clientele of wealthy Asians, many of whom share their class position and international jet-set status. They are into the business of producing 'class' for the same circles as their own and, often, in sites outside their nations. They already possess confirmed national status and seek success in 'the West' to consolidate their class capital across the borders, at the same time further legitimizing their markets and social lead within their own nation.

Bridge-builders between East and West: reintroducing the past

The design identity of Sehyr Saigol, the Pakistan-based designer behind Libas, is inspired by her own beginnings as an artist. Her publicity states that she uses 'craftsmen, artists and designers who lack exposure outside their respective countries'.

Saigol's clothes, like Ritu's, are presented as art clothes, highly crafted 'concepts in body dressing', as her publicity puts it:

> The Libas Collection label presents the creations of Sehyr Saigol, the contemporary and dynamic fashion designer based in Lahore, Pakistan ... Sehyr designs, weaves, prints and tailors in Lahore, Pakistan, using fabrics from around the world, designing not only for the fashion-conscious women, but increasingly more to meet the demands of her Western audience, using the shalwaar (trousers) and kameez (blouse) ensemble to create new concepts in body dressing. She has achieved imaginative variations by combining Western influences with the rich traditional motifs of Asian and various other countries.
>
> (*A Brief History of Sehyr Saigol*, 1996)

Saigol, like Ritu, her Indian counterpart, is a purveyor of national commodities which encode the rich traditional motifs of Asia, handblocked Mughul and durree motifs, heirloom embroideries translated through designs that are, 'classic ... alive ... as an ensemble mixed and matched with western style' (publicity material given to author in 1996).

However, unlike Ritu's, Libas clothes are made using imported fabrics and European textile industrial technologies, including computerized embroidery sewing machines, before being worked on by Pakistani craftspeople. Sehyr translates old and classic motifs into contemporary vocabularies in her clothes. She is a cultural legitimizer of reinvented traditions, such as the ambi design of the Paisley shawl, that are designed to sell in markets outside the subcontinent.

Mrs Zaineb Alam, former manager of the Libas shop, emphasized a point about the current assertiveness of British Asians in relation to the revivalist design agendas of Sehyr Saigol.

> Today we have arrived. We don't have to make a statement. I can be as ethnic as I like.... Now we have gone backwards. Now we are happy to introduce cultural things like the old Mughal angarhka style that the Mughal men used to wear. There is a woman's version to that. Libas is bringing the cultural things and old things back.
>
> (Zaineb Alam, interview with the author, 1996)

Libas's defining design signature is of bringing the old into the new. *Libas* magazines are full of articles and photographs of the old-into-new design vocabularies of the maharaja era and the Sanskriti collections; the traditional, classic, class-coded design aesthetics and sensibilities that give pride of place to royal monarchical designs, present maharajas and past Mughal kings, courtly clothes and embroideries, Islamic calligraphy and architecture. This is Raj nostalgia. The magazine features designers doing similar work to Sehyr Saigol, such as Ritu Beri (*Libas International* 8.2 1995:12). There are pictures of her 'Sanskriti collection' which is referred to as 'a narration of the ensembles inspired by the mode of attire in the four major periods in Indian History – ancient, medieval, British Raj and contemporary'.

Antiquity, ancient, old, age, historical – these are key words in the *Libas* lexicon. This is very much part of a nationalistic agenda, whether it be the revival of Muslim embroideries, Mughal architectural motifs or ancient calligraphies. All commoditize the nation, in particular the national heritages of royalty. For example, in Princess Diana's lifetime, Libas did stock copies of her suits. So this elite design avenue ends with another royal woman's clothes, in this case a British one now deceased, whose style borrowed from and also entered the design vocabularies of Libas.

As well as recontextualizing the ancient East, however, Libas is also very sensitive to contemporary European fashion design, monitoring developments closely and following seasonal cuts and colour trends. This is truly an aspect of borrowing from the shapes popular on the European markets and catwalks: they are transferred to Pakistan for production and circulated back to Britain to be sold. It is a two-way traffic. It is much too simplistic to think that the East is simply being exploited. There is a desire on the part of subcontinental elite designers to combine European designs and outlines to create something that is 'of the East but combines with the best of the West'. This is not just one-way appropriation as it is often presented in the literature, 'the West exploiting the natives and indigenous arts and crafts, appropriating subcontinental styles and prints'. There are, in fact, multiple traffics, appropriations, recontextualizations and, indeed, exploitations that flow in many directions (as compared, for example, with Ritu re-appropriating Indian designs kept at the Victoria and Albert Museum).

Like Ritu, Libas does not co-construct designs with customers, nor make made-to-measure clothes. Their clothes are sized in three sizes: small, medium, large. Some customers will order clothes over the phone, having seen them in the magazine:

> It is a global market. We get orders here in two weeks and you can order as much as you like. We have our own factory. They have a five-acre factory and people can order as much as they like. Everything is under the same roof.
>
> (Ibid.)

The young British Asian market was never Libas's market nor did they cater significantly for weddings, unlike the other shops I describe for whom the wedding market constitutes the bulk of their business. Libas clothes were always extremely expensive (£300–4,000 and more): 'They [young British Asians] can't afford it. They can only dream.' (ibid.)

Mrs Alam also talked of Libas 'trying to educate' British Asians into better taste (for example, not wearing red as a bride if it does not suit you). This educative role is a salient feature of all the subcontinental elites. They want to educate the local public. In the case of Libas, this continues to be done primarily through the dissemination of *Libas* magazine.

Yazz international: promoting the de-ethnicized language of class

Yazz – the shop and its markets

Yazz, the shop, sold art clothes and artefacts on Baker Street in central London from 1995 to 1999. Yazz specialized in the clothes of well-known and established designers from India and Pakistan[1] selected by Yasmin Hydari, the shop owner.

Mona, shop manager and Hydari's daughter, explained the shop's philosophy:

> Yasmin ... wanted to provide women here with the taste; we don't do just clothes, we do artefacts, antiques. Forget fashion and what is very fashionable at the moment, we have embroideries that are centuries-

old that are becoming a dying art. She is very much into promoting the culture. She wanted to be able to do it in a very high-class way. Class sounds a bit... It's not right but in a very classy manner ... She is an artist. She does mostly textiles ... She has also changed the image of Asians here. She wants to create a market.

(Mona Hydari, interview with the author, 1996)

Here the elites' subtext of wanting to change the image of Asians and distance themselves from local immigrant British Asians again recurs.

We talked about Yazz's markets and whether they had been able to decode their customer bases. Mona said:

We have clients from all parts. We get approached [by] people from Southall and Wembley, from magazines that just ... predominantly cater towards Asians. All these people and they come to us, they say, 'Do you want to stock our stock? Do you want to be in this magazine, that magazine?' They don't understand that we are not really trying to get the Asian community. We are trying to do something completely different. We have got English clients. We are trying to get certain types of people. But our clientele base is not connected with a particular group. People who can afford these things are a small minority of rich, in comparison, to the general population and a small minority of Asian women who will be able to afford to buy this kind of thing and who know the labels.

(Ibid.)

Initially Yazz was targeting high-class Asian women and some English women who had been exposed to Asian culture, those who would be able to afford top designer wear for Indians and Pakistanis:

We were creating a niche. There is no other place really who does supply top designers' ranges from India and Pakistan, the kind of quality that we provide. Obviously people who would be able to pay for that kind of quality and the name.

(Ibid.)

By 1996, it seemed, a majority of their customers were indeed English:

Slowly more and more of our clients are English women ... 60 per cent. Our English clients are women who are a bit daring, a bit different, a bit eccentric. They might not use the trousers but will buy the dress to wear on its own. We have Malaysian clients, we have Asian clientele. We have beautiful embroideries which can be appreciated by certain people. We do a lot of intricate thread embroideries which take months to do and we know some people whose mentality is such that they can't understand this. They say it is so plain even though it's fully embroidered. You need a certain kind of person who can appreciate that. Now we are going towards English clients who can afford to pay this kind of money. We are talking about the Jemima Goldsmiths and that kind of society that has been exposed to and doesn't feel at odds with our culture, with our clothes, and who can carry it off.

(Ibid.)

I asked about their British Asian clientele. She explained:

We get professional women who can afford who always come in and say, 'I don't really wear this stuff. I don't really have the occasion to wear this stuff' – Women who can afford to buy fairly expensive outfits. They always come out of curiosity and have a look. They buy something once in a while.

(Ibid.)

So, their clientele is not so much British Asians as transnational Asians and wealthy whites.

Yazz wanted to differentiate themselves from the rest of the local boutiques, as did Ritu, yet they both participated in Mala Rastogi's Thread of Fantasy fashion show,[2] which allied them with the other British Asian and Asian entrepreneurs and their markets. It seems that they did not have a separate circuit that could sustain their enterprises and that, despite their desire to stand apart, their dependencies were on ethnic media and ethnic fashion shows and magazines. Mona was talking about the plans they had of advertising in Vogue to capture 'other' markets, in particular Asian women who did not tune into the ethnic media and so had not heard of the shop:

We are going to strike up something with Condé Naste [sic]. We might be in Vogue, Tatler and Harpers. We are heading in this direction. If they see it in Vogue, they will be ten times more inclined to come here.

(Ibid.)

So, in some ways, Yazz did want the ethnic market of young women who read these upmarket magazines, while maintaining the boundary between the children of immigrants and the elite Asians.

Interestingly, Mona was unhappy with the desire of some of their white clientele to mix the form of Yazz's clothes:

They want to be able to say, 'If we are going to be wearing your dress we want our input into it, you know. We want a new fresh form of salwaar-kameez. We don't want what you are wearing. Let's find a medium and then we will be prepared' . . . That's what I find the mentality is. That's what they are saying, that you meet them half way.

(Ibid.)

She would have preferred the local whites to accept the 'pure form' that Yazz wanted to market through the arts and revival discourses. It seems, from Mona's statement, that the de-ethnicized form of clothes that they were selling was market-driven because the English women they sold to wanted a form of suit that did not reflect its origins, its ethnicities. Or perhaps the English women wanted to negotiate. They wanted to co-construct and design a form that integrated elements of their own with what Yazz wanted to market to them. But Mona saw this is as a negative compromise. This is in strong contrast to the diasporic designers whose aesthetic of crossovers, continuously negotiated and stitched, is true to their daily experience.

At the same time, she was not fully familiar with the local British Asian scene, suggesting that there were no changes in Southall and Wembley. She saw them as almost static sites:

If I go to Southall, I see that we have not moved one little bit . . . In Pakistan and India, in terms of fashion they are much ahead of us here. They are doing something really spectacular. Here I find that they have not moved an inch, they have not changed a bit.

(Ibid.)

Yazz clothes ranged between £250 and £5,000, although there were few clothes in the £250 area. Like Libas, Yazz was not particularly into the wedding market. Since Libas and Yazz have an art clothes agenda this is not what they are about, even though wedding-day clothes are the outfits many young women want from these boutiques. Mona told me:

We have just everyday things more than wedding things because if you just want wedding dresses, we have very expensive dresses more in the £2,000 to £5,000 range. Not everyone is willing to spend that kind of money. We have a reputation of being a bit expensive, which marketing-wise is not a bad thing because you have to keep a certain image, but our prices compare reasonably well.

(Ibid.)

Expensiveness adds to the exclusivity of the shop, as already mentioned in the chapter on Bubby.

Negation of ethnicity: ambiguous markets or market ambiguity

Yazz's business card (see Figure 6.1) had on it an impression of a woman which I found hard to decode. The image resembles an Edwardian woman. I was also struck by the caption on a Yazz advertisement that appeared in *Libas* magazine which read 'Yazz: The language of class'.

I commented on the image during my interview with Mona. Mona said it was designed to suggest sophistication, an image of an elegant, sophisticated woman. I asked Mona if the model was an angrez (a white woman). We discussed the ambiguous picture which was similar to a painting in the shop.

Figure 6.1 The image of a woman on the front of Yazz's business card.
Source: Mon Hydari.

I was told that Yazz wanted the image to be fairly abstract because their markets were not clear to them. Mona said:

> Until you are absolutely sure of your market and of what you are selling, you want people to keep guessing, not only that it intrigues people, something they don't know and they cannot grasp immediately. The embroidery is typical but the outfit is not.
>
> (Ibid.)

So the difficult-to-decode picture is a deliberate marketing strategy to keep customers guessing about the products Yazz plans to sell, stalling until they themselves are sure of their image and market. Their market messages are rife with contradictions (as many messages are), but it is the negation of ethnicity that I was most struck by here:

> Whenever we say 'East meets West', we cringe. That is such a cliché now. We are trying to move away from that and trying to come up with what it really is. We are still working on it. When people ask, we don't want to say these are Asian clothes because they are not really. We want to say something concise. Yes, this is what it is and I think it will take a bit of time before we are sure where we are ourselves.
>
> (Ibid.)

So they were not sure which markets they wanted to reach. Of course, it would have included wealthy people but this is why their publicity images were not sending a clear message. The ambiguity arose because Yazz, I am sure, wanted to spread its net as far as possible to capture a class-coded, high-status and very rich clientele. Mona's view was that there was still 'too much ethnic stigma' attached to wearing Asian dress: 'It is drowning in this ethnicity and you need to say, "it's fashion, forget being ethnic, it's fashion".' So to attain an extensive market, they wanted to negate the ethnicity of the clothes.

I thought at the time that their market nervousness and ambiguity was a confused marketing strategy which, I wrote in my fieldnotes, would fail to win them a large enough customer base. Their message was too unclear. Yazz was in many ways like Tarun Tahiliani's shop, Ensemble,[3] in Bombay, which sells his own clothes and those of other leading designers in India. Yazz was another form of Ensemble but in an out-of-place situation, in London. Ensemble is owned and run by a local designer who sells the clothes of the exclusive, well-known local designers in a retail site local to his class network. It is, as Bourdieu says, a shared habitus (Bourdieu 1977) that plays itself out in commercial domains which are used by and determined by the same cultural aesthetics and sensibilities. Yazz, on the other hand, did not have a single design identity, although it was clear that what they stocked was produced by established and upmarket designers who had 'names'. They wanted to sell to white Europeans, yet there was a contradiction in their uneasiness about English women who only wanted to wear the clothes on their own terms. Yazz was having to grope for change in new, fast-changing cultural and commercial markets. These complex dynamics were perhaps reflected in their ambiguous design message for the impure markets they wanted to capture through selling 'national purities' in commercial commodities. However, Yazz did not succeed in the London market because it did not fully understand local markets. Their commerce did not grow out of the local scene and they failed to project clear images to produce strong market responses. This, to me, is the result of a form of ethnic timidity by people who are not sure of themselves in 'the West', where they want to succeed.

CONCLUSION

National elites versus diaspora design entrepreneurs

All these fashion entrepreneurs are making strong political statements – their commerce and commodities are highly politically charged. All of them engage in a discourse of cultural pride. In the case of Bubby, the damage done by racist taunts and stereotyping galvanizes her to create a defiant hybrid style that is both true to its context ('I do not want to lose it now,' she says) and responsive to the youthful sartorial mores of her subcultures. Geeta Sarin responded to English racism by being 'proud of our culture' in a British context, playing a pioneering design role in the suit economy. In Ritu's case, her design agendas emerged, not out of hostile encounters with racism, but through responses to the damage of imperialism and also through her own transformative personal experiences of being educated in the West, which prompted her to learn about her own cultural background and the arts and crafts of her country. Libas and Yazz share the revivalist arts and crafts agenda that is also the hallmark of the Ritu design identity. Wheareas Bubby and Geeta engage in a racialized narrative of cultural defiance and pride, that of the three subcontinentals is of reinventing traditions in contemporary form, the revival of old forms, ancient crafts and arts, some destroyed by British imperialists and others displaced by the machine processes and commodities of modern mass-production. Ritu, too, is making a political statement, reacting against the destruction wrought by former colonizers. She makes a nationalist design statement, intimately connected with the Indian nationalist movement, whose most influential members spearheaded the revival movement. She is definitely part of these powerful, opinion-forming elite groups, as a second-generation, contemporizing design interpreter. However, Ritu's frame is more politicized and nationalistic (having responded to the Indian Congress government's desire to revive languishing skills) than either Yazz or Libas. Libas performs interlocutor functions in presenting products that represent, as their publicity states, the 'high traditions and craft skills ... the finest from the East with the best of the West' (publicity material, 1996). Yazz's agenda, similarly, was to give wider exposure to contemporary 'top designers of India and Pakistan' (advertisement, *Libas International*, numerous issues) in a commercial space defined by a high art discourse.

All of them want also to engage in a form of cultural pedagogy through the market, taking Asian design to a wider public. The market for all of them is as much a medium of cultural flow as it is of economic and commodity exchange. The elite fashion entrepreneurs from the subcontinent state this as their explicit agenda in a way that Bubby and Geeta do not. Ritu explicitly states that she is part of 'an education process that there is an alternative ... this is what India is, we will not change'. This is directed both at local white and Asian populations. Yazz and Libas also aim to educate the local populations. Libas is explicitly geared towards the overseas market, as their clothes are not sold in the Pakistani markets. Bubby and Geeta already have the British Asian market since they are part of the communities amongst whom they initiated their enterprises. They created these markets by 'doing their own thing'. They created a style for themselves which found a market niche. They asserted their cultural agendas and voices through style and have found lucrative commercial markets. Their discourse is not explicitly educational but they have performed this function indirectly through an assertion of their hybrid styles which have found many spaces in a postmodern time. They express their agenda in more explicitly commercial terms. They clothe European women, not because they wish to educate them about Asian culture, as Ritu implies she does, but to make a profit. They do not negate market interests, nor engage in an arts and crafts agenda. Bubby and Geeta do not adopt a 'teaching' approach, because of their egalitarian co-designing and the fact that they are market-driven: they need to make a living.

In some respects, all of these designers are dynamic *national* actors, in the cultural and commercial zones in which they choose to operate. The design aesthetics of Ritu, Libas and Yazz are about an ancient nation, a past-orientated discourse of contemporizing an ancient nation's languishing craft skills and design vocabularies. Ritu, in particular, talks of representing India, of performing an ambassadorial function to present 'a unique style reflecting the ancient traditions of Indian craftsmanship in a contemporary vocabulary', as stated in her publicity material. The same applies to Libas, as is obvious from this statement about the owner Sehyr Saigol who, I was told, was designing 'classical things, reintroducing the past into today's world. She is a revivalist' (Mr Alam, manager of Libas shop, in interview with the author, 1996). They are signifying what is already significant. Diasporic fashion entrepreneurs like Bubby and Geeta, on the other hand, are engaged in future- and present-orientated dialogues of forming the nation as they go along. In contrast to Ritu, they are, in a way, *anti*-nationalistic. For them there is no national heritage and ancient past to preserve and revitalize, only a new nation to be formed and an emergent national space to negotiate. They celebrate the syncretic forms which enables them to assert themselves in the market. This agenda, which comes out of their cultural location, naturally has a close fit with the market moment. Their influential and often subversive designs are transformative, transformative of the nation shifting the sartorial, cultural, and commodity landscapes of Britain. They are generating new forms of Britishness and new identities of European-ness through a clothes economy of locally negotiated diasporic designs, which are themselves tempered by and transferred through global economies.

So, while Ritu, Yazz and Libas are preoccupied with the purity of their design aesthetic, for Bubby and Geeta an impure hybridizing form is formed all the time, without imposing the design templates of inherited and ancient data banks. The Ritu, Yazz and Libas design ethic stands aloof from – and remains suspicious of – such hybrid forms. Ritu refers to British Asian style somewhat pejoratively as 'gypsy clothing' while Mona at Yazz dislikes the tendency of white European customers to alter the pure form of the clothes they buy from the shop (despite the ethnic ambiguity of Yazz's publicity material). Yazz, Ritu and Libas wanted to sell what are and look like ethnic products to a non-ethnic market, through an anaesthetized rhetoric which wants fashion to forget ethnicity. The cultural aesthetics and commercial sensibilities of the diasporic designers, on the other hand, are products of their context: this, by its very nature is impure, as it deals with newness all the time. The elites are having to respond to the desire for impurity of form in locations in which they are themselves like new migrants, uncomfortable at dealing with their migrant status, albeit often a temporary one.

'Impurity' is in fact an integral part of the British Asian diasporic way of working, of their improvisational aesthetics. Bubby and Geeta respond eloquently to their customers through co-construction and customizing: these skills define their diasporic aesthetics thus creating the new licenses of participation. Both Bubby and Geeta deal constantly with their varied range of customers directly and are in their shops on a daily basis, even though they have assistants, whereas Ritu, as she told me, never sits in the shop in India or Britain. Since she professes that retailing is not her thing, she does not deal with the shop work but instead leads the design aspects: it is her staff who run her enterprises according to her design signatures. The same applies to Yazz and Libas. The owners, whose design philosophy the shops embody, do not dirty their hands with retailing. They remain distant from the day-to-day running of the shops and do not co-construct or engage with their customers directly.

At the same time, as I suggested earlier, Bubby and Geeta are much more explicit about their market and commercial interests. Bubby wanted her own label and to sell universally beyond ethnic domains, while Geeta openly says she wanted to sell to Europeans, especially in her Knightsbridge shop. Their design narratives are not contradictory in relation to the market. Their co-construction and customizing are features that also characterize the fast capitalism and new capitalist processes which constitute the economic terrains of our times (see Introduction). As locals, situated within a British milieux, they represent an authentic diasporic voice with a firmly grounded aesthetic which is cognizant of the local market. Ritu, too, represents an authentic voice but one that is in tune with Indian markets, rather than British. She presents herself as a consecrating belief producer in the Bourdieu sense defined by 'a refusal of the "commercial" ... a collective disavowal of commercial interests and profits' (Bourdieu 1977) in the economy of symbolic texts, the cultural goods of arts and crafts. Her London enterprise perhaps closed because her cultural moments of revivalist arts and crafts were out of synch with the market moments outside the perimeters of her nation. Yazz and Libas closed soon afterwards, I think for the same reasons. Their global commercial and cultural trajectories emerge from the arenas of the subcontinent, where they are powerful national actors, but their power no longer holds in settings where they are not local actors nor of the local. Hybrid locals like Bubby and Geeta, on the other hand, whose design enterprises are based in locations where they have lived all their lives, have the commercial advantage. They, too, are global actors in their ways. They use all the communicative relays and the cheaper subcontinental production sites that many larger capitalist enterprises also rely on. However, they draw their signifiers from their own settings, their lived locations, in which they have their markets. Unlike the elite design entrepreneurs, they do not signify what is already significant in their nations to translate for new markets of which they are neither products nor residents. They live in their own national locations with a different set of cultural and racial politics.

On a basic level, Ritu, Libas and Yazz, as outsiders, simply lacked the local knowledge necessary to make a long-term commercial success of their enterprises. More particularly, as members of their national elites, highly educated, they have the ability to classify their own domains but also the desire to classify and frame any landscape they are situated in. They are marketing their commodities from that classifying domain which confirms their power in their national arenas, presenting a pure authentic form. Crucially, they lack the negotiative principle of co-construction and improvization that defines the design vocabularies of diasporic design entrepreneurs. For elites, any negotiative interjection by local 'wealthy classy white people' who frequent their shops, is disturbing for their all-encompassing classificatory systems.

Moreover, subcontinental elites seem quite divorced from the ethnicized cultural battles that diasporics have gone through and now assert in commercial domains. The diasporics' designs encode these ethnicities, hard fought for as public registers of their recognition. Yazz, Libas and Ritu, and their personnel are oblivious to this or perhaps refuse to acknowledge these struggles. This is further reflected in their fascination with (and surprise at) European women wearing Asian dress, something which locally based Asians raised in a multicultural society would not bat an eyelid at.

The shop personnel of Yazz, Libas and Ritu did not perceive fundamental changes in the UK market because they have entered the market recently and did not know what had gone on before. Their understandings did not come from local experiences acquired over time, but from the superficial class-coded knowledges commonly articulated in their class circles. Also they entered the scene in the late-1980s (Libas) and mid-1990s (Yazz, Ritu) when the other shops in ethnic areas had been around for more than a decade. The groundwork was already in place. People used to buy the cloth and get it stitched into suits. There have been suit boutiques selling ready-made and designer clothes in

London since the early-1980s. As outsiders, they had missed the definitive movement from a fabric-and-sewing economy to one of ready-made clothes boutiques selling alongside the designer ready-made clothes. The later phenomenon of top Indian and Pakistani designer ranges sold by Ritu and Yazz was another aspect of selling exclusivity within exclusivity. It was a graded market in terms of exclusiveness with different classes of consumer and in geographically varied locations. This is not to say that there were not exclusive top designer ranges within ethnic areas, there were (and are). Variety Silk House in Wembley had stocked many of the top Indian designers like Madhu Jain, Xerxes Bandena, Zandra Rhodes, Ritu Beri, JJ Vallaya, Suneet Verma and so on since the mid-1980s. These enclaves of exclusivity were already established in East African Asian-dominated commercial spaces developed by multiply-migrant diaspora Asians who had already educated British markets into ethnic commodities.

Yazz and the others of this ilk are in a way 'foreigners' in British markets, holding stereotypical notions of British Asians from whom they remain distant and hold in disdain. Mona talked in terms of culturally lost and confused local Asian immigrants, as did Ritu and Libas personnel. I do not think British Asians are, after all, so confused. I think that the elites themselves are quite confused about how to respond to new markets in fast capitalist situations in a global city like London, in which they have much less familiarity and genuine self-confidence and little political and cultural clout. The diasporic fashion entrepreneurs are absolutely clear about their market messages, which they assert strongly and which emerge from their racialized experiences as locally based British Asians and as second-generation progeny of immigrants who have had to negotiate dissonance all their lives, mostly from positions of disadvantage. This is an opposite location from the Indian and Pakistani elites who are new to dissonant situations especially outside their national strongholds.

In the meantime, there is great vibrancy in the diasporic shops and others run by locally based entrepreneurs who sell in their local sites, where many of them were raised and remain resident. Some are flourishing enough to become chains of stores. They all exploit subcontinental production and purchasing sites and design expertise. They all use global communications to transfer clothes, to market them in Britain and to get local co-designed clothes manufactured in India, Pakistan and Bangladesh. These local enterprises have enormous site advantage – they are local Brits from migrant backgrounds who sell, politic, and do their cultural and commercial work in their local sites, whilst using global markets.

Part III

SUIT MARKETERS

INTRODUCTION

In this section I describe a trio of fashion entrepreneurs who are marketers of suits produced in large numbers by suppliers in the subcontinent. Sometimes these clothes are manufactured exclusively for them using the label of the enterprise but these mass marketers do not, on the whole, perform direct design functions, nor sell exclusive art clothes or co-constructed clothes, as do the fashion professionals whose commercial and cultural narratives I have presented in the previous section.

The definitive feature of their commerce is that they are locally based people who have a great deal of command over market information, both in Britain and the subcontinent. They know what sells locally and what they should import from the subcontinent. They know their customers well, often having shared their migration trajectories, and live amongst them as British Asians. They are residentially and commercially located in the midst of their markets. In having this grass-roots information on a day-to-day basis, they perform many indirect design functions by advising their subcontinental producers of 'what works' in their local British markets. Since they travel to India many times a year and are in constant contact with their suppliers, they transfer this information back all the time and thus have an impact on the designs produced for their markets. Although they do not engage in design functions directly with their customers, they are creative recontextualizers. They are savvy marketers who are intimately in touch with the street and their customer bases. They sell ready-made, mass-produced clothes made to British Asian specifications, clothes which have British Asian codes inserted into them through transferred market information. Although these marketers are not co-constructors of innovative designs, they are transferrers of design information by their circulation of market information back and forth to their Indian suppliers.

In Chapter 7, I outline the movements within the suit economy through the story of Daminis, a department chain store whose development parallels the settlement processes of British Asian communities. Daminis transformed itself from a small fabric and sari shop into marketers of ready-made suits manufactured under their own label. Their shops have multiplied in ethnic areas as well as, most recently, in a central London location.

In Chapter 8, I then describe two enterprises based in Southall, west London. I tell the marketing stories of wholesaler Komal Singh, the owner of Bombay Connections, who markets her clothes through a catalogue (a commercial text); and Mala Rastogi of Creations Boutique, whose commercial narrative is initially about selling from home – 'suitcase suit shops' in the private domain – moving on to a wholesaling and retailing enterprise in the public domain of Southall Broadway.

7

DAMINIS

A commercial community mama's shops

Daminis is a chain of four clothes department stores owned and run by Mrs Damini Mahendra, henceforth referred to as Mrs Damini, and her son, Deepak. I met Mrs Damini in 1996 at their newly opened shop in Green Street in east London (a few doors down from Bubby's shop, Chiffons, in fact). There are two other London shops, one in Southall Broadway and the other in the Edgware Road (opened December 2000), with the fourth branch located in Leicester in the East Midlands.

Mrs Damini started her first shop in east London in 1969. Her narrative is particularly illuminating because it reflects the story of the suit in Britain, encoding the cultural and commercial settlement processes amongst Asian communities in Britain that have moved beyond ethnic circuits.

A commercial matriarch: a networking community mama

Mrs Damini was widowed at twenty-five, soon after migrating to London, and was left with two small children to bring up in a new land. Her success in setting up an enterprise on her own (which in the 1990s has become a chain of four shops) is for me a compelling cultural and commercial narrative. Mrs Damini is a really likeable, warm-hearted person. She is very popular amongst her huge network of customers. She is a skilled saleswoman and adept at dealing with people from many walks of life. She is located in a community of which she has been a part for over thirty years. She knows her markets intimately. Her customers invite her to their weddings and engagements, to their children's functions, to endless family occasions within her extensive networks. One of her relatives visiting from India had to inquire of her, after seeing great numbers of people who greeted her fondly, if there was anyone in the world she did not know! She explained that this is because of the shop and 'saray andhay jandhay' (people come and go). Hence I call her 'a commercial mama of the community'. She performs the functions of an honorary kinswoman in a personalized, community-mediated, commercial context. Many people call her by a kinship term like 'aunt' or the Punjabi equivalent 'masiji', or even 'penji', the term for sister. Komal Singh of Bombay Connections whom I write about in the next chapter, a wholesaling suit entrepreneur who knows her through community connections, knows her as 'aunty'. So do my cousins who live around east London, who have been buying fabric and clothes from her for many years. They bought their own wedding clothes and those that they wore at their brother's wedding from her earlier shop on Romford Road. I first heard of her from them twenty years ago. But I only met her personally and saw her new Green Street shop during my fieldwork in 1996.

Her pivotal position in the community is obvious from the interactions in the shop. For example, when I was in the shop, a Punjabi Muslim couple came in and asked her why she had not attended their daughter's wedding the previous weekend – they would have so much liked her to have done so. This was one of the endless invitations which she could not have possibly accepted or, having accepted, actually attended. This couple had bought outfits worth £3,000. They were not rich, she told me, but really 'good-at-heart people'. Another loyal customer came in with her brother and sister-in-law from Canada. She had come to introduce her relatives to Mrs Damini and to look around the displayed merchandise.

Daminis' transformative commercial trajectory

Mrs Damini traces the development of her shop from the time she started it in 1969. As a single mother with small children it was 'very hard to start the shop', she says. The late 1960s was when Asians were just beginning to come into Britain in greater numbers. Previously the common pattern of migration had been of men migrating on their own but now the process of reconstituting families got under way. Mrs Damini came from the Punjab. When she opened up the shop there were few Asians in the area. She says she was lonely and 'if I saw one [an Asian] I would grab their arm and invite them to my house'. She started a cloth-sari shop because she herself liked to wear good clothes. Also, she had a way with clothes. She had no business knowledge because she had been a housewife. These days, she talks with pride of her 'business-minded' son who joined her in the early 1980s when he left college. Now in his mid-forties, it is his drive that has taken the shop into ready-mades, transforming it into a department store; he has computerized the stocking systems to keep track of merchandise in all the stores; and also experimented with new retailing computer technologies. However, Mrs Damini remains the one who buys the stock, signs the cheques and controls the money. She is also the overseeing matriarch who supervises the activities in the Green Street shop.

At the time when she started her shop, Green Street was a derelict place and not the sought-after street it has become now.[1] It was a dilapidated street similar to, say, the Broadway and King Street in Southall, Ealing Road in Wembley or Tooting High Street in south London, which have all now been transformed into vibrant, booming commercial arenas.

The suit fabric shops in the initial stages of the business in the late 1960s had real difficulty in finding stock from wholesalers because the commercial infra-structure of wholesaling was not yet established. There were a couple of whole-salers in 1969 which were, Mrs Damini says, 'tootay pajay', literally, broken-down places with limited stock. As well as fabric on the roll, she stocked saris, sari blouses and petticoats and some dresses. She sold Japanese nylon saris because this is what people wore and she sold a lot of them. She sold Japanese polyesters that were used to make suits then – these are still popular for domestically stitched suits by seamstresses.

By the 1980s, however, the cloth and sari market was no longer as profitable and Deepak, in particular, felt that their returns were too small for their expen-diture on rents, rates and shop assistants' salaries. So, with the development of an economy of ready-made clothes, in their new shops Mrs Damini and her son have moved away from fabrics to the more profitable, mass-produced suit sectors. She says, 'We had Benarsi silk saris, French chiffon saris, we kept every-thing. We had a very good business for twelve years; then, the lease for that shop finished.'

The new store in Green Street now focuses almost exclusively on ready-made clothes. Wedding outfits and menswear are on the first floor; ready-made women's suits are on the ground floor, together with children's clothes. Cloth and fabrics are relegated to the top floor.

It is an impressive store in terms of size and fixtures and it benefits from the old and established clientele developed over nearly thirty years. The shop is on the corner site of a former petrol station and was built according to Deepak's design specifications, glass-fronted, with wooden floors; this is his 'dream shop, his lifetime's work', his mother explains. He has modelled it on London and Indian department stores, like Sheetal and Roopam in Mumbai. A staff of six or so young shop assistants work with Mrs Damini. Mostly young British-raised Asian women, they wear a uniform of black and green salwaar suits. They often have high black platform shoes; they transfer all the street styles they generally wear in interpreting their green and black suit uniforms.

Fast global connections: ready-made suits from India

Although Mrs Damini came from India as a young married woman and had her extended family living in India, she did not have commercial connec-tions with wholesaling cloth merchants or clothing manufacturers. Like the majority of other London-based enterprises I write about, she had to struggle to establish connections with wholesalers in India who could export what she needed.

When she first started her business, and for many years afterwards, her sup-pliers were selling saris and not ready-made suits as this economy had not emerged. So, in the mid-1980s, when Daminis wanted to 'go into ready-mades', again they had to seek out new suppliers. Initially, they were few and far between though now the design economy has been professionalized by designers trained in the Indian state-sponsored design schools. Mrs Damini paints the scenario thus:

> We had to find exporters. We found them ourselves. Luckily they were very good people, now the father has died, a Gujarati people. They still send us everything. We just go and choose whatever we want . . . They sell ready-made clothes now, but in the early days, even they only had loose material and that is what we had in our shops, that is what we bought from them – crêpes, shamu satin – and we used to have local tailors who would sew the clothes here if customers wanted them to . . . But then there was the ready-made trend. The trend just started seven to eight years ago. But at that time, in 1989 to 1990, it was very difficult to find designers in India who were making these clothes. But then there was a flood when every person in India said they were designers. Recently, everyone says they are designers, everyone has become a designer.
>
> (Mrs Damini, interview with author, 1996)

Mrs Damini and her son Deepak visit India much more frequently now, every six weeks, which is 'six to seven times a year because the styles have changed every two months', she says.

She says she does all the buying in Delhi, Bombay and Calcutta. She developed the links with her suppliers in these places gradually. Some of them introduced themselves because:

> . . . especially when you are buying big, people come to you. They come looking for you. You do not have to look for them. Suppliers come of their own accord when they hear you are in town to buy. But in the beginning you have to search them out yourself. A lot of suppliers have their own retail showrooms.
>
> (Ibid.)

She says that she also learnt from her buying mistakes on many occasions and that she has done:

> . . . wrong buying because India is full of thieves who cheat. Also I have made mistakes myself. Once we have bought stuff in bulk and it's here, what can we do? We cannot send it back. We have paid for it, paid VAT [value added tax] and freight costs.
>
> (Ibid.)

She explained how she buys the merchandise and how she decides on the colours and styles. I asked her if she watches fashion trends. This is a big facet of both Bubby's and Geeta's commercial style:

It just comes to your head if you are seeing so many things. They do not suggest but we let them know before we go to India that we are coming. At least ten days in advance, we inform the designers that we are coming. So they get the maximum number of designs together before we get there. If we like these designs we order. Otherwise, we suggest the lengths, colours, width, embroidery ... Like the lenghas, especially the wedding lenghas, it's not like our days. We wore ordinary lenghas, whichever ones we were given. These were often stitched at home. These days it's not like that because *girls want lenghas that no one else has worn.* We struggle for that. We try to get the designs and colours that no one else stocks. We give them many suggestions. If we buy ready-made stuff they have made we cannot sell that here. We have to get things made to our specifications and many times they get things wrong. They already have designs and we suggest adaptations, changes that would sell here. We say this is too traditional or this has too much embroidery. We say we want something different ... Like Benarsi [in the past considered to be timeless, classic saris] are out of fashion now. But shamu satin and crêpes with embroidery[2] are in fashion now.

(Ibid.)

The other retail processes that have changed are the rapid speed with which they can get outfits from India and the ease of telephone contact, which is cheaper than ever before and with clearer connections. Also transport costs have come down with the establishment of many competitive international courier services which operate with increased speed and efficiency. Daminis, like Bubby's and Geeta's shops, has constant visits from couriers bearing packages from India. They get courier parcels of specially customized clothes arriving several times each day, in addition to what is already in the shop stock. The garments that arrive from India can have small alterations and fitting changes made to them in London by a network of seamstresses Mrs Damini knows. In fact, a seamstress who does this for her came to the shop whilst I was there and Mrs Damini explained to her the small changes that needed to be made to the neck and the waist of the outfit to give a personalized fit for the buyer. Also clothes can be individually sized and made to customer specifications though, unlike Bubby and Geeta, Mrs Damini does not negotiate a design. She says:

We can get the pieces in the shop made to size for anyone. We get three to four pieces that arrive from India every day. We have our own people and designers working there. We know the number and the colour and can get it made very easily. We just fax them. We have an office in Bombay and she can get things done. We have people in Bangalore, Calcutta, Delhi. We buy different things from many places. We have our own label, Daminis. There are many designers who make for us but the label is our own. In the past we used to have to deal with one courier company to send our things to England. Now there is so much competition. We used to have to spend £20–30 on one suit. Now it's cheaper and very efficient and it's so easy [it costs around £8 per suit]. We used to think twice about calling India, now we call India fifteen to twenty times a day and the calls go through very quickly. People were laughing at me in Bombay. I could not get a local call through but got the international one in *one second*. We fax India every day and we get suits every day for odd-sized people or special requests. Someone is tall or short and we charge the same amount because otherwise we would lose the customer.

(Ibid.)

Flooded markets and rapid obsolescence of suits

Mrs Damini says that the market is now 'flooded' with designer clothes, 'nothing like the early and mid-1980s when it was very difficult to get hold of suits' (ibid.). Mrs Damini's explanation for this flooding of the market by ready-made suits is that women now wear a new suit just a few times rather than passing it on or wearing it on many occasions. The suits become obsolescent fast. She explains that:

> ... the first generation did not spend so much money on clothes. They used to make a few suits and wear those all their life. I am talking about India in my time [she is in her mid sixties]. India's young generations and also those here in England, they want to go to one party and they want a new suit. They do not want to wear that again a second time. So naturally there would be demand. It's the same here. Like, for example, I had a customer in the shop yesterday. They bought four suits for their small kids for £400 each. I told them to get them made a little big so they can wear them for a while. She replied immediately that they will not wear it a second time. In the past, they used to make one suit do the rounds for four weddings.

(Ibid.)

This point about the increased consumption of clothes, the lack of recycling of clothes and their rapid redundancy, is a characteristic common to many consumer markets. We talked about how consumer attitudes have changed and how people do not reuse clothes as they used to even in the very recent past. Also, there are many more social functions to attend now; in fact there is a dramatic increase. These parties started a long time ago in the early 1970s but the young generation, she says, have parties every weekend. In addition, there is the increased number of social functions surrounding the wedding ceremony, each requiring a different outfit of clothes. Mrs Damini estimates that she would supply four or five suits to each wedding family member. In common with the other successful entrepreneurs I spoke to, weddings were the mainstay of Mrs Damini's business and ensured that it and similar suit shops flourished even during the recession of the early 1990s when other Asian businesses foundered. Mrs Damini puts it thus:

> The recession in the early 1990s had affected so many Asian businesses. They have closed but not the suits businesses. Most of these shops that used to sell Japanese materials started keeping ready-made suits and did well. I have sold so much cloth for many years before going to ready-mades in the past four to five years. The recession did not hit the suits business much at all; in fact, the suit shops increased.
>
> (Ibid.)

Mrs Damini is also keenly aware of the impact of women's increased economic independence. We talked about the earnings of young women and the difference this has made to the market, together with decreasing family size. She said:

> Naturally, parents are not going to spend £200 on a suit easily but the girls have no problem doing that. These days there is no good piece below £150–200. Girls in the past, in my time, did not make a fuss about their clothes. They wore what their parents gave them. Their father earned and was the only earner. Girls did not have their own money. There were more children, sometimes six children, and they had to pay for their education and everything else. There was less money to spend on clothes and people had to reuse their clothes for their younger children, pass them down to get wear out of them.
>
> (Ibid.)

A beautiful young Asian woman in denim jeans and a white blouse came into the shop while I was there. She was talking on her mobile phone for a long while as she was investigating the shop merchandise. Mrs Damini sold her some gold-plated silver jewellery and said she was not a 'time-waster' because she bought with no fuss. She knew she had 'apni kamayi', her own earnings. However, another young woman, a teenager who tried on ten outfits, was a classic time-waster. Mrs Damini told the shop assistant not to spend any more time with her and to attend to the other customers. There are, apparently, many time-wasting teenagers who do not want to buy. They have little cash but go into these shops to try out outfits they cannot possibly afford. They fulfil their desires for these clothes temporarily by trying on as many outfits as they can get away with.

The Princess Diana suit moment in Daminis

Princess Diana was receiving widespread coverage for wearing salwaar-kameez suits during the time I was visiting Daminis in 1996. One particular picture taken of her at a charity gala in aid of Imran Khan's cancer hospital had shown her wearing a cream suit. There was a great deal of publicity about this salwaar-kameez suit on television, and on the front pages of popular and serious newspapers as well as in various magazines. The next day a Muslim woman in her late sixties had came into the shop to ask Mrs Damini if she had an outfit similar to that worn by Princess Diana. Mrs Damini encouraged her to look at some outfits she told her were like Diana's suits. Actually there were no suits I could see that were similar to Diana's but I think Mrs Damini was simply encouraging the customer to see what was in the shop. Mrs Damini said Diana had made a great deal of impact, with many people asking about her and the suits she wore:

> She is beautiful, elegant and she can wrap a piece of cloth around her and she would look beautiful.... Anything can suit her. Jemima [Goldsmith-Khan] has made a big difference also. People ask about her suits also, naaldhay [similar] suits. We did ask our people in India to make a couple of suits like hers. We knew the material she was wearing so it was not difficult to get them made.
>
> (Ibid.)

Soon after this, a photographer from the *Independent* came to the shop to take pictures for its fashion pages because of the interest generated by Princess Diana. I shall return to her impact again in the diasporic sewing cultures chapters which follow.

Second generation interventions: cyberizing the suit economy

As I have already indicated, Deepak Mahendra, a British Asian son, has significantly extended the business established by his mother. Like all the other prominent entrepreneurs I have written about, he too expresses a desire to break into the mainstream:

> Ultimately ... we would like to aim upmarket and break into the European market with our Asian clothes.
>
> (Deepak Mahendra, quoted in *Libas* 1997:139)

He pushed for Daminis to be included in the prestigious London Festival of Fashion in 1994, earning praise from *Libas* as:

... the only [Asian] representatives in a mainstream British event ...
rubbing shoulders with designers like Vivienne Westwood ... [and] top
super-models like Naomi Campbell to model their clothes.

(*Libas* 1994, Vol 7:111)

Deepak has already successfully taken the shop into the ready-made, mass
market. The shop represents a commoditized market at a time when the suit
had been popularized and worn by many people. The ways in which Deepak is
marketing reflect his second-generation British location: the shop is designed by
professional architects and is a computerized commercial space, even experi-
menting, as we shall see, with new forms of retailing using specially designed
software. When I was in the shop, there were glitches with the new computer
system and Mrs Damini was not sure if it was worth spending so much money
on this elaborate system. She said it was her son who had wanted it and that he
was now spending a lot of time with the suppliers to get it sorted out. Deepak
could see its potential in a business he will inherit from his mother. He keeps up
with new British retailing systems and is also supremely au fait with Asian consumer trends.

Daminis are not innovators but mass marketers within ethnic circuits.
Deepak explicitly states that in most cases suits are bought ready-made and
directly transferred from India to Britain without any design input. In this
respect, Daminis is a direct recontextualizer. Some of their suits are specially
designed in large numbers for their four stores. Mrs Damini provides much valuable design information and market inputs to their Indian manufacturers about
what is required for the British market. Although Daminis sizes clothes for customers individually and gets them made in the colours they want from the
design template of a garment already in the shop, their clothes are not exclusive
like those sold by Bubby Mahil and Geeta Sarin who, in addition to the standardized merchandise that they stock in their shops, also co-design made-to-
measure clothes for their customers.

The other second-generation British Asian input is from Dakshad Govind,
who manages Mrs Damini's Leicester store and works closely with Deepak. Born
in Malawi, she is now in her mid-thirties. Her parents own a grocery store in
Leicester. She works in Daminis on Saturdays and during her holidays and has
done so for seven years. In 1996, when I interviewed her, she was studying for a
Master's degree in Business at Leicester University, specializing in computers
and interactive retailing. The only member of her family in the clothes business, she wanted to 'study something in the fashion line' while her father
wanted her to 'study something that would get her a job', so her Master's is a
good compromise. She is also efficient at managing people and good at building
staff relationships. She organizes outings for the staff 'twice a year by hiring a
van and taking them to some place of interest and picnics. This builds good
rapport between the girls and they come to know each other better,' she says.

Unlike Mrs Damini, Dakshad sees clear regional differences between the

London and Leicester markets. The latter is a predominantly East African Gujarati community with, Dakshad says, 'a lot more money, a higher standard of living.... We can't sell the same clothes in Leicester that we do in [east] London because it is a much more sophisticated market. It's much more an African Asian market.'

Dakshad Govind, who herself comes from a multiply-migrant background, was working on the new concepts of interactive retailing which will lead to the 'cyberization of the suit'. Since the late 1990s there have been a number of websites, often entering the market from India, where Internet users can co-design a garment on the Web. But what Dakshad was doing at the time was to develop in-shop computer software packages. She has been using her academic background to create or adapt a software program that can help customers try on clothes 'virtually'. She said:

> You will be able to see suits on a virtual model from different angles. So instead of trying on an outfit, the customers will be able to see the suits on a virtual model ... this gives them an idea, without trying the clothes on, of what they might look like as well as being less taxing on the wear and tear of clothes which is a big headache for retailers. The virtual model could be sized to the customer's body type, this was not difficult to do. You could also video the outfit from different angles, just like taking a picture from different perspectives and angles, and feed that into the computer. This prevents wear and tear on the clothes and the customers get views of the outfit from different perspectives.
>
> (Dakshad Govind, interview with the author, 1996)

Dakshad feels they have to pay careful attention to all these new technology aspects because in future they will be selling suits to a highly computer-literate population.

Interestingly, she saw the ready-made suit economy as resulting in a loss of culture and identity. She says Indian designers trained in New York, London and Paris are '... becoming Western ... they are taking up Western trends and losing their Indianness'. When women stitched their own suits, they kept their cultures alive, unlike the women now who are losing these skills and, with them, their identities. When women made their own clothes there was a design egalitarianism and not a design hegemony imposed by industrially-made boutique suits. This is a theme to which I shall return in the following chapters on sewing cultures.

Concluding remarks

This case study illustrates the transition and change of a woman's business and of the suit itself, in the setting of a changing community. Daminis is a localized enterprise that remains local but works through the global markets of fast capitalism. Mrs Damini's story is that of a struggle to set up a business in a new immigrant location. Her business know-how, her ability to exploit her personality and her networking skills are all illuminating processes of the suit story. Daminis' shop narrative encodes the different phases of settlement as well as the changing cultural and consumer patterns. The development of the shops also reveals the developments in Indian markets and the ways in which British Asians are using their increased cultural confidence within their own areas of Britain to access Indian production and design sites to their advantage. The fact that these diaspora people have maintained and asserted their cultures in Britain, where they have established commercial spaces and local markets, at the same time benefits the Indian producers. The latter have found new markets outside India for their products, markets which they are supremely keen to cultivate and from which the Indian government wants them to extract valuable foreign currency.

Daminis is now located in mainstream arenas and is also an established enterprise that has been around for almost the same length of time as Asians have been settled in London. It is using all the processes of the new technologies – the faxes, courier services, frequent calls to India, regular visits to purchase merchandise from India, the made-to-measure sizing, the customization according to customer specifications – to make it a business located within the global markets of the world that is at the same time absolutely localized. It uses department retail store techniques, combining them with British computer technologies and retail architecture, professionally designed, to sell to British customers the shopping experience, the surroundings and the products. Deepak is using the department store format and combining it, with the help of Dakshad, into a computerized, co-ordinated chain store. In developing interactive virtual cyber-technologies to sell their merchandise, they are stepping into the future because they anticipate correctly that many future buyers will be computer-literate.

It is interesting to compare Daminis, as a diasporic business, with the diasporic enterprises of Bubby Mahil and Geeta Sarin. Although there is not the same level of negotiation of design through the sketches that Geeta and Bubby engage in, Daminis too know their markets thoroughly, as long-standing locals with an established customer base. They benefit from the same ease of communication with India which facilitates the flow of goods and their ability to meet their customers' exact requirements. Daminis are highly customer-orientated in their made-to-measure, but also with the approach of 'here is an outfit already made and we can get the same thing made for you in a different size and colour'. Their suppliers and Bombay office can co-ordinate this made-to-measure approach because they have information at hand about the clothes that are stocked in England and can replicate them with ease. Faxes, couriers, constant phone calls and frequent visits to India aid all these processes of fast capitalism enormously.

As Deepak says, he wants to move into the mainstream where Asian clothes are worn by everyone. The development of the shop from a peripheral suit fabrics and sari shop to a chain of four in the main established Asian centres of Britain, and the recent expansion to London's Edgware Road, already reflects the establishment of Asian communities as culturally and ethnically confident entities who are appropriating cultural and commercial spaces in Britain to assert new forms of Britishness. These dynamics are thus already impacting on the cultural mainstream and creating novel textures. Furthermore, there are the inputs of second-generation British Asian young people who are coming of age in a global world connected through all kinds of communications technologies. These locally raised young are transferring some of these new cyber technologies to transform a once negatively coded ethnic economy into the future of cyber-designed shopping. These are the people once on the margins of commerce and culture who are negotiating a new, mainstream cultural, capital and commercial world. They have been produced through migration and movement by entre-preneurial British Asian women like Mrs Damini, a commercial, community mama who connects the world together through her locally based, globally con-nected markets.

8

NETWORKING MARKETERS OF READY-MADE SUITS

In this chapter, I describe a duo of fashion entrepreneurs based in Southall, west London: Komal Singh of Bombay Connections who has always been a wholesaler of suits, and Mala Rastogi of Creations Boutique, who transformed a 'suitcase suits' enterprise, selling from home, into both retailing and wholesaling through her current shop. Like Daminis, the redistributive, selling functions of these two enterprises are more central to their businesses than design functions. Their design interventions are implicit in their role as London-based importers, locals in their local markets, but with enormous access to multiple sites of production and design in the subcontinent. They are, in a way, 'organic marketers', who are located and raised within the communities they sell, the equivalent of Gramsci's 'organic intellectuals' (Gramsci 1971).[1] Like these intellectuals who have a grounded aesthetic which is encoded in their intellectual pursuits, being close to the communities that have produced them, these marketers live amid and understand intimately the markets in which they sell. These entrepreneurs are products of locations in which they initiate and maintain their markets. This local residence and knowledge gives them commercial durability as suit marketers. They are also racialized as British Asians and use these experiences implicitly, not explicitly as does Bubby. Their paramount agenda is the marketing and selling of ready-made suits, mass-produced suits.

Performing connections: Komal Singh of Bombay Connections

Based in Heston, an area neighbouring Southall in west London, Komal Singh imports ready-made suits wholesale from India which she sells on to shops all over the UK. Her hallmark is Bombay styles, epitomized by synthetic fabrics with beadwork and plastic embellishments. She describes them as 'bordering on the brash' (see Figure 8.1). Komal recontextualizes these 'semi-mass-market' clothes through her catalogue, Bombay Connections. Komal is unusual in not having a shop in combination with a wholesaling enterprise. She is the only person I have found who is a wholesaler with a regular catalogue which individual customers and retailers can view before buying her clothes. Customers

Figure 8.1 Chiffon mania – the easy-to-maintain synthetic chiffon dress-like kameez is inset with a boldly embroidered panel, studded with red 'stones'.

Source: Komal Singh.

can go to shops that sell her clothes whilst wholesalers buy from her west London premises directly. As I describe, the catalogue catalyzed the success of her wholesaling enterprise by giving her enormous legitimacy in the market.

Komal's suit narrative in Britain

Familiar with Southall and its vicinity since her childhood in the early 1960s, Komal knows well the transformations in the suit, having seen them unfold under her very eyes. Southall was and is still populated mostly by direct migrants who did not have the traditions of sewing at home to the same extent as the multiply-migrant suit-wearing women. Komal's experience was largely of directly migrant India-raised women who were used to a professional sewing economy of tailors in the subcontinent who stitched suits for them. Komal describes how most women living in Southall at that time would buy their suit fabric while on holiday in India and either have it made up by a tailor there or once back in Southall. Both, she says, were mostly unsatisfactory:

> ... [in Southall] we would be crying and saying, 'But you have ruined my fabric!' And the usual thing, that things were never made on time. This was going on with everyone. That's the only way suits were made in those days ... You would find someone who was stitching at home who had two children screaming on top of their heads and who was not particularly good, or you had professional tailors in India – who were very over-worked and who would say it would take a week but never give it to you. So that was what was happening. Ready-made suits were not available in India or here.
>
> (Komal Singh, interview with the author, 1996)

Komal describes also the semi-ready-made economy which emerged for a time, a five- or six-yard length of fabric that had the borders and the edges of the suits embroidered, i.e., the sleeves, or the ends of the sleeves and the side splits. These pieces of cloth, usually the traditional silk, were then stitched by tailors or by seamstresses at home who worked within the constraints of the existing design.

Then, when in Bombay during 1986, Komal met an enterprising woman who used synthetic fabrics like chiffons, crêpes and satins. Unlike silk, these were crease-resistant and easily washable. Komal was inspired by them and the innovative ways in which the woman had placed the embroidery. Komal had an instinct that these new styles and materials were going to become 'a big thing'. So, in 1987, starting with £10,000 capital she had been given by her brother, she had some suits stitched to bring back to Britain:

> ... I did a fashion show and I advertised all over. We hired out a hall and we got a young choreographer. We managed to get some young

people. I had black models wearing the salwaar-kameez and white and Indian models. The music was completely Western. This fashion show was a great success and that is what gave me the motivation to continue because I realized how much of a buzz it created in the audience. It was big for me. I was expecting 400–500 people but there were more.

(Ibid.)

Success was far from immediate, however, and it was only with the catalogue that Bombay Connections really took off, as I shall describe below. Nonetheless, the market moment was ripe. The suit-wearing trend was by this time very much in place in Southall, as Komal also describes:

At that time, girls would go to school in uniform but come home and wear a shalwaar-kameez. If your parents went for lunch or dinner somewhere you would wear one. I was very familiar with a shalwaar-kameez, it was nothing extraordinary.

(Ibid.)

This is a significantly different suit-wearing profile from Bubby, for example, raised in the east End of London, who was reluctant to wear a suit because of the racist taunts she was subjected to there.

An image-conscious recontextualizer

Komal is a translator and an interpreter. She is not a designer herself but works with teams of designers. She sells through a text which is about the visuals, the pictures and the words, the story of Bombay clothes as told though her British Asian design vocabularies. She says:

Designers in Bombay often have the gift of the gab. They can make things look expensive and the gift of the gab is played in the clothes ... We work with a lot of different designers and manufacturers in the subcontinent. We work with over fifty different designers in India, Pakistan and Bangladesh and lots of boutiques and companies.

(Ibid.)

She is a transnational diasporic and captures this phenomenon by her hybrid style of synthetic clothes, blending elements that do not spring from co-construction but from Komal's own multiple-sited experiences. She avoids the traditional silk which is hard to look after, either requiring starching at home or dry-cleaning:

We can't do starching things here. I really stay away from this fabric. I prefer chiffons, georgettes, linens. I basically use clothes that have polyester content and do not crease up so much and they are easier to wash and maintain.

(Ibid.)

She also identifies differences in the Bombay Connections style in the cut of the suits: 'Almost nothing I make is a basic kurta cut. I make dress styles where I have combined dresses.' She combines dresses (i.e., a European dress silhouette) with salwaars. The salwaars she uses are of different kinds with a variety of cuts depending on the current styles. She also uses parallels, the straight trousers, with the dress-type kameez tops, instead of the regular, classic salwaar.

Like the other transnationalized locals I have described in this book, Komal Singh has a complex, rounded understanding of her British markets and those in India. She can therefore successfully analyse the styles of designers who fit her design and marketing templates:

> Bombay Connections is not about producing ten beautiful outfits but about producing 1,000 different outfits for a semi-mass market, not a mass market but the closest you could get to buying designer wear at high-street prices. I consider my clothes to be ready-made because designer wear is like the haute couture retail. At retail my outfits sell at £125–295.

(Ibid.)

Her retail market is 95 per cent Asian, maybe even 98 per cent. She says that: 'Many non-Asians love our clothes, black people love our clothes. In places like Tooting, Croydon, [in South London], where there is a black community, 20 per cent are black customers.' In fact Channel One, a London cable TV channel, did a programme on the suits in 1996, using black models. She supplies stores in all the major British cities – Birmingham, Bradford, Glasgow, Leeds, Leicester, Manchester. She says generally there is a problem with Asian retailers because they are not presentation-aware or image-conscious and do not spend money on displays. She chastised them for not spending money on window dressing and display props for their shops, the very mechanisms needed to display wares at best visual advantage to attract customers. As I have mentioned in the chapter on Daminis, a great deal of their time and money has gone into creating visually effective shopfronts and interior displays. The second-generation retailers are generally more alert to presentation and shop aesthetics.

Catalogue marketing: fashion as text and images

Komal's catalogue is her textual instrument of fashion which dictates her visions for her clothes. She did not bring the catalogue out till 1990, almost three years after she first started the business in 1987. Although her fashion shows and exhibitions of her clothes were well received, they did not enable her to break into the well-established, male-dominated retail markets of Southall and elsewhere. The male entrepreneurs were seemingly unaware of the emerging trend in ready-made suits and, moreover, dismissive of Komal as a woman. Although she had total belief in the quality and saleability of her clothes, Komal was not interested in setting up a shop herself, preferring the relative freedoms of wholesale:

> I do not like the idea of opening the shop at a particular time and shutting it. I like to travel. I like to buy and sell and move about and I also like a quick turnover which retail does not have. I like to work for me.
>
> (Ibid.)

Then, while putting together the advertising for her clothes, Komal realized that one of her strengths was presentation:

> Not that I photographed anything myself but I had the knack of getting the best photographers, and picking up the best photograph, and getting best printing done to really get high-quality glamour images ... We advertised in both *Stardust*[2] and *Libas* magazines, glamorous images and, lo and behold, shops started to ring me up and wanted to see my collection.
>
> (Ibid.)

Initially, she wanted to launch a magazine herself but did not have sufficient funds. She did have a marketing precedent in Geeta Sarin's Rivaaz catalogue, however. In fact the Bombay Connections catalogue was much more successful than Komal had anticipated. It enabled Komal to build up an image of, as she puts it, 'a high-funded designer sitting in some prestigious office', which brought her far more clients than turning up at the shops in person:

> I had to create a distance and image and that worked immediately. It was amazing. I had three clients right away. Two weeks later these people were asking me for stock and then I had ten clients and then thirty and so on, all around the early 1990s. I had my own office and people had to come to me. I realized I had to turn the game around and had to be in a more powerful position.
>
> (Ibid.)

She talks about her catalogue representing her 'vision' of what her clothes should be. It is her ideal vision statement presented in textual form. She writes in the catalogue, 'The vision of Bombay Connection is a cosmopolitan look ...' (Bombay Connections 1995).

She is also emphatic about representation, the photographic images and the models, the people who present that image. Her marketing strategy is 'clothes as text and text as clothes'. Her catalogues demonstrate her sharp understanding of the critical issues of representation and presentation, the Roland Barthes notion of 'written clothing and image clothing' (Barthes 1990), the visuals as text and the potency of the text as an instrument of image commerce. The textual elements constitutes her first interface with the public and the entrepreneurs who buy from her wholesaling, mass-producing enterprise. These potential buyers look at the pictures and the discourse accompanying them in the Bombay Connections catalogue before they come and see her clothes in her wholesale unit in west London. The text catalysed her sales and also legitimated her credentials in the market. Its publication gave her exposure to wider markets, establishing her emerging business in the developing ready-made suit market.

Crucially, Komal's ability to create a glamorous image and her understanding of representation changed the commercial and gender balance of power, in much the same way that the Rivaaz catalogue had done earlier for Geeta Sarin. The focus shifted from her gender to her publication, giving her the space and the distance to project the clothes she wanted to sell. The catalogue neutralized condescending male attitudes and also allowed her to reposition herself: retail entrepreneurs then had to come to her to view the clothes, on her terrain and on her terms. Komal is thus able to sell her clothes through a decontextualized commercial text that makes her design identity explicit but her 'female genderedness' implicit.

Capturing movements in clothes

I found Komal's discussions about clothes fascinating, especially in her emphasis on 'movement' and 'connections'. Her narrative emphasizes the fluidity and the movement in her clothes, just like her own constant movements across national boundaries and also those that characterize the story of the suit .

She described how she captures the movement and the connection in her clothes by relating it to her autobiography. She was six years old in 1962 when she came to London but went back and forth between England and India till she was in her late teens because, she says, her 'mother could not decide where to settle':

> Had I come in 1962 and stayed here . . . and just gone back home for a three-week holiday like a lot of Indian families do, I would have been a lot more British but because I had so much of my schooling and exposure there and so much exposure here, you know I consider myself to be a truly cross-cultural type of product.
> (Komal Singh, interview with the author, 1996)

She says the suit business became all the more important to her as a means of maintaining the link between London and India:

My going into shalwaar-kameez was particularly because I wanted to keep up the connection between India and London. When I grew up I wanted to go into a business which would mean trading between the two countries so that I could keep up this lifestyle that I quite liked. My moving about between the two countries has strongly influenced the clothes that I wear and the clothes that I market and design and trade.

(Ibid.)

Her focus on connections is also obvious from the terms she prefers when referring to the suit as two separates joined or put together. She dislikes it being called a Punjabi suit: 'I never called it a Punjabi suit. I feel that has been its downfall. It's such an unromantic name. I like jhoras as they say in Pakistan. Jhora refers to a connection, an ensemble, jhora means a co-ordinated set.'

I am very struck by how much these fashion entrepreneurs' commercial lives and design agendas reflect their own biographies. All of them have developed enterprises that encapsulate their migration patterns, their class and cultural locations, and their experiences of race. Their enterprises are fundamentally a reflection of their lives and travels. Komal captures these experiences, the ruptures and the sutures, the pains and pleasures of her multiple journeys:

I am not very British at all and at the same time I am not very Indian at all. It sounds very easy now I am grown up but when I was young it was very very traumatic. It was very upsetting because when I came to England and when I went to my first year in my senior school, we were two Indian girls in my class. My hair was past my knees and everyone was wearing miniskirts and had blonde hair. We stuck out like a sore thumb and yet when I was a little more sophisticated and I went to India, I stuck out like a sore thumb because I looked too advanced. I was expelled out of school in India just for having my top button open on my shirt. I used to feel hot so I had two buttons open, my principal expelled me. It was quite hellish because I was a misfit everywhere.

(Ibid.)

She laughs. Komal also talks about the influences on her personal style and the designs that she is interested in exploring as a consequence of her multiple border crossings. These connections are about the sites, locations and movements that have produced her, and which she translates into market impulses. Her clothes represent her identity through style and design. It is, as she says, a cross-cultural and cross-border experience. Bombay Connections reflects her fractured and multiple-sited biography:

> It is the connection that I maintain with India ... I have always loved the word connections ... It sounds really strange to people but to me the shalwaar-kameez really and valuably presents all my upbringing for some strange reason because I combine the look that is required here.
>
> (Ibid.)

Although hers is not a politicized narrative in the way that Bubby's is, Komal is nonetheless a product of her racial and cultural politics. Her enterprise is about creating connective threads between the multiple sites of her experiences. Her clothes as represented in her images, in her spoken and written text, are the threads which stitch together these multiple borders, edges and cuts.

On East–West clothes connections

Again, in common with the other entrepreneurs I have written about so far, Komal sees wider markets for her clothes. In her desires to go beyond the East/West formula and terminology, Komal says:

> I see shalwaar-kameez, it is going to be a much more cosmopolitan and international dress, wearable by many women across the board and ages and all countries of origins. That break is already there. We approached Liberty's, Harrods and Marks and Spencers [the mainstream retailers]. Times have changed amongst mainstream retailers and I know European people would be willing to wear these clothes. I am not saying that they would wear them in the typical way the shalwaar-kameez is worn, with gold embroidery, but some of the things that I am showing are completely clear. They do not have a pinch of embroidery and are cut more classically and may have long trousers and tunic. Even *Vogue* and *Harpers* have long tunic and trousers which is what a shalwaar-kameez is and that is very much an in-fashion look. The shalwaar-kameez is not a limited look.
>
> (Ibid.)

We talked about Princess Diana and Jemima Goldsmith-Khan, since they were on the front pages of magazines and newspapers wearing the suit at the time I interviewed her. She said, 'You have seen how well they have carried it off. They have helped create a new market.' But she did not like the style of Catherine Walker, the haute couture designer who designed Princess Diana's suit for a trip to Pakistan, in a light turquoise-blue. Komal felt the jacket was too streamlined and too 'achkan-type' – it looked like the kind Nehru wore: combined with the narrow trousers, she felt it looked like 'Pakistan International Airways Uniform'. She liked Jemima Goldsmith-Khan's clothes better because 'Jemima was a little bit more Eastern and feminine, but this could be my [Komal's] bent towards feminine clothes.'

Komal does use the East/West terminology in some of her publicity material but is conscious that it does not capture fully the dynamics of suit design and its complex cultural and commercial markets. She attempts to go beyond this interpretation, talking about an 'international' and 'cosmopolitan' look. In a way what she does is truly East/West, however, and she cannot avoid using this dualism because it does capture some essences of her markets and her own biography with precision. There really is no clear and fluent vocabulary to capture the complex phenomena, the cultural and economic dynamics that are producing these new markets and that encode the multiple influences of and on multiple sites. These binaries of East and West are like ciphers and codified aesthetics, a formulaic performance that does not capture the fluid and nebulous cultural and economic processes on the ground. I am reminded of a comment, in another context, by Robert Solow, the MIT Nobel Laureate:

> There is not some glorious theoretical synthesis of capitalism that you
> can write down in a book and follow. You have to grope your way.
> (Solow, quoted in *New York Times* 29 September 1991)

How can we grope to discover the emergent twenty-first century economic, political and cultural terrains and to educate ourselves into the terminologies of the borders and the fast changing borderless terrains we attempt to live in and conceptualize?

A creative commoditizing networker: Mala Rastogi of Creations

Mala Rastogi's shop, Creations, is located in Southall Broadway, the main shopping street of the Punjabi capital of Britain. There she sells ready-made suits designed and made in India. In her early forties now, she came to Britain in 1986 after her marriage. She is a new British Asian in comparison with the locally born and/or locally raised entrepreneurs and, unlike many of them, she has strong family and business connections with India.

Home 'suitcase markets' to a shop

Mala started selling suits from her home a couple of years after she arrived from Delhi. Her family there still acts as her India-based agent. Her shop on Southall Broadway was opened in 1993 when suit commerce generally was well under way, led as it was by local British Asian entrepreneurs. Nonetheless, there were still few suit shops around in comparison to now. Mala entered the public retailing of suits when the trend was on the ascendant but not yet fully fledged. Although not an innovator, she is a facilitator of the suit commerce, making ready-made suits readily available.

She started, in 1988, by bringing home 'twenty-odd suits' in a suitcase after a visit to India, which she then sold quickly from her home to a circle of friends. Later she doubled this number and from there:

> ... it boomed and boomed. The volume just became bigger and bigger. I didn't have a shop for a long time because firstly there were just the circle of friends and their friends and their relations. Then it grew so much that the house became a shop and it got out of hand. That's when I decided to have a shop.
>
> (Mala Rastogi, interview with author, 1996)

These 'suitcase suit economies' (Khan 1992:66) are still in existence and have been around in many cities for a decade or so. They reflect the different stages in the suit's commercial progress, depending on the location and the maturation of Asian settlements in the diaspora. This is how women who are sellers (not design innovators) have often started their enterprises. I have been told of the same phenomenon in Nairobi, Kenya, of women who travel by air in first class for the extra luggage allowance so they can lug suits back from India. Asian women commonly use the same strategy in Massachusetts where I live and many other cities in the USA. In Durban, South Africa, suitcase entrepreneurs have their own term, known as 'bag ladies' or 'aunties'.

This method of transferring goods has been going on for as long as the ready-made economy has been around and is almost entirely conducted by women. According to Mala, 'home businesses' in London are even now more extensive than the 'public boutiques' to be found in the main Asian shopping areas:

> It's much bigger. If there are five shops there are fifty home-selling. It's like Tupperware teaparties. When I was doing it from home, we used to pack up our suitcases and take it to other people's homes and the person who hosted it, she would get a suit free. If there was a sale of £1,000 or £1,500, she would get 10 per cent, either a suit or cash. This is when I started seven to eight years ago. My friend Z.. in Birmingham is in that stage; she is still doing this and doing it very well.
>
> (Ibid.)

There are many home businesses that have never transferred to shops and have not gone beyond this stage of development. (Such transfers are not always successful: they go under or the initiators of such enterprises prove not to have the stamina, the patience or the will-power to sustain them). As Mala indicates, it can be very profitable to remain outside public commercial domains even though it is a nuisance to have as a sub rosa market a private domain, i.e., your home, which then has to function also as stockroom and shop.

In the initial stages of her enterprise, Mala tried to sell her imported suits to the predominantly male-owned suit fabrics and sari shops in Southall, but without any success whatsoever. As Komal Singh also found initially, the male owners of these shops were uninterested in ready-mades, not at that time seeing the potential of this emergent trend. By the early 1990s, however, the trend was unmissable and the established shops did start buying Mala's clothes. This, together with the fact that, as her home-selling networks had expanded, her 'suitcase' business had become simply too big to handle from home, convinced her that she needed to have her own shop.

Like Komal Singh, Mala is not a design innovator because she is essentially a creative importer who makes no design intervention. At one level she is a straightforward importer, transferring clothes from one market to another and benefiting from market price differentials. She is also 'a winner of a market dis-equilibrium' (Thurow 1999). She is able to exploit her Indian connections, being a direct migrant from India who has been in Britain for a relatively short period, in contrast to the locally born and raised entrepreneurs who share her market space. Mala's family, mother and brother help with the movement of suits. It is a family business. They have benefited from the rapid expansion of the Indian ready-made sector, as Mala's brother describes:

> ... We once gave an ad in the paper for a salwaar-kameez designer. I got 150 calls in one day. People are desperate to sell. Too many people.
> (Interview with the author, 1996)

Mala's micro-markets

As I have stated, Mala's modus operandi is not to negotiate individual designs with customers. She is a marketer of clothes in a straightforward retailing mode. When asked about processes of co-constructing a garment with a customer, she says, 'That would be too much headache to do. The body should be allowed to rest.' Neither does she size or get suits made in the colours customers want. You get what is in the shop. She is not a negotiator but a direct seller who engages in the traffic of commodities. However, this is not to say that there are no inno-vations in distributive recontextualization because the latter can involve cre-ative processes. As in the case of Mrs Damini, they are about transferral of market information – this does have design impacts because the manufacturers design what sells in particular markets. So, although Mala does not make a direct design intervention, she is indirectly having an impact on the design process by passing on information about the kinds of line that sell, which clothes are 'hot items' in the markets she serves.

I was impressed by Mala Rastogi's understanding of her markets. She deals with customers directly all the time in her shop. She is not patronizing or con-descending towards 'immigrants' and British Asians as are many elite Indians and Pakistanis who want to market their clothes in London. As a relatively recent immigrant herself, living amongst her British Asian customers, she talks about her markets in more discerning, non-judgmental ways. Mala understands many of the customer complexities.

She describes the generation now entering their twenties who were ten or so when she started:

> ... They would wear jeans and their mums would buy cloth and sew it up for them. This is the generation that you used to see in jeans all the time. Come weddings, festivals, gurdwara visits, they will wear a salwaar-kameez. These are the young people who are also getting married. They are very traditional when they come to the special occasions in their lives. This generation of the mid-1960s has been coming of marriageable age and is a boon to the market.
>
> (Mala Rastogi, interview with author, 1996)

Mala suggested that their parents represented:

> ... a smaller market. This is a much bigger market of Asian kids who are hanging around everywhere. You see them in the media and doing well, better than their parents' generation, who were mainly in the labour class. They came as factory workers and builders and they put up corner shops. But their children are professionals, a lot of lawyers, doctors and chemists, engineers are abundant.
>
> (Ibid.)

Mala's markets have benefited from an established second generation in Britain that is not only larger than that of earlier phases but, crucially, culturally more confident and economically wealthier. This locally produced category of young people in Britain is a growth market of consumers in many domains, including the suit economy.

A commercial networker

Perhaps the most striking aspect of Mala's enterprise as a retailer and wholesaler is her role as the entrepreneurial networker who is connected with many other women entrepreneurs. When I interviewed her she was busy organizing a fashion show, Threads of Fantasy, in collaboration with Zee TV, the Asian cable network, whose offices are also located in west London not far from her shop. The show took place at the Grosvenor House in central London in September 1996, tickets costing £80, and was later broadcast to a Europewide audience of subscribers to Zee TV. It was organized to showcase locally based Asian fashion houses and to fundraise for The Foundation for the Study of Infant Deaths, a British cot-death charity. Mala brought together well-known Indian and British Asian models, a choreographer from India, Asian media 'celebrities', members of the Asian business community, and marketing and PR services. Through the show, she connected six well-known Asian fashion enterprises, of which four were owned or promoted by women (including both Yazz and Ritu).

In addition, as I was standing in the shop, other women entrepreneurs appeared, both those based at home and those with boutiques. Bubby walked into her shop to pick up a parcel that had got mixed up at the airport. She also mentioned that she had run short of halter necks and wondered if Mala had any in her recent consignment.

Of the entrepreneurs who came in to buy wholesale, one was a locally based Gujarati woman who lived in west London. She sells from home to a whole network of Gujarati women who traditionally wear saris but who have taken to wearing the suit during the last few years. She was one of Mala's home business-women. Two other suit entrepreneurs came to buy from Mala's wholesale stock for their shops in Coventry and Leicester in the Midlands. Both also reported an increase in the numbers of European women coming to their shops, as a result, they thought, of Princess Diana's interest in the suit.

Mala Rastogi is one agent and one part of a chain of women – consumers, public and private entrepreneurs – who are making many journeys with these highly charged and potent clothing commodities. I only saw women customers and entrepreneurs in Mala's shop.

These entrepreneurial women in both public and private domains are making the global connections and transnationalizing this economy. As Mala points out, London – and Southall in particular – is well located for this, as:

> [it is] a centre point for Asians living in Europe, South Africa, and Canada. I have had people from Holland, Malawi, South Africa and lots of them. They buy many outfits, twelve in one go, when they are visiting here.
>
> (Ibid.)

Women who buy from her wholesale, whether as shop-owners or home-entrepreneurs, extend her distributing capacities further, as distributors in their own right locally, nationally and internationally. For example, the women who sell from home often sell to friends and relatives who may be based within Britain or visiting from Canada, Australia or the USA. In all these countries there are boutiques and suit shops in the major cities but not in the smaller towns, and even the ones established in the capital cities do not have the variety and choice found in a major global city like London. So, in Mala's case, it is indeed about a creation of markets, as her shop's name, Creations, suggests. Her activities are about an appropriation of commercial spaces, of women asserting themselves in economic markets, in previously male domains. They are representing themselves in commerce using global communications and transfer technologies which have facilitated their distributive functions as entrepreneurs who operate in niche markets.

Concluding remarks

While the design entrepreneurs I have discussed – Geeta Sarin, Ritu, Libas's Sehyr Saigol and Bubby – have both ethnicized and feminized mainstream sartorial landscapes, the marketing suit entrepreneurs have feminized ethnic business landscapes.

For most of the established sellers of cloth and saris, these enterprising women suit marketers have engaged in the disruptive innovative processes described by Clayton Christensen (1997) in his book *The Innovators's Dilemma*. He describes how often outstanding companies lose their markets by unwittingly bypassing opportunities for new markets. In the 1980s, these British Asian women were, on the whole, not part of established enterprises. They were outsiders who created new markets through their recontextualizing activities. They emerged from the margins and have now managed to establish a strong foothold amongst established business locations, thus destablizing and also making defunct those existing enterprises which did not transform themselves. (Daminis, of course, provides an example of a successful transformation.)

The suit commerce is a highly gendered commercial circuit occupied by women who are making their commercial connections and asserting themselves as economic and cultural agents in the market. Their friendships are part of the connecting functions of this commerce. The market is being used by them in complex ways. While colluding with capitalist processes – as Doreen Kondo (1997) says, they are 'complicit' in their agency in the market – they are also using the markets as a mechanism of economic self-assertion and cultural negotiation, as a site of female connections through consumer exchanges. All these novel dynamics are at the same time impacting upon the sartorial and cultural economies of Britain.

None of this detracts from the pathbreaking role of immigrant mothers and their daughters who wore suits in unfriendly public domains and stitched them in the domestic domain according to their own designs, both classically and syncretically in hybrid forms. They kept the cultural and sartorial frameworks vibrant. This is not say that there were no women entrepreneurs in these economies. Clearly there were. Mrs Damini is one example, a woman initiator of a cloth and then a clothes enterprise. There were and still are women who manage enterprises funded by their husbands or kinship group and who have been facilitating others in ethnic enterprises. There are also women who have initiated their own enterprises from their own capital. (The biggest growth area currently for women running their own businesses is in all facets of the wedding economy, florists, henna treatments, party arrangers, etc.) However, the number of suit boutique retailers dealing with ready-made and designer clothes has increased dramatically in the 1990s, catalysed by the processes of fast capitalism. Transformed global communications have made it possible to operate in and from multiple sites that women suit entrepreneurs, in particular, are able to utilize in importing, distributing, and redistributing clothes in localized global markets.

Part IV

SEWING CULTURES
Sketching and designing

INTRODUCTION

This section is about designing diasporic landscapes through domestic sewing and the culture of sina-prona*, the generationally transmitted cultures of domesticity that are so potent for diasporic cultural production. It is about women making connections to the market through a *private* domain of diasporic design. I examine the source codes and the precursors of the diaspora commercial sewing economies of previous chapters in the aesthetics grounded in domestic sewing cultures.

In Chapter 9 I shall explore the democratizing functions of pattern making and some of its history, as well as examine in some detail the whole notion of sina-prona and its significance. In Chapter 10 I shall then present the sewing biographies of four London domestic seamstresses, all of whom are members of a multiple-migrancy community, having grown up in East Africa.

---

* Sina-prona is also referred to as seenha-paronha. I am using a phonetic pronunciation derived from the dialect I speak, which is shared by other British Asians. There are regional and urban-rural variations of representing this term. I am not following any official format here.

9

DIASPORIC SINA-PRONA

Sewing and patterning cultures

In this chapter I want to concentrate on sewing patterns as a means of democratizing fashion, both commercially produced paper patterns and those generated at home from multiple design sources. I will give some background to the American commercial patterns which were developed in the nineteenth century as an integral part of the American diasporic cultures of migrant seamstresses, and draw comparisons with the patterning culture of Asian women in East Africa and Britain. I will also begin to explore the use of patterns within the private domains of the home sewers, the innovative forms they negotiate and circulate through similar networks to those of the commercially based fashion entrepreneurs.

In the second part of the chapter I will describe in some detail the culture of sina-prona, a dominant notion in the socialization of women within the East African Asian (in particular Punjabi) diaspora.

Democratizing fashion through patterns

There was a phase in my life when I was much into patterns and pattern books. I spent many a Saturday afternoon after working on my part-time Saturday job at the local library, poring over countertop pattern books at a local fabric shop. I bought these patterns often and made many sewing and pattern mistakes before I learnt to use what suited me. I still have these patterns now. My older sisters and many of the women I know now, and knew when I was a child in East Africa, sewed using these commercial patterns. They used them 'purely' to sew what was in the pattern itself and also 'impurely Punjabifying' them for making the salwaar-kameez suit. The domestic seamstresses, whose work I deal with in more detail in the following chapter, all make use of commercially produced patterns to extend their design vocabularies for producing the suit. We all had these patterns in our homes wherever we migrated and settled.

I want here to make the connection with the early American sewing cultures which benefited first from the development of commercial patterns. These patterns, together with the introduction of the sewing machine, were critical in democratizing American sartorial economies.

My reasons for writing here about American commercial patterns and sewing machine development are that, in February 1997, I went to an exhibition at the Fashion Institute of Technology in New York, entitled *Dreams on Paper: Home Sewing in America*. Valerie Steel of the Institute took me around the exhibition and I was really struck by how similar the developments in American home sewing were to the diasporic sewing cultures of Asian women, developed in Africa in similar, pioneering circumstances and also in England in a much more developed format. I had not realized till I saw this exhibition and learnt something of the history of these patterns and home sewing, that the patterns were actually originally developed by American tailors, such as Ebenezer Butterick, Madame Demorest and James McCall, who had commercialized them and created their markets.

Like Asian women in East Africa, American pioneer women had to sew to produce the material bases of their culture in frontier settings with no professional service. Previously, to the extent that I had thought about the origin of commercial patterns at all, I had, wrongly, assumed that they were British:

> The commercial paper pattern is an American phenomenon. By the mid-19th century, patterns and drafting systems were a popular component of woman's magazines. With the development and the rapid spread of the sewing machine to the home, the demand for sewing patterns was so great that paper patterns sold separately became successful commercial enterprise. Today, this American industry has developed into a $2.5 billion business ... Truly a democratic development, paper patterns allowed women across the country access to the same styles, at the same time, and sometimes even the same designers, as society women they admired.[1]
>
> (Williams 1996/7:1)

What is significant is that these early pattern makers created a new space and new way of creating a design economy that was available to the general public. Paper patterns made the fashions of the rich available to ordinary people, even though they had to rely on their own labours and sewing machines to make them rather than the professional tailors of the wealthy elites. Paper pattern makers created new market niches through their innovations and also new niches in the print media that were the most influential instruments of information dissemination in their time. The pattern makers published magazines containing information on various topics but which also, most importantly, advertised their sewing patterns. They created new design vocabularies which they made available from the specialized domains of the professional tailor to the home sewers and seamstresses in the domestic domain. These design texts facilitated access to clothes styles worn by Europeans:

The demand in America for English tailoring resulted in menswear patterns published by tailors eager to market their individual drafting systems.

(Ibid.)

The patterns appealed particularly to new settlers and immigrants seeking to improve their circumstances (Kidwell and Christmas 1974:75, cited in Craik 1994:209). The availability of commercial patterns thus dented class barriers, a tailoring project in social class engineering through pattern distribution. The development of paper patterns not only made it possible to replicate the fashions of the elite, but also, 'trends in fashion emanated from non-elite groups in competition with elite fashion' (Craik 1994:206). It also provided the opportunity to reverse the flow of fashion ideas from Europe to America. Although sales of American paper patterns in Europe 'did not match those at home, they pointed the direction for future exports of American consumerism there' (Walsh 1979:31, quoted in Craik 1994:209). I am sure these design exposures would also have added to female domestic labour, by increasing the pressures on women to sew, partially eased by the introduction of treadle machines in the 1900s and the electric ones a decade and half later.

In some ways, diasporic fashion entrepreneur Geeta Sarin's pioneering catalogue also performed very similar design functions. I found her catalogue in the houses of many domestic seamstresses and I have already related the incident in Lahore when a Pakistani ready-made suit manufacturer had appropriated her catalogue designs to make suits for his local markets. I have related, too, how the catalogue increased design knowledge about the use of fabrics like raw silks to make newer, more interesting styles, in addition to the classic silhouettes. Her catalogue thus extended design exposures and ideas in many economies, a democratizing and design distribution role similar to the American pattern companies.

The patterning form developed in the mid-nineteenth century by immigrants and their descendents in America was further taken up and 'ethnicized' at another period by a different set of diasporic people in locations both in Africa and Britain. In twenty-first-century Britain, as I shall show in more detail in the following chapter, Jini, a proficient pattern user, uses the actual patterns whilst Surjeet, Hardev and Pami scan pattern books all the time and draw a pattern right onto the fabric or draw a sketch from the pattern and then cut the cloth accordingly. These pattern books are made by pattern companies for retail in magazine format, the abridged version of the substantial $1 \times \frac{1}{2}$ foot counter catalogues used in fabric shops or departments. Most of these seamstresses have both the abridged and the countertop version, which fabric shops sell off cheaply at the end of the season.

In some ways, these women are using the pattern books as guides in exactly the same way as the early American tailors who went on to initiate the widespread use of paper patterns:

Early patterns, unsized and unscaled, were intended as guides for professional tailors and dressmakers. Tailors patterns appeared in print as early as the 16th century ... By the late 18th century, instruction books for making clothing had become available, both for the professional tailor and the home seamstress. Women's magazines and tailors journals were publishing garment designs as both unscaled diagrams and full-size patterns by the mid-19th century.

(*Dreams on Paper: Home Sewing in America* exhibition brochure)

The diasporic tailoresses similarly use the pattern books and magazines simply as a guide. They really do not need the full tissue patterns and pattern instructions to cut and make their clothes – they adopt the 'freehand method of home dressmaking', (Tulloch 1999:115).[2] Many do use patterns, nonetheless, and adapt them all the time, while others are able to use them as design templates and decipher the pattern picture in the same way that they can decipher many other styles by eye.

In East Africa, commercially produced patterns were commonly used by the younger women in the capital cities by the early 1960s. The patterns were easily available at the fabric stores in the main shopping areas of Kampala, Nairobi and Dar-es-Salaam. More generally, fashion magazines and, before women's magazines became available, newspapers, were scanned for ideas and dress patterns for making tops, the kameez part of the salwaar-kameez, and also many other clothes. The use of patterns amongst the younger women was also encouraged in the needlework classes that young girls had in secondary/high schools, which systematically trained them into 'more professional' sewing skills, expertise they used further in their domestic sewing.

Their combinational sketches and patterns included elements from these American patterns but also produced patterns that were part of their own contexts. So patterns were (and still are) individually created by borrowing from different design economies, as I shall show in more detail in the next chapter.

I have suggested that the American patterning industry, another diasporic expression of a continent full of migrants, is one significant design economy that was appropriated by multiply-migrant British Asian mothers and daughters. The design economy into which, as girls, they were socialized from an early age – sina-prona – I shall elaborate in the following section.

Diaspora sewing economies: sina-prona

I have stated earlier that the sina-prona economies were and are need-based, functional economies of the diaspora. Diasporic women had to sew and perform all the tasks of migrant households in frontier contexts to create the domestic infrastructure of diasporic communities, unsupported by specialized service providers. This need-based collection of craft and sewing skills was necessarily an innovative economy: they learnt, copied, borrowed, imagined and made. They were forced to create.

The notion of sina-prona – literally translated, sewing and beading – is a metaphor for the many skills that constitute the making of a home. Sina-prona becomes a code for femininity, the making of a suchaji (skilled) and exemplary woman with a commanding expertise, with the appropriate skills of domesticity. It is also about a creative domestic femaleness, the characteristics that define conventional womanliness, the sensibilities that govern the making of a competent homemaker and household manager. There is no doubt that it has aspects of servicing the household, of reproducing and producing the family, and, in particular, of servicing the men, of validating patriarchy, with many elements of drudgery.[3] I do not want to idealize sina-prona socialization because clearly there were and are many oppressive aspects to it. There are many fine feminist critiques of equivalent sina-prona expectations from women who were forced to engage in these activities and who thus had other ambitions thwarted. But there are also creative aspects of this domestic economy. These are some of the source codes defining the improvisational aesthetics of both the diasporic fashion entrepreneurs and the seamstresses who have taken these domestic skills in interesting design directions, cultural and commercial. These are the fundamental sensibilities of diasporic cultural production.

Sina-prona encodes aspects of the smooth functioning of the home, particularly with reference to the stitching and craft skills connected with women. It is also, however, a reference to the facility with which women exercise their skills, the domestic stitching and crafting prowess of women who needed to perform the functions of reproducing diasporic households in new and dislocated sites. Sina-prona is also used in conjunction with the discourse of 'haath kul javay' which is, literally, 'the hands should be opened'. This discourse of open hands is that hands should be practised, have familiarity with tasks, should know the tasks, and have repeated them many times, to repeat them with facility and ease, using the stored databases of tasks previously performed and practised. These are notions about repetition in which the regular practice of a task or part of a task makes it do-able on another occasion, naturally, without having to struggle and be forced to remember. Also applied to conventionally masculine tasks, but most used of girls or women, it is about creating economies of familiarity that reproduce a skill pool, a version of domestic femininity and, also fulfilling the notion that 'practice makes perfect'. Many of these tasks were part of the burden of running a household, the chores that had to be done, the clothes that had to be stitched that could not be bought ready-made, the food and meals that had to be put on the table. All these were the jobs and activities that needed to be done to maintain a family, to feed it, to clothe it, to create the homeliness of a home: these created the aesthetics of people's living spaces that were true to the cultural backgrounds that they or their parents and grandparents had migrated with and that were rearticulated anew in the new contexts. However, there were many aspects of sina-prona which women and girls participated in that were pleasurable, that expressed their voices and built relationships between them, as reflected in statements from a seamstress such as

Hardev who states, 'I was fond of doing this work or craft and I used to enjoy sewing and did it with pride and care.'

The migrant women's skills thus constituted a databank of expertise on which to draw. I have lived in such economies in my childhood in various towns in East Africa, as well as London. I am reminded of a similar context for domestic sewing described by L. M. Montgomery in her novel *Anne of Green Gables* set in Prince Edward Island in Canada, an economy of Anglo-Saxon diasporics. In the novel, nosy, interfering Mrs Rachel Lynde 'ran a sewing circle'. Young Anne wanted a puffed-sleeve dress but Marilla Cuthbert, Anne's adoptive mother, refused to make it for her, instead borrowing patterns from neighbours for simpler dresses that took less material. Marilla also borrowed patterns from the mother of Diana, Anne's bosom pal, to make Anne a skirt when she decided to keep this orphan girl. Later in the novel, Matthew Cuthbert, Marilla's softer-hearted brother, resolved the puffed-sleeve dress expectations of Anne by asking Rachel Lynde of the sewing circle to make Anne a puffed-sleeve dress, 'in the very latest fashion'.

These dynamics of sharing sewing tips and patterns are very familiar to me and central to the sina-prona economies I am describing. There were many people who shared their skills in this way but it was at the same time a competitive economy. Those women who wanted to be ahead of the game and know more than others, kept their sewing and craft secrets to themselves. Often people learnt from them nonetheless. Hardev, whose sewing biography I describe later, narrates a story of how she learnt an overlapping, imbricated lace that a woman was crocheting. Hardev did not want to ask for instructions because she knew if she asked she would not get them; moreover, it was not appropriate to ask for other people's designs, but to wait for them to be volunteered. Hardev watched her, came home, figured out the pattern and did not sleep that night till she had crocheted a sample. So she reproduced the design anyway from observing, regardless of whether she was taught or not. In the case of bridal trousseaus, young women about to be married often did not reveal what they had made in case someone else copied.

Yet people did copy all the time and also, in many cases, voluntarily shared with – and taught – each other. I remember many occasions when women would come to my mother to learn to make various mathais, Indian sweets, at which she was expert, as well as to learn how to cut a certain garment. We also went to learn from other women what they knew. There were many sina-prona generosities that drove these economies and, on the whole, in the closely networked communities of the diaspora, people were kind and gave freely of their services and skills to their neighbours.

The economies of sina-prona that were highly developed in the diaspora in the earliest migrant settings of East Africa have been reproduced again in Britain, where their second-generation daughters have developed them yet further. In the 1990s, some of these skills have been diluted in the young British-born diasporic children, many of whom do not sew. But I have been surprised at how many are creative in many other, additional expressive forms such as music, art and drawing. However, there is no doubt that traditional sina-prona of the older sort is on the decline as the ready-made economy develops and as more and more women work outside the home, with less time for domestic activities. It is not as tenaciously reproduced as it was in East Africa and in my generation of women in their forties in which it was, and remains still, strong. Many of us are good at sina-prona in a way that the eighteen-to-twenty-five-year-olds are not and do not need to be. The young have far greater facility with the skill economies of their context, computer technologies in particular. A couple of them I know actually use this computer dexterity to create suit patterns and have sewed them quickly in simple, clear silhouettes. But for them, there is no equivalent to the need-based economy of the previous migration setting. There, sina-prona skills were absolutely critical if you wanted your children, yourself and your men to be clothed and the home to have cloth on the bed and on tables, etc.

The critical technology in the sina-prona economy was the sewing machine – the central piece of equipment that most diasporic Punjabi women possessed. The machine was around in every suit-wearing household I know and part of most marriage gifts. The machine was less common in Gujarati households of sari-wearing women who needed to sew less, although their other domestic skills were just as developed. However, the suit is in vogue amongst Gujarati women and they get them stitched and buy them ready-made, both in Britain and in India. Some of Mala Rastogi's suit-selling women are Gujarati women.

The type of sewing machine varied across the generations according to the technology available. Most women of my mother's generation, women who are now seventy to eighty years old or more, sewed on hand machines. These were black Singers with gold embellishments, which were kept in small wooden cases. Some women also had the treadle machines by the late 1950s. My sisters and cousins were bought electric machines in their late teens in East Africa in the early and mid-1960s, machines they migrated with and still use today. These were mostly the German Pfaffs, the British Singers and the Italian Necchis. My mother got a secondhand Pfaff from another East African woman when she moved to London in 1968, leaving behind in Kenya the hand-operated Singer machine she had used since 1942. She used to say the Pfaff moved too fast at first, but uses it fluently even though she is now, at eighty-four years old, only partially sighted. She uses her index finger as a guide and sews often. My eldest sister grew up in Kenya using our mother's hand machine till she graduated to her own higher status 'automatic', the Pfaff bought for her when she was twenty. She still uses this machine thirty-five years later as it has moved with her from place to place. My older sister has a Swiss Bernina which she was bought in her early twenties before her marriage and which she used all the time till last year when it needed to be repaired. She now has a computer-ized, basic Swiss Elna, passing the repaired Bernina on to her eighteen-year-old British-born daughter who is being peripherally inducted into the sina-prona culture. I was bought the same model of Bernina as my sister when I was twenty, on which I sewed all the time till I moved to the US and bought myself an early 1960s American Singer at a local estate sale, a light browny-beige machine in a Formica-covered cabinet. This is my 'combine harvester', a solid machine with a 'there there', a machine you 'can do business with' on which I stitch the sutured and ruptured landscapes of my multiply moved, located and dislocated existence. It is through this technology that I stitch the diasporic subjectivities, aesthetics and sensibilities of the sina-prona cultures that I have moved with and which I reproduce, into which I have been inducted and into which I too bring new influences. I present this family narrative of sewing machine history to represent the stories of this crucial piece of technology that has helped to translate and create the many aspects of the sewing and sartorial economies I explore in this book. This story of sewing machines shows how diasporic women generally have mended and stitched the ruptures of our location and dislocation in the many parts of the globe in which we are now resident at the beginning of the new millennium.

I do want to emphasize that sina-prona is not exclusive to diasporic women. It is also the domestic ethos of many subcontinental women and of those who are the direct migrants from that context in British and other locations. It is a dominant ethos, highly developed in the subcontinent but less so, I would argue, than in migrant contexts in which the lack of tailoring professionals meant you had to know how to make clothes yourself, otherwise you were in trouble. Just as the multiple migrants, experienced at the game of migration, were skilled in the management of their minority status, so they also reproduce and develop the sina-prona economy with greater ease than do women who have not had to learn these processes in an earlier phase of migration. They have relied on specialized service providers to fulfil their needs because they stayed in their homeland bases and moved directly. These directly migrant women, in my experience and observation over many years, therefore do not develop these skills easily in the new migration context.

In the chapter that follows, I will describe in more detail the sewing activities of the domestic seamstresses who operate from their homes and who engage in so many of the same processes that I have described for the major diasporic fashion entrepreneurs in the market. These women are from the background of sina-prona and haath kulna (opening hands) conventions that I have described above, that have been transferred and transformed by them in London. I describe their sewing biographies and how they innovate and borrow to make the new spaces of sina-prona.

10

DESIGNING DIASPORAS
THROUGH SKETCHES

The deep-rooted cultures of sewing and inventiveness that diaspora fashion entrepreneurs have emerged from, the commerce they have developed and the negotiative styles that represent their modus operandi (as discussed in Chapters 3 and 4), are also present amongst the diasporic seamstresses who sew from home. They use exactly the same improvisational techniques in their sewing crafts. As I have described in the previous chapter, these design aesthetics had their basis in the domestic domains of previous economies of settlement prior to migration to Britain.

In this chapter, I present in detail four sewing biographies of diasporic seamstresses. The economy of these seamstresses who sew at home for themselves and for their clients for cash remains vibrant. Good seamstresses are constantly in demand and over-booked most of the time. The typical, one-size-fits-all boutique suit does not fit women who are not of average height and size. These non-standard women, amongst many others, keep home seamstresses swept off their feet. Although it is not possible to reproduce boutique suits exactly without the appropriate industrial machines and embroidery skills, boutique suits are copied all the time and often quite well, with much individual design input. There is a great deal of boutique suit espionage. I have engaged in some of this myself, having replicated – more or less – a couple of designer suits I had.

I have already mentioned in Chapter 1 the effects of women's entry into the waged labour market: even women who are proficient sewers no longer have the time to devote to making their own clothes but do have the money to pay a seamstress to sew their clothes. Wage-earning women who can sew and those who cannot keep these private economies of the stitch robust.

In this chapter, then, I give glimpses of what was developed in an African Asian context, and show how it is now reproduced on the British scene in the domestic suit economy. I will make clear the similarities between this and the commercial suit economies, the latter led, as we have already seen, by hybridizing diasporics who are continuing to redefine these African (British) Asian aesthetics.

One key similarity – and a feature that I have already highlighted when writing about designer Bubby Mahil, in particular – is the constant drawing and sketching these women do, to create designs. Drawing creates the new becoming. This is its power, not that of reviving a dead past, but creating new design vocabularies of the present. The lines of their drawings constitute a here-and-now design syntax, which emerges not through established vocabularies of power, making the significant more significant, but through the new significance that emerges from capturing local, current contexts. These sketches of clothes-to-be-made are potent inscriptions of the moment.

Surjeet's story

Surjeet is one of the seamstresses whom I interviewed in Southall, west London. In her mid-forties, she lives close to the Southall boutiques and fabric shops which she visits frequently because she sews constantly. She has a full-time, non-sewing job but also sews for people, both for money and free of charge for close friends and relatives.

Surjeet's sewing room is right at the back of the garden of the house in which she and her husband live with her in-laws. She shared the sewing room with her sister-in-law, a professional seamstress, until the latter married and moved out of the house. It is a very pleasant space, a room of about 10 foot by 12 foot, which is like a well-insulated, warm greenhouse. She has both a standard and an industrial sewing machine, a Toyota. She also has a separate interlocking machine to finish the seam edges. She has three large tables and a rail on which she hung her own, individually cut, thick tracing-paper patterns, alongside many fabrics, borders and edging laces and reels of thread. The room also has a paraffin oil heater to keep her warm when sewing at night and in the winter. Her sewing space is like an artist's studio. It is an almost sacred space of cloth, stitches, threads, patterns, cut cloth, semi-ready clothes and samples of women's clothes that she has for size and from which she will generate new outfits. She pays homage in her sewing temple every day, performing tasks she enjoys. All the women of her maternal family sewed, including her sisters and also her sisters-in-law, who have been sewing since they were nine or ten years old in Kenya.

When her family first moved to Britain in the 1960s, she got work as a machinist in a factory. Raised on a farm in rural Kenya, her English was not fluent and the only jobs available for women who spoke little or no English were in the rag trade. This was in Leeds in the north-east of England. She worked in a ladies' underwear factory at first and later moved to a men's suit factory where they trained her to do some of the hardest jobs, such as putting arms into the armholes of men's jackets. She learnt fast and did these tough jobs well.

She thus elaborated in an industrial context the sewing skills she had learnt at home. She is proficient and sharp at analysing how clothes are put together and knows the standards well-made clothes should meet. She told me: 'If I buy a man's suit, I check first to see jacket sleeves and armholes. I have to see how well they are made. If I don't like it, I just tell them this is not good.'

She can make 'a proper jacket with lining and everything' easily and has done this many times. She used a commercial pattern to make a blazer for her sister-in-law. She showed me the kind of jackets and clothes she had made. She learnt first to cut clothes by watching her mother and sisters, then copying. She started cutting on paper when she was seven years old, making clothes for her dolls. Nobody taught her directly but 'we all learnt somehow. We were not forced to learn. We just picked it up.' She and her sisters also learnt knitting on broom 'needles' – long bristles taken from the broom used to sweep and clean the floor.

As a result of her industrial experience, she is good at using any type of machine connected with tailoring – overlockers, hemmers and seam-edge finishers. There is a special machine for crisply top-stitching collars which has two needles – it is a machine I am told most people find difficult to work but she uses it with ease. She used to make factory samples – so-called 'cabbages' – the prototypes made to smooth out pattern and design problems before clothes are mass-produced. She has never done a needlework course but observed professional cutters and design personnel making patterns in the clothes factories where she worked, as she had previously watched her mother and sisters. She did industrial machining for many years before she got a better-paid office job. She still does some industrial samples for friends who own clothes factories.

'I have to sew for half an hour every day'

Surjeet loves sewing and misses it if she does not sew regularly:

> I used to sew all the time. I learnt to cut and also sew apnay suits [our Punjabi suits] all the time. I never stopped sewing. I want to stitch every day on the machine. If I don't sit with the machine, I feel like something is missing. I have to sew for half an hour every day.
>
> (Surjeet, interview with the author, 1996)

If she is stitching an outfit, she manages to do the different stages of the suit in half-hour time slots she can find in between doing her full-time job and housework.

Surjeet hardly ever uses what she calls an 'inchi-tape', i.e., a measuring tape:[1]

> When I cut my shoulder width on cloth, I never use tape, I just take two giths which is sixteen inches and I add a finger extra to that for the seams. One finger is half an inch – that comes in the seam. Most average women are about fifteen to sixteen inch shoulder.
>
> (Ibid.)

She prefers to get an already stitched kameez top from a client and takes the size from that. Also, she does not have notebooks and, unlike other seamstresses I interviewed, does not keep records. Once she has the kameez size, she can cut 'any pattern'. She can elaborate many kinds of patterns from that basic garment. She showed me the various styles that she makes, some of which were lying around in her sewing room. It was Surjeet I cited in Chapter 1 for the remarkable speed at which (some, at least) seamstresses can work: a simple suit from a 'princess cut' takes her a maximum time period, from cutting to wearing the suit, of approximately three hours. A 'simple suit' she can sew in one hour. The suit she was wearing had been sewn in two and a half hours. Other duties permitting, she only stops when she gets to the end, including putting on the buttons and hemming.

She sews for older women a lot and for free for some of them:

> They like my style. They like the old style that is more fitted. Suits are often cut from a pattern now. In the past, you had a straight cloth, you put pleats and embroidered them and wore them, a simple suit.
>
> (Ibid.)

She also makes clothes for women of her own age group, in their early forties. The older women used to sew themselves and many still do, for example her mother-in-law, who sews her own 'simple' suits. While her older sister also wears simple suits, her younger sister buys from boutiques but only for special occasions. Surjeet says the boutique-bought suits the younger ones wear are actually simple in shape; the complex parts are the embroideries and embellishment, products of the well-established expertise of subcontinental craftsmen.

Surjeet's charges for 'a basic suit' are £10–15 and for a suit with lining, £15. For the lengha, a bias ankle-length skirt, she charges £15. I told her that she was under-pricing her labour. She responded:

> I don't sew for people who are headaches but I am happy to do it for other people I like and sometimes I don't accept any money. My sisters-in-law give me money, even though I am happy to sew for them free but they say they will have to pay someone else and that they should pay me instead. After all I do the work, they say. My sister-in-law charged the full amount when she sewed full time. She used to do the designing and had notebooks of all the designs she did and many of clothes she made. She has still kept most of these notebooks ten to fifteen years later.
>
> (Ibid.)

This business of 'liking the person for whom you sew' is one that comes up again and again. All these women sew from home and, unsurprisingly, do not like to deal with unsavoury characters in their home terrain nor do they like people who haggle over the prices they charge. As it is, they all undercharge for the services they provide and if they were to charge as much as the equivalent English seamstresses, they would have to more than quadruple their prices.

Surjeet has worn a suit all her life and has no problems about wearing it in any context. She has always been confident about wearing the suit:

> I never feel ashamed, I don't care even if there are only whites around and I am the only Indian there, I will wear my Indian clothes. They can stare at me if they like, I will wear my clothes. It doesn't bother me. If you say to a gora [white person], that you should wear an Indian suit, they will not change their clothes. They stick to their clothes. They will wear what they will wear. I will wear what I want to wear.
>
> (Ibid.)

At work she wears skirts and blouses which she was initially given by the organization she works for. She copied these and made some from other fabrics in the same style by adjusting the patterns and adding minor variations.[2] Using one of the patterns which hang on the clothes rail, she then calibrates and adjusts measurements as she cuts. This is the process I mentioned in the previous chapter, whereby professional tailors used patterns not as measured sizes for each individual but as guides to produce the final garment. Some of the patterns that Surjeet has are of clothes she has liked the shape and style of and has therefore cut them out on durable paper for future reference. She makes a pattern in thick tracing paper that hangs well, does not tear easily and can be reused many times. She has some princess-cut shapes – a basic style used for many kameezes in the 1990s and currently.

She described some of the patterns she had cut and also a pink suit she was wearing which 'had a bodice on both sides':

> This is like an English dress. If you want an English dress and don't want to wear a salwaar with it or you can wear a salwaar with it. It has bodice and kaliyan [gores].
>
> (Ibid.)

We went through all her patterns and she explained how she used what and where. There was one pattern with a long drop waist with pleats around it. She said such drop waists suit really slim people. There were various versions of princess cuts and the kurtas with many kaliyan. There were many kaliyan-walli (gore styles). She had cut her own pattern from a commercial pattern and added her own inputs to it to suit her figure and personality. She said, 'When I sew this, I am going to make it my own, how I want it.' She was going to change it by lifting up the waistline to just under the bustline. She has all kinds of patterns which she adjusts all the time. She 'takes something out or adds something. It takes no time and it's not difficult'. She personalizes a pattern and uses

146

a combinational design strategy of borrowing pattern vocabularies and adding her own, including that of her customers, as discussed below. She also borrows from the boutique suits which she investigates thoroughly at the shops. She copies as well as innovates all the time. She might already have a dress, the design of which she reworks to produce a new pattern. At other times she uses a pattern to cut another pattern but one that is different from the original because it has her input and combinational freedoms. A pattern is used as template in multiple ways.

She also designs and interprets, thus 'Punjabifying' English magazine clothes and patterns all the time. For example, she said her sister, who is very trendy, wanted a lengha. She saved her sister £150 because she made one by copying an evening dress design in a net fabric from an English magazine. She bought a similar material, all in one colour, and added a lace top. She copied the top in the magazine, but added sleeves. She half-lined it, again as in the magazine. She told me that the net material was £35 and the chuni was £15, making just £50 in total. Her sister wore the lengha at a reception and everyone admired it. Surjeet also sewed a similar outfit for her brother's wife.

Boutique espionage

Surjeet and many other women like her do not give their custom to the boutiques economy, on the whole, but they do borrow styles and design ideas from boutique suits. She or one of her friends might buy one or two suits between a whole group and then copy the style and share the pattern amongst themselves. The domestically replicated suits are worn at the same social functions as the boutique originals in overlapping fields of clothes, but with adaptations. For example, one boutique suit might be used by a bunch of women to make similar outfits, maybe without the embroideries, or with simpler embroideries, or they might embellish them with ready-made borders. One or two boutique-borrowed patterns might circulate within an extended kinship group or friendship circuit. These much used patterns are often cut out in paper for future adaptations.

For example, Surjeet saw a lungi salwaar suit at Geeta Sarin's shop, Rivaaz, in Wembley. She had a look at it in the shop and copied it:

> It was in her showroom. I used to go and look all the time. Now I wear simpler suits. But when I saw the lungi salwaar in Rivaaz, I really liked it and I said, 'I will try to make that one.'
>
> (Ibid.)

The styles in boutiques are used as sources of design ideas to make home-produced suits more stylish. Possibly this actually enhances suit purchases by younger women who buy from boutiques, inspired by the stylishly dressed, suited women. Komal Singh, the owner of Bombay Connections whom I have written about in Chapter 8, believes that it is no longer possible to produce a stylish, well-made suit at home because the level of sewing and cutting expertise has become much more professional for the boutique suits. But the home-sewers do borrow design ideas from these professionally produced suits. It is a circular economy in which ideas flow from boutique to home and from home to many other design conduits, including the boutiques themselves.

This view that home-produced suits look home-made is not acceptable to some seamstresses who do not subscribe to boutique commerce, either because they do not want to pay the price of boutique suits, or they simply do not care about higher standards, or they are actually good at producing boutique-like suits, without the embroidery. Surjeet does not like ready-made suits from India, seeing them as over-embellished and gaudy. Also, rarely can she wear them without altering them. She does not like their linings and, to her proficient and discerning eyes, they are not so well stitched: 'The tension of the stitch is not good. I don't like the stitching. They use big stitches.' It is true that if you sew yourself you are very conscious of the tension of stitches and the finishing, finer points you do not notice if you do not sew.[3]

According to Surjeet, boutique suits are not that complicated to make once the basic shape has been decoded. I was telling her that the suits had become more complex. She disagreed:

> Aaj kaal, these days, the suits are actually very simple. There is nothing complicated about them except embroidery which is really good. But the suit itself is not difficult to make. It's not difficult to make kaliyan walay kurtay – the kurta top with multiple panels.
>
> (Ibid.)

I tried to convince her that fine pin-tucks and pleats are time-consuming and difficult to do, also that they are well made in India because of exploitative labour practices which allow the making of elaborate suits using sweated labour. But she did not think pin-tucks were difficult – 'you just do it'. There is no doubt that the boutique suits produced in India do feed the design economies of these seamstresses in the private economies of the domestic domain.

Surjeet regularly visits the boutiques to examine suits sold for £200–400. She thoroughly examines the outfits on the display dummies and the racks:

> If I like something, I cut it straight onto the fabric. I can't wait to cut on the paper first. I haven't got the patience to cut it on paper. I want to cut and sew and wear it. If it fits me nicely than maybe I will cut a paper pattern. I always have cloth at home because I hardly buy cloth. Someone has always given me the cloth. I will try it on some material that is not expensive. Like I bought this material of six yards for £4. I can try a new pattern on that cloth. I don't believe in buying a £200–300 suit. This is an average price. I don't believe in spending so much because you wear it at a party once and you can't wear it again.

You think you have worn it already and don't want to wear the same thing again with the same people again.

(Ibid.)

Also what she makes for herself is cheaper and unique to her own style: 'It's different. I can wear it and I know nobody will wear one like this.' She likes the styles she stitches through her own design interventions and creativity. These are simpler suits with clear lines and minimal embellishments, individually crafted. Drawn from many sources, peculiar to Surjeet, they encapsulate the present moment and rearticulate diasporic skills through her own design intervention.

Paramjeet's story

'Our cultures show in the sewing'

Paramjeet, Pami as she is called, sews in her dining room where she has a Brother industrial sewing machine and also a standard domestic Singer on which she does buttonholes. She lives in an area of south London where there is no concentration of Asians. However, there is a dispersed Asian community in her vicinity. Her mother, who lives close by, also sews. She taught Pami, starting her at eight years old when they lived in a small town in northern Tanzania. However, Pami now has a much wider repertoire of sewing skills than her mother because she has become much more experienced in stitching many different styles of clothes for her multicultural clientele. Her mother can make basic 'old style' suits whilst Pami can sew anything and in any style at this stage in her sewing career when she has been 'at it' for almost twenty-five years. Like Surjeet, she is in her mid-forties:

> Our cultures show in the sewing. It's like keeping a good house. The India walliyan [the directly migrant Indian women] don't sew. They buy suits in India and sell them here. We were told all the time, 'If you do not know sina-prona, what do you know!'
> (Paramjeet, interview with the author, 1996)

Pami moved to south London in the late 1960s and has worked in many places. She started off doing clerical work in an office, then worked in a boutique selling English clothes, at British Home Stores, and in Tesco's as a cashier, and as a machinist in various local clothes factories. She stitched at home for the rag trade when her children were small, making skirts, blouses, trousers and children's clothes for a factory near her house for many years. She no longer does this type of rag trade sewing. Her own customers now range from little kids to old women who wear the basic suit of the 'old' type. Her customers are mainly women of different Asian ethnicities, along with some black and white women. These Asian women are Muslims, Gujaratis, Punjabi Sikhs and Hindus. Pami commented, 'Everyone is wearing suits. Teenagers tend to wear culottes with the kameez and not a salwaar but the tops are the same for many women whether they are apni [Punjabi] women or not.'

She said she is recommended to them by the main high street shops in her local area, which has a few Asian fabric shops, and those in Tooting in south-west London, which has emerged since the late 1980s as an Asian shopping area. There are also suit and sari shops which send her customers.

She has become an experienced seamstress both through her rag trade work and through servicing her own clientele. She started sewing Punjabi suits and the variations of the suit in the early 1980s, when younger Asian women started wearing ethnic clothes more often than before. By 1983, she was fully into making suits. The suit economy was beginning to take off at this time, has since become fully fledged and seems here to stay.

She initially learnt how to cut cloth to make clothes at home (cutting, as it was called, in Tanzania when she was young) at ten or eleven years old, when she had already been sewing for two or three years. She was also sent to a sewing teacher to learn basic stitchcraft. This was not a formal sewing course in a college. She went to the woman's house to learn because the woman used to teach some of the local girls. There were many other women who taught sewing in the main towns and who ran small sewing schools sometimes from their homes. I myself, aged 14, went to such a local sewing school in an Asian suburb of Nairobi for a short period during my summer holidays. These sewing classes were often held in large rooms where there were young women and girls at different levels of skill learning to sew, cut and embroider, also other crafts, such as crochet or knitting. I learnt to make sculpted cushion covers that were fashionable at the time. The women who taught these courses had done semi-professionalized dressmaking courses and they were expert seamstresses. My teacher could show us how to make our own patterns on thick brown paper and many other practical dressmaking skills. These sewing schools still exist in Nairobi, Kenya, and have been professionalized since the 1970s. Most girls also took needlework in school as part of the compulsory school curriculum but needlework classes in school were different and more academic.

Now Pami sews whatever people bring her: wedding dresses, school uniforms, bridesmaids' dresses, sari blouses, many types of clothes, curtains. She can make wedding dresses without a pattern by just looking at a picture of a bridal gown. For example, a client of hers who wanted a wedding dress brought in a bridal magazine. She analysed the gowns shown and copied one for her, making some adaptations. She thus created a composite design. She advises clients on where to get reasonably priced fabrics and buys thread, bias bindings and buttons from the local markets, which are cheaper.

Pami cannot follow commercial patterns, finding pattern instructions diffi-cult. Nonetheless she makes self-generated patterns all the time. Like Surjeet, Pami uses the hand and finger measures of gith and giras much more often than a tape measure. Another reason for her dislike of commercial patterns is that they require more cloth. Diasporic women make much of this business of not wasting cloth and have enormous 'cloth respect and thrift'. They say that you try not to lose 'a finger-length of cloth'.

Pami cuts her patterns on brown paper and has the basic size patterns of regular customers. She sometimes uses newspapers to make patterns as well, taping the sheets together to make a sufficiently large piece. Newspaper is easy to use as there is always some at home. She makes sketches but also uses her home-made patterns all the time.

Pami also has many pattern books and magazines at home for her clients to scan. Like all the home seamstresses, she compounds and combines designs to create a new design:

> I add to it and take out something and make a suit. When I started, I used to make plain suits with darts, the plate-wallay suits. Then A-lines, princess cuts, the long kameezes with long side slits, churi dhar pyjamas, kameezes with churi dhar sleeves [sleeves with bangle-like folds near the wrists], lenghas and lungis, whatever is in fashion. I can make all of these.
>
> (Ibid.)

Her customer base has come to include many more young girls, between the ages of fifteen and nineteen, in the past six years or so. She says they are wearing Punjabi suits more often now. This reflects the general trend for suits to be worn more by younger women now than was the case in the past.

Pami never advertises but gets customers through word of mouth. She not only makes clothes for private customers but has also made boutique-type clothes for a woman who ran a boutique-cum-beautician's shop for a short period. This business is no longer around. She made East–West clothes for the fashion shows that this entrepreneur organized at Asian fairs, the melas in big public parks. She has stitched many kagras (multiple gore skirts) for local Gujarati women and the same type of skirts for white women. These skirt-forms can be translated in many directions. Also her non-Asian women suit-wearing clientele wear their suits in their own ways:

> A number of the black and white women wear their salwaar in reverse because they do not know and they like it that way. Also a number of them wear the salwaar above the ankle, not like the fashionable Pakistani style that was in fashion a little while back, but because it feels like standard trousers and does not trail on the floor as a salwaar does sometimes.
>
> (Ibid.)

Her white women clients get suits made mostly in cotton whereas Asian women have their suits made in many mixed fabrics such as synthetics, cottons, mixed polyester and silks. She inevitably does many more of 'our Asian wedding clothes' in the summer when the wedding season is on. She makes more office party clothes around Christmas, often for white women. She makes black skirts, also off-the-shoulder and sleeveless dresses, i.e., 'black things in different styles'. She has also made many nursery clothes for children and makes school uniforms regularly at the beginning of the school year in September. Since she used to make skirts for the rag trade, she can churn these out rapidly and does so often, utilizing her former industrial sewing experience.

In common with other home-based seamstresses, who have a local and a transnational customer base, Pami has her US-based Indian customers. One of these is a Punjabi woman who had lived in her local south London neighbourhood in the past and, despite moving to Miami a decade ago, still gets her clothes stitched by Pami. She knows Pami's sewing styles and skills and has stuck with her over the years. There is no Miami-based expertise in making salwaar suits and, as Pami says, 'she is used to me'. Pami also has customers who know her through her kinship and friendship groups but who live in other towns and other parts of London – Birmingham, Southall, East Ham. She sews their clothes and sends them by post. It is her clients' long-term familiarity with her that keeps her national and transnational stitching in progress.

Like Surjeet, her charges are low: £15 for a basic suit ('a simple suit', she says) and £18–25 for any elaboration. A princess cut is £15, whilst suits with buttons, collars and lining are £18–35.

Pami said that the ready-made economy has not led to a decline in demand for her sewing skills because people cannot find their sizes, or do not like the ready-mades. Also they might buy a few ready-made suits and get the rest stitched. They find that there is too much embroidery on the ready-made suits and they do not like how they are made.

Micro-designing: sketching and drawing

Pami and I looked at the Bombay Connections catalogue published by mass-marketing suit entrepreneur Komal Singh. Pami had copied a suit from the catalogue. That is, she borrowed the shape and cut and, instead of the embroidery which was there on the original, she put a ready-made embroidered patch that can be easily bought from Indian fabric shops and she put some border edging in between the seams. Pami likes Bombay Connection clothes because they use the synthetics easily available in the markets and stores which seamstresses use all the time. She also gets magazines from Indian shops in the main ethnic shopping areas. In addition to the Bombay Connection catalogues, she had *Libas* magazines, commercial pattern books, *Movie* and *Filmfare* magazines, as well as, of course, the Rivaaz catalogue. Her customers bring magazines as well to show her the style and pattern they want her to make and leave them behind for her to keep. They also bring Bollywood videos for Pami to freezeframe on a particular style they would like copied. So the conduits of patterns and commercial suits and home sewing are all linked, with the design flows going back and forth and in various directions in these ready-made clothes and cloth economies.

Pami regularly makes drawings of outfits that her clients wants stitched. She showed me some of her drawings and narrated how she had made them, the sources she had borrowed from and also the design inputs she made. Two of her drawings had titles like 'Variety Silk House Suit', referring to an early entrant into the suit market that sells some of the Indian designers' work and which is in fact led by a diasporic couple from an East African Asian background. Another diagram is entitled 'Bombay Connections catalogue' with page references, to remind her to look at the catalogue when making her client's suit. However, there are other elements that go into a drawing and the suit that is later stitched for her clients:

> They usually have an idea of what they want. For the style they want to choose, they look at my pattern books and tell me that they want such and such a collar and this or that type of cuff and point out the shapes. There are so many sleeve styles now. It's no longer a simple sleeve. There are tulip sleeves, an overlapped sleeve, puffed sleeves, and churi dhar sleeves recently. We decide on the basis of the material, what suits the material. We make a new design always when I draw but I also copy a suit exactly that they already have and in a style they like to wear often.
>
> (Paramjeet, interview with the author, 1996)

She keeps notes of the sizes of her customers and often remembers what she has stitched for them in the past. She only draws the top and measures the salwaar size. She says that the salwaar does not change much as 'it's the same most of the time'. I looked at her old notebooks and also her recent ones. We went through the detail of drawings – the darts, the puffed sleeves, the kaliyan, the placement of the gores – features she needs to know to get the outfit stitched correctly. We also looked at the sketches she made for the fashion show in 1984 when the ready-made suits were just emerging and were still hard to find.

This process of micro-designing is common to all the cases I describe. All the many elements are incorporated into the sketch first and then produced on cloth. The combinational variations are endless. Multiple sources are raided, added to and subtracted from to draw and sew a form that is negotiated in complexly formulated ethnic and non-ethnic spheres.[4]

There are many fabric connections and flowing threads in Pami's sewing narrative: a woman who has lived in south London visits from Miami in the USA to get her clothes stitched by UK-based Pami. Pami herself was born in Tanzania where she learnt her sewing craft: in Britain, she ethnicizes commercial patterns and anglicizes Gujarati kagras, borrowing from many design economies to create a composite design that is true to her context and biographical trajectory. Her designs – the product of many mixings, tensions, combinational freedoms and restrictions – capture a living landscape in the clothes.

Hardev's story

Hardev is in her sixties, older than the other seamstresses whose cases I have described here. She has the classic sewing history of a diasporic, born and raised in a small Kenyan town near Mount Kenya called Nyeri. Hardev describes Nyeri women as:

> ... very clever girls. In a small town with a competitive economy where there was a great deal of emphasis on acquiring and developing all kinds of domestic, sewing and craft skills.
>
> (Hardev, interview with author, 1996)

Hardev herself started sewing when she was ten years old. Like Surjeet, she and her sisters started by making dolls' clothes under the tuition of their mother. Typically, they only learnt to cut once reasonably proficient at sewing. Later, her mother would cut the suits they wore themselves. She would tell them where and how to put this seam on cloth and get them to complete their suit, thus teaching them gradually the different stages of putting together a garment. They could complete a whole suit by the age of thirteen or fourteen. There was a real work ethos amongst the families in their neighbourhood:

> Nowadays we have telly. At that time, we did not do that, sit around and watch. We were told off if we were sitting around doing nothing. There were a few families living close to us. They would all sit together and embroider, sheets, pillows, and do cross stitch and satin stitch embroidery.
>
> (Ibid.)

This surveillance of girls 'sitting around doing nothing' was common. You were supposed to work most of the time. It was the ethos of 'having something in your hands and working' rather than sitting around chatting.

This ethic of working hard is very prevalent amongst diaspora women and also a common immigrant ethic. Women of the diaspora, when they have gone back and spent time in India, often come back and say that Indian women of an equivalent class group 'sit around and talk all the time'. Many of these subcontinental women have servants to do the household chores and cooking and therefore have ample time to develop their 'talk discourses'. Hardev said her friend's mother, when they were playing and talking too much, took bicycle spokes off an old bike, sharpened them to make knitting needles and started them on knitting and crocheting. They learnt a great many skills in this manner. She said:

'Apna fashion appi banadaysi, apna damaag use karday si – people made their own fashion. They used their own head and brain.'

Hardev has gone back to Nyeri many times since she moved to London more than thirty years ago:

> In Nyeri, the women are still very creative. They do so much crocheting and needlework still. My mother lives there. She just does it without asking. They are making raffia things, making khapus, baskets. These women were very creative. They had to be, otherwise, can you imagine buying clothes for eleven children! All of us kids from a big family. You had to know how to make them to manage on the money people had then. The next generation [in the UK] is getting lazy. You can get it in the shops and ready-made, so they think why should they do it. I told a family member that she should sew more often. She can do it but she told me, 'I can buy clothes everywhere. There are plenty of clothes in Marks and Spencers and it's not going to close down soon, is it!'
>
> (Ibid.)

'We were inventive. We made our own fashions'

Hardev talks about the high level of skills that people had in East Africa. She wonders:

> Why did everyone do art, make clothes for themselves? Why did they all sew? Some went to business with the creations. Most Asian women from Africa, in fact, every woman, each and every one could sew clothes. If not really elaborate styles, the basic ones they could make and had to make. They used to say, 'What kind of woman is she if she does not sew!' Every house had a sewing machine, every woman I knew, even the really old women, could sew. They used to stitch pyjamas, shirts and trousers, underwear, the bias-cut undervest, etc., and they made their own clothes . . . All their clothes, our mother used to sew.
>
> (Ibid.)

Hardev also described the hybridizing forms of the young women in her London social circles:

> Now the daughters of these women are creating the businesses. But the third generation will not do this. They are doing different things. My husband's brother's daughter has done dressmaking. She creates designs. What she wears, you will wonder about what she is wearing. The fashion is this and that and she is wearing her own thing. She wears English-style blouses with a lengha. She is creating fashion.

> She is like us when we were young in Kenya. She lives in London now. She works for a firm. Also have you seen R . . .'s [a woman at the temple whose British-born daughter-in-law is in her mid-twenties] daughter-in-law? She wears a blouse then she wears a pink skirt and she puts chuni on top. Her clothes are half-Indian, half-English, and she mixes every design. The new generations are doing this. We used to do this as well in our time also. We used to wear a frock with a salwaar and I made a printed twist dress in the sixties with a matching plain colour salwaar.
>
> (Ibid.)

She used to wear this to the gurdwara, and similar combinations with the New Look and twist dress, as in Chapter 1 I have described myself wearing.

Hardev started her sewing career sewing straight seams on items like pillow cases. By fourteen or so, she had made baby clothes with 'smoking'. (Smocking is called 'smoking' by most diaspora women.) By her late teens, she could both sew and cut fluently. When she got married at twenty she had made everything in her daaj (dowry), her suits, the bed sheets (which were embroidered) and everything else that needed to be stitched, with the help of her sisters and mother. Daaj clothes were often made exclusively by the bride, and, even if not, they were presented as such to demonstrate her domestic prowess. Of course, as stated earlier, many women found this to be oppressive but it was the predominant ethos.

Hardev stressed that all these domestic expectations of young women meant that they did learn and become accomplished. They were innovative in what they did:

> We used to learn a lot from everyone. We used to copy and invent. We would see a design and come home and make it immediately. People used to invent a lot. Nowadays they look around to get their designs. At that time we were very inventive. If someone had a design, they never gave it to anyone.
>
> (Ibid.)

She recounts the story that I told in the previous chapter, of the imbricated lace that she learned to crochet simply by watching carefully:

> The competition was a good thing because we kept improving. We kept watching how the other was doing. I read *Talking Points*, a craft magazine I get all the time and all the art work we used to do is all coming back . . . the person who knows how to sew knows that there is an art in sewing, if there is no art, how can you sew?
>
> (Ibid.)

This is a point that revivalist designer Ritu Kumar makes, too, in a different angle on art, about Indian traditions of wearing art, of laying it on the floors they walk on, of not having the concept of art divorced from living, hung statically on the wall. Hardev suggests:

> If there is no art, how will you make and wear your clothes? If you look at someone wearing clothes, you think, how she looks. Sometimes the clothes look really good. It's not that the cloth was expensive but it is the way they wear it and the style they wear it with and the style they have made it with. It's in the sewing and in the ways you put it together. Everyone has their own style of wearing it and also a separate style of making it.
>
> (Ibid.)

Like Pami, Hardev had some sewing lessons from a local sewing school in her town. She used her skills to make clothes for herself, her husband and children but only started sewing for individuals outside the family in the 1980s.

She sewed for friends for free at first. Then, in 1985, a fabric store in her area asked her to sew for their customers as the suit was being worn by more and more women and the shops were being inundated with inquiries. She started sewing for them and still does. A lot of the patterns in her notebooks are from that time. She also has a number of black customers in Tooting, south-west London, which has an established black population who shop in these Asian shopping centres, a point also made by Komal Singh of Bombay Connections. Hardev says she has more black women clients around thirtyish and white women who are younger, with a sprinkling of older ones. She also makes suits for Muslim women from Pakistan who, like many direct migrants from India, do not tend to sew at home. Word of mouth is what has made her home sewing enterprise multiply. One person tells ten other people, she says. She only sews for people who are recommended to her and only if she likes them. She checks them out from the recommender. Like the other seamstresses, she is fussy about whom she allows into her home.

Apnay designs: the powers of drawing and sketching

Hardev showed me the catalogues she sewed from and her eighteen sketchbooks which I looked at, along with samples of her scallop-shaped filigree cut-work for use around hemlines and necklines. We talked about the patterns she forms by talking to her clients, which is what she records in her notebooks with all the client measurements. The effects of Nyeri's climate of design secrecy are still in evidence: she never shows a client what she is 'making for someone else'. Where possible she avoids duplication and maintains confidentiality. This is why she would not to allow me to take photocopies of pages from her actual notebooks. Instead she rapidly copied a couple of sketches.

Hardev's notebooks, like Pami's, reflect the improvisational aesthetic of the diaspora. She explained one sketch she had made of a picture of a dress in a magazine, how she translated the sketch into the dress, the folds she made and the overlaps, etc. She made a salwaar with it. She called it 'a Thai overlapping skirt, a lungi type'. She too can make anything. Although she no longer makes men's trousers (in Kenya she used to make men's and boys' trousers all the time), she uses her trouser-making expertise to sew pyjama-type trousers to go with some of the long kameezes, instead of salwaars. She makes many skirts, especially one called 'double umbrella with which you can wear boots because it is long'. She often makes blouses as well and adapts blouse patterns to dress and kameez styles.

In common with the other seamstresses, she had a wide range of source books, including a substantial collection of the countertop Simplicity, Style, Vogue and Butterick pattern books. She also borrows ideas from both European and Asian magazines, including *Vogue*, *Woman*, *Libas* and the Indian film magazines, as well as clothes catalogues of all kinds:

> Mostly this is what I do, look at magazines and make the kameez designs. They [the clients] tell me to make such and such a design and make salwaar with it, that is how I do it. They make this dress and this frock in such and such a way and add this and that, pointing out the design from one magazine or sometimes two or three. I just make it from these pictures.
>
> (Ibid.)

We looked at a magazine picture together and she decoded how the dress was structured, transposing the visual into a verbal form which would later be given material form as a suit. Truly this was the notion of 'shifters' used by Roland Barthes (1990) – the translation of structures and the circulation of fashion relying on a transformation of the iconic, the technological and verbal structures.

Hardev copied many suits from the Rivaaz catalogue almost exactly:

> I copied necklines and shapes and borrowed from the catalogue the colours that were matched in the pictures. I copied the same styles for people, the same colour and everything.
>
> (Ibid.)

She thinks that the suit magazines and catalogues made more, younger women start wearing the suits, even before the advent of bhangra. The Rivaaz catalogue, in particular, enabled her to make trendier younger styles. She commented that '[My business] has ticked along on the back of Rivaaz which has made it move along. Otherwise we used to make simpler suits.'

It was the first time that she had seen suits in an Indian fashion catalogue. The process of scanning magazines for designs was one she was familiar with from her East African background, both in Kenya and, after her marriage, in

Uganda. Then she used *Woman, Woman's Own* and *She* to make her own and her children's clothes, relying on her sisters in more fashionable Nairobi to keep her up-to-date by sending her new ones and even pattern catalogues.

Clients may also buy one dress from a local boutique on her high street. They ask her to make that same style of dress with a salwaar. She says this is because:

> ... the dresses we make and they [the local whites] wear are the same. The only difference is that they have shorter sleeves and we tend to wear longer sleeves especially in the temple. They ask me to make a dress and the salwaar. All my young clients do this. The women I sew for are Sikhs, Gujaratis and Muslims.
>
> (Ibid.)

The Princess Diana sketch

Hardev had made many sketches of the Diana-style suits, copying from pictures of the suit that were published in *Hello!* magazine (see Figure 2.1). She gave me the sketch that she made of the picture with the size details (see Figure 10.1). She made the same outfit in a similar material and colour, a light turquoise blue. She showed me two sketches of the Diana suit clones she made, one with straight trousers which she had sewed for a white woman and another one with a salwaar she had made for a Punjabi woman. Hardev and I talked about how it did not 'look right to Punjabis'. She said the kameez was right but the trousers were 'off balance'.

The Princess Diana suit and sketches made by Hardev were for me a really fascinating phenomenon. This light turquoise-blue dress designed by Catherine Walker represented a style which Hardev borrowed, drawing both on the Diana style of suit interpretation and on the design skills of a haute couture designer. Catherine Walker had clearly borrowed the style herself, adapting the salwaar-kameez worn by British Asian women. The style was then reappropriated by Hardev and her fellow Asian seamstresses who made for it their clients. Some wanted a straight copy, others wanted to change the trousers, and some others copied the sleeve style which had fabric buttons with fabric button loops, etc. This interesting and complex process of multiple appropriations and rearticulations cannot simply be read as top-down percolation, the trickle-down of design. The other dimension of this is that the designer has borrowed from the clothes that immigrant women and their daughters have been wearing for many years on the British scene.

Hardev gave me her opinions of what she thinks of as East–West styles. She said she made a lengha for her daughter-in-law for which she adapted a commercial wedding dress pattern. She bought lace and fabric to line the lace, making the wedding dress pattern into a lengha (an ankle-length bias skirt) and kameez. I showed her Surjeet's 'English catalogue' dress with the net bodice off

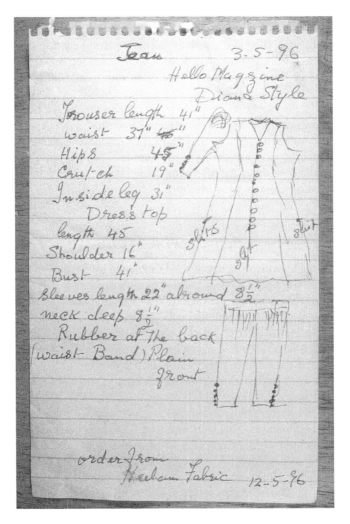

Figure 10.1 Hardev's sketch of her adapted version of the Catherine Walker suit worn by Princess Diana (see Figure 2.1).

Source: Hardev.

the shoulder, her strategy of 'indianizing angrez clothes', asianizing European clothes. Hardev said:

> This is when East and West meets, that is what they call it, East meets West. Burda patterns and *Hello!* magazine, they are all East–West mix, they are doing this. All our cable fashion shows on AsianNet cable are called East/West.
>
> (Ibid.)

160

She also says:

> Even Western dresses have gone to the knees and so have our dresses.
> The kameezes that come from India are also long because they are
> making clothes for Western countries now ... Many more Indians
> come to visit England more than we go to India.
>
> (Ibid.)

The implication is that dresses are long in India because of the influence of
European fashion; that just as in Britain fashion manufacturers influence and
borrow from each other, so do Indian fashion manufacturers who are 'West-
orientated' because they 'visit England more than we go to India' and 'they are
making clothes for western countries'.

Jini's story: a professionalized pattern manipulator

Jini came to London in the mid-1960s aged sixteen, soon after leaving high
school in Nairobi, Kenya. She went to a local college, the North London Poly-
technic, initially to study Economics. However, she soon realized this course was
not right for her artistic inclinations and her liking for wearing and making 'good
clothes'. She had been able to sew proficiently since she was a young teenager.
So she changed to a two-year Fashion and Design Diploma course. This was not
just a clothes-making course but one which exposed her to the manufacture of
industrially produced clothes, textile design, pattern making and grading.

Soon after acquiring her diploma, she got a job with a prestigious ball- and
wedding-gown maker in Bond Street, in Central London. The ballgown maker
professionalized her fashion school training and gave her the tailoring
experience she now uses for making Punjabi suits, in addition to wedding and
ballgowns, among other garments. The owner of this ballgown shop, a Greek
gentleman, was a hard taskmaster and an excellent teacher:

> He knew his stuff. He fully trained you and he'd make you use every
> machine and you had to know the in and outs of the machine and
> then he would take you on this visit where they made special skirts and
> he would take me around on his rounds.
>
> (Jini, interview with the author, 1996)

His specialized shop made gowns for many famous clients and BBC drama
series. From him Jini learnt to how to make a pattern from scratch, how to put a
garment together, how fabrics drape for particular patterns, their suitability for
certain designs and not for others, and so on. It was the best experience she
could have had, she says. She only started stitching at home because after her
marriage she soon became pregnant and her husband did not want her to travel
to the centre of town to work.

161

Making wedding clothes for her aunt and also for her husband's sister gave her the necessary confidence in cutting and making suits on her own. She then made a christening gown for a good friend locally which turned out really well. The friend encouraged her to charge for her labour appropriately, giving her well over £100 instead of the £50 Jini had asked for initially. Frequently complimented on her own stylish (home-made) clothes, her business snowballed by word of mouth. She tapped into her local networks that have connected her to many other clients in other places through their own, extended networks.

Jini's sewing room is full of patterns which are neatly filed and organized into boxes, along with many of her sewing materials. Many small shelves hold storage boxes with buttons, decorating accessories, spools of threads, a bunch of scissors, etc. She has drawers full of patterns and magazines. Her machine is a standard Bernina and she has an overlocking machine to finish the seams. She has a radio and a double-cassette tape recorder with lots of music cassettes for background music. The room is lovingly maintained, like the rest of her house, which is full of beautiful objects – lampshades, picture frames, Japanese flower arrangements – which she herself has made or assembled. She is multi-talented.

Patterning 'anglicized' and 'ethnicized' designs

She is very imaginative, a transferrer and translator of design syntax across borders to create new patterns and design languages. She is one of the domestic seamstresses who sews and creates with eloquence and fluency for both her Asian and essentially white clientele (she lives in a predominantly white area) and shifts the design codes of these economies all the time to create new design vocabularies.

Jini had always used commercial patterns before she learnt to use patterns professionally. She used Butterick patterns and also made patterns for the kameez top. She always adapted the commercial patterns. If she did not like a design element like a bow, she says she 'just nipped it or did something else'. At the ballgown shop, she learned how to make her own patterns, from start to finish, and individualized for each client.

She told me how she now develops commercial patterns, for example, for a Gujarati Patel bride who wanted an indianized version of a European white wedding dress. This dress was a cause of some controversy and conflict, a battle fought on cloth and style between a set of parents and their daughter who was getting married to an Englishman. The daughter requested that Jini sew her a fishtail train in her wedding dress because she did not want the traditional lengha, but a cross between apna, our dress, and an English white wedding-gown's train. The dress finally consisted of a champagne-coloured, figure-hugging dress, fitted at the top, with a short train at the back. The dress was sculpted and lifted up at the front to show the knees a little. Jini had to sew 150 buttons going all the way down the back. Her experience at the ballgown maker's had taught her how to cheat: she admitted 'You didn't have to make the loops but put the buttons on top of the zip so that it went in a straight down, sort of hiding the zip under the buttons. No loops, but it gives the looped effect.' For this dress, then, Jini 'indianized' a commercial pattern and borrowed elements from a 'European' bridal garment to create a cross-over 'anglicized indianized' wedding dress for a locally born British Asian bride.

In the following example, however, she crossed over in the opposite direction, anglicizing a Punjabi suit top, the kameez, to make an off-the-shoulder black evening dress for her daughter. Her daughter wanted to look trendy and 'regal' for her school graduation ball, which is why Jini interpreted this dress with long, elbow-length white gloves, which went just above her elbows. Jini used a version of the very fitted kameez that was worn in the 1960s and 1970s, back in fashion, but longer, in the late 1990s. She omitted the shoulder straps and instead put gold organza tissue fabric to give an off-the-shoulder, arm-revealing dress. With it her daughter wore some chunky gold-covered Egyptian jewellery, similar to Indian jewellery (see Figure 10.2).

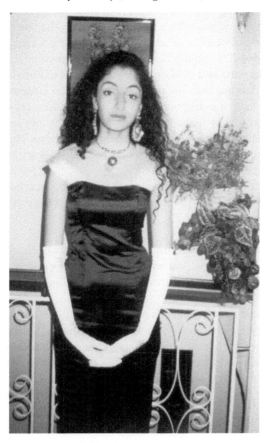

Figure 10.2 The dress Jini made for her daughter's graduation ball.
Source: Jini.

In this case Jini anglicized (so narrow a term for what she is doing but I do not know how else to describe it) an Indian garment, a kameez with which she was very familiar. We talked about how white gloves were worn in East Africa by women with Punjabi suits and also saris at British colonial functions. (This was mandatory if you wanted to shake hands with royalty, I think!) But there were other trendy 'Westernized women' who wore white gloves for dinner parties and functions in 'Westernized settings'. So Jini's daughter was here putting her own late twentieth-century, third-generation British Asian inflection on regality.

With this dress, there was no pattern involved at all. Jini created a design and cut straight onto the cloth, adapting a very familiar silhouette. It is a variation on a sewing practice that is drawn from economies of familiarity that are worked upon anew for a new generation. It innovatively recontextualizes an established Punjabi style. In the next example, however, I describe how Jini uses commercially designed patterns in an 'ethnicized indianized' way.

Her drawers contain over 100 commercial patterns, all neatly filed with customer names on them. Some have the size details on the patterns also. Lines of modification and elaboration, of addition and subtraction are drawn on many of them, extending and reshaping hemlines and necklines, adding collars, taking away bows, using skirts and blouses or jacket patterns to form a dress. The additional design inputs are both her own and those of her customers. As with customers of other diasporic designers, they do not have to accept the form as it is presented to them; they make an input through the lines and talk around a pattern. The drawings emerge through the conversations, the dialogic of discourse and the doodles made on the patterns, the lines within the lines that generate the patterns within patterns.

Take, for example, one of her patterns that we chose at random from her collection. One is Butterick 4415 for sizes 8–10–12 (see Figure 10.3). The description on the back is as follows:

> MISSES' DRESS. A fitted, straight dress, lower calf, evening and floor length, has side panels (no side seams), back zipper and long sleeves with stiffening at cap and button/loop at lower edge.

The front cover of the envelope shows three variations of the same pattern: a simple version in plain pink with no embellishment; a bridal gown with princess cut and a skirt in a lined net fabric and a plain skirt like the lining material; and the third with a human model (as opposed to a sketch), with see-through net puffed sleeves and lined net all the way through, worn with a big bow from which drops a short veil. Jini used this pattern in three ways.

1 She used the pattern exactly as intended by the pattern makers without any changes.
2 She made a three-quarter-length long dress, extending the graded skirt which almost showed the knees into a straight, floor-length skirt hem.

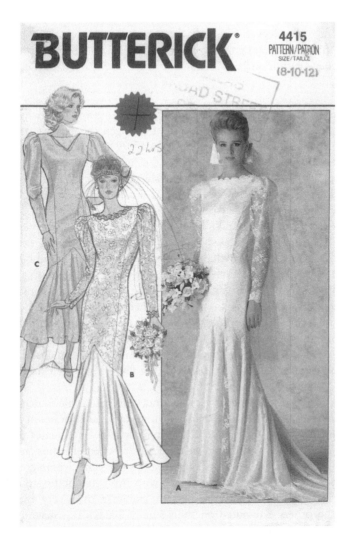

Figure 10.3 Butterick 4415 – showing Jini's 'Punjabifying' lines on the pink dress on the left-hand side.

Source: The McCall Pattern Company: Butterick, McCall's and Vogue Patterns.

3   She made a V-neckline instead of the round one shown and reduced the puff on the sleeve to make it into a knee-length kameez to wear with a salwaar in the temple for a Punjabi woman and for herself.

She is a design and pattern manipulator par excellence.

Jini has also made patterns through espionage as in the case of the wedding dress I describe next:

The wedding gown was £1,300 and [the client] went to see it and she didn't like the sleeves. She said, 'I am not going to tell them I don't want that gown. I am going to make it. So I am going to tell you, can you see me with it on?'

(Ibid.)

So Jini was prepared for the new interpretation of the gown, originally made out of lined tulle. She used the same style but changed the sleeves and also the fabric – to a duchesse satin which she got for £5.99 a yard. The outfit was made for a quarter the price and with the sleeves the customer liked.

Jini explains that she also does what she calls 'designer clones', designer gowns and dresses that she copies by getting a commercial pattern close to the original designer outfit, then adapting it as necessary.

She shops for the fabrics and all the sewing notions and accessories from the shops she has come to know as specializing in these sewing products. She goes to a few shops all the time including one in Southall called Rainbows, which has a good range of fabrics which are reasonably priced. Her English clients love to go to this shop because it is nothing like the kind of fabric shops they have been to before. Most of them also pay her for her shopping time, as her purchasing expertise is one of her consultancy skills. She can, if necessary, make all the clothes needed for the bride, the bridesmaids and the page boys, the cummerbunds, men's cravats, and the hankies to match the bridesmaids' dresses, etc. She can 'do the whole lot including doing the flowers and table arrangements', she says.

Jini has powers of adaptability that are drawn from multiple sources, from her professional training with a famous ballgown maker, and from her manipulation of – and facility with – a commercial pattern syntax. She creates new design vocabularies to service both her Asian and English clientele, thus creating new pattern languages. Her style of working contains the same dynamics as those of Surjeet, Pami and Hardev. The difference with Jini is her ability to utilize and manipulate the patterns and the pattern grammar to a very high degree. Whereas the others elaborated on their sina-prona skills as machinists in an industrial sewing context, Jini had fashion-school training and worked for a professional ballgown maker. Living in an essentially white neighbourhood, her English clientele is now larger than her Asian 'ethnic sewing' clientele. However, both customer bases persist and she sews for both. I was introduced to her by a Punjabi woman whose Indian-made wedding dress she had adapted. Her expertise in shopping also allows her to 'border cross' with her clients, taking her English clients who have never before bought from Indian fabric stores to shop for their material. As she says, they love this as they have never seen such a variety of vibrant colours in the mainstream fabric shops.

She really is the suturer of many sites, through the connections she creates with her multicultural customer base and her own abilities to create the patterns within the patterns. These are the micro-worlds that constitute the fabrics of the local. These at the same time animate and are animated by the global. Jini, for me, is a mixer, a combiner. She is a living example of the formula that the commercial fashion entrepreneurs use in marketing their ready-made and designer suits, 'East–West combinations', they say. Jini and the many other domestic seamstresses live and make authentic East–West combinations all the time. These novel combinations and complex textures are ones that the east and west binaries just do not come near to capturing.

Concluding remarks

The domestic seamstresses of this section embody, at a fundamental level, the processes of (re)producing diasporic culture. They are at once reproducing the culture of sina-prona, by continuing to sew (and in fact reworking it, by using their sewing skills not just to service their family's clothing needs, but to earn money and thereby gain some economic independence); and, at the same time, reproducing the material culture in the form of clothes – reworking the design of the traditional salwaar-kameez, among other garments. The crossovers, the hybridities, the compounding of designs and influences borrowed from different sources have been fundamentally determinant factors in producing diaspora cultures. These seamstresses are design innovators in their own right, who negotiate their culturally complex locations through cloth, threads and stitches. They acquired their sewing skills from living in East Africa, skills that were later transplanted to Britain where they are now combined with a multiplicity of design sources and codes to create their own original designs. Their improvised/improvising sewing cultures emerge from an inherited cultural base, which has subsequently become the commercial modus vivendi of diasporic fashion entrepreneurs such as Bubby Mahil and Geeta Sarin.

Like Bubby and Geeta, the domestic seamstresses are also participants in the wider cultural battles that are shifting mainstream consumer and cultural economies. These migrants and the clothes they create are products of movement, dislocation and also strong location, within the London scene in which they are now settled as British Asians with a multiplicity of identities. Many of the seamstresses have a multicultural clientele, albeit with a preponderance of Asian women. The traditional and fusion clothes they make thus emerge naturally from their everyday lived experiences. They suture the multiple ruptures of dislocation and location to create new cultural and commercial tissues. Their markets are not only ethnic ones but ones that cut across (and thereby re-form) communities. These connections are animated by the multicultural, multiply-migrant sites of local and global landscapes in which they are situated. These are the textures of migration, movement, settlement, displacement and replacement that also animate the commercial enterprises of their diaspora daughters.

The domestic seamstresses are, moreover, simultaneously democratic and subversive in their work. Like American pattern makers, they make previously exclusive designs available to ordinary individuals, copying designs through boutique espionage, from catalogues, from Bollywood films, from magazines, as, for example, Princess Diana's Catherine Walker outfit. In the same vein, American tailors of the nineteenth century made their patterns available in the market. They were democratizing agents in making new designs and styles accessible to the general public, thus puncturing the design hegemonies of previously exclusive economies reserved for the rich. When women construct or co-construct their own clothes by means of the dialogic sketch there is a design egalitarianism rather than the design hegemony imposed by industrially made suits. Angela McRobbie (1998) describes how, in Paris, designs were made from original sketches which were reworked before the production process.[5] In the case of these domestic seamstressess I have described, their sketches are not meant for any larger scale production but for individual garments that are produced in dialogue with their customers. The sketches – a series of straight and curving lines – are the tools that produce new designs incorporating the multiple inputs of both seamstress and client. They are a potent tool, a means of engaging with fashion economies though one's own agency, combined with the expertise of a design professional.

My interviews with the domestic seamstresses have shown again how diasporic sewing economies and commercial fashion economies benefit from the eloquences captured in their drawings and doodles. In addition, it is at the level of the sketch that the process of cultural negotiation and reworking of identity is most clearly seen (not least because most of the garments themselves have long since vanished into the wardrobes of the clients). As with Bubby and Geeta, the seamstresses' sketches constitute new narratives of discovery. Their lines and the curves encrypt the dialogues, the diasporic memories and imaginations, the tapping of multiple design economies within magazines, catalogues, pattern books and film, on the street, in boutiques. The sketches are thus potent encoders of multiplex design codes, with powers that establishment discourses of classification and verbal syntax cannot capture. The seamstresses' sketchbooks are vibrant vocabularies that draw their strengths from the negotiated new, the emergent and the unfolding, in the patterns and drawings of dialogically produced egalitarian conversations. These are not the verbal languages of power, but they have their own eloquence nonetheless, encoding the multiple influences to which their oft-moved designers and their clientele have been subject.

The fashion markets these women have generated in selling their combinational styles are thus true to their contexts and represent their sensibilities. These are the complex textures of global capitalist markets in which culturally mediated products are innovated and sold by politicized marginals who both subvert and also collude with new capitalist processes.

CONCLUSION

Disruptive markets from the margins

At one wedding I happened to attend at the time of my fieldwork, the groom (a blond Punjabified man) wore a Nehru-style achkan and a pink turban. At the wedding of British Asian film director Gurinder Chadha, her cousin's black husband wore a white kurta pyjama, while at a third wedding I attended at around the same time, the English bride of a British Punjabi computer consultant wore traditional Punjabi bridal clothes. These border-crossing clothes and ceremonies reflect the changing textures of the world to which the fashion economy I have described in this book is in part a response. The rituals and ceremonial frames of the weddings themselves also generate new textures that incorporate the dissonances and the newnesses. They have traces of their erstwhile sites, containing older memories and practices of performance, but they are articulated anew in the new sites of the early twenty-first century.

Many of us are responding to similar influences. My niece, Hartaj, then aged five, requested me to sew Punjabi suits for her many Barbie dolls. Her father, my brother, is an East African Asian Punjabi man raised in Kenya, Uganda and Tanzania who has spent his adult life in London, Stockholm, Paris, Helsinki and Zurich, while her mother is Swedish-Norwegian, raised in the USA, Norway, Spain and Sweden and now living in London. I stitched the doll suits for Hartaj in four different styles in different textured fabrics. I sewed them by hand because they were tiny and so fiddly to make. I realized that I, too, through this activity, was again engaged in creating emergent sartorial economies of the suit that reflect the complex hybridizing dynamics, creatively rearticulating established cultural practices and skills for dealing with the new and the dissonant. These negotiative mechanisms result from dislocation, movement and settlement.

The entrepreneurial designing, marketing and stitching women of this book work in a similar way, innovating complex material cultures for the body. The processes that they engage in involve a whole range of actors, memories, inheritances and expertise. The vocabularies to capture these multidirectional dynamic forces have yet to be fully formulated, to express the flows of the new connections, the multidirectional threads, the agencies of transmission and transferral, the intermeshing and intermixing, the symbiosis and the synergies, the pulses and impulses that they are generating in the local sites of their global worlds. I have described potent micro-activities that create micro-markets in marginal micro-spaces. These design processes are absorbed from multiplex economies. The micro- and macro-processes of global markets and communications are crucial, processes which are raided and yet resisted, accepted and yet negated, undermined and yet celebrated, which have both established and emergent locations, which have strong power and weak power and which are located and dislocated, emerging from all over the world. These are the complex geographies of space and place and connections that I have described the women stitching and unstitching in the clothes they design, sell and sew.

The success of their particular British Asian fashion economy is inextricably bound up with the struggle, conscious and unconscious, to forge new cultural identities in the late twentieth and early twenty-first centuries. Localized global citizens asserting their voices through identity-coded products, they are at the same time reinscribing the nation. Whether using a diasporic inheritance of improvisation, or newly negotiating migrant status, they are working to constitute a dynamic sense of self in their British contexts. In so doing, they create new signifiers which are about negotiating a new nation, new forms of Britishness, new ways of being European. They are renarrating the nation according to their own terms through the discourses encoded in the fashion economy of suits (cf. Hall 1997b[1]). They produce the nation from the potent margins, the sutured domains of the ruptures, through the intermezzo, interstitial zones which are vibrant and produced through a complex personal and racial politics of the minority from which they come.

The complex new spaces they have created are both cultural and economic. The ethnic gendering of commercial fashion spaces runs parallel to the cultural and commercial ethnicization of mainstream Britain generally. The economic and cultural activities of local British Asians are potent and transformative of the cultural and commercial terrains within which they are located. I have shown how a particular group of fashion entrepreneurs have asserted their own cultural agendas in the markets they have created, with many local, national and global impacts. Making connections from the margins, they have created new commercial landscapes that are transforming many mainstream capitals. They engage in a form of subaltern marketing, if one can use such a contradictory term. Global spaces have emerged through the working out of some complex and difficult cultural politics and identities of the local. They represent no easy globalization of commodity markets and exchanges but represent much more deep-rooted, long-term cultural and economic processes. From a superficial perspective, their cultural and commercial activities might seem to have been easily and recently produced. It is true that the space and products they have made have indeed erupted into markets dramatically and have only recently acquired wider public registers. But they have in fact been in the making and simmering in the peripheries – both vibrantly and not so vibrantly – for many decades, as the preceding chapters have made clear.

I am not talking here, therefore, about an instant globalization or a Disney world global mush or a McDonaldization that has been transplanted rapidly by outside agencies. The political and cultural groundwork of these new consumer dynamics has been ongoing for a long time and has strongly grounded aesthetics. These spaces look easily achieved but they have actually emerged from complex local politics and cultural work, commercially interpreted and inflected. This particular fashion economy is not about the simple transferral of commercial goods, but encodes more difficult cultural and political struggles. Their 'consumption scripts' (Mort 1996²) are products of complex processes of cultural formation and commercial interventions that are about the assertion of immigrants and their progeny to form themselves as viable markets and image economies. The new terrains of design, marketing and image-making are products of years of gendered cultural battles in difficult racialized and masculinized landscapes. Their particular design and marketing processes spring from the cultural politics and the experiences of movement that have defined the identities of these women. Similar dynamics apply not only to the fashion entrepreneurs but also to their clients, themselves creative interpreters and influential consumers of the suit. These assertive women have created new image economies, around which these markets and styles have been generated and through which they assert their own cultural and commercial agendas. These are the identity-coded consumption scripts that women in the mainstream are now also buying into and internalizing.

These British Asian locals have had to deal with the disruption of movement in difficult terrains where identity cannot be taken for granted or implicit. The taken-for-granted has to be formulated at every stage despite disruptions and disequilibriums. The ruptures have to be sutured and stitched at every stage and the stitching is continuous at every stage to produce new garments and the new perimeters and parameters of cultural and commercial production. There have been many instances in which there are and have been attempts to break their ethnic confidence. Their markets have emerged because they have had to deal with this negation of their ethnicity on many fronts and on a daily basis. They are products of hostile environments in which they have had to resist attempts to encroach on their cultural bases and their ethnicities. But their resistance has not been through pushing a pure form (as in Ritu's response to her Western education) but to produce their cultures through negotiating frames that are not 'ethnically-absolutist' (Gilroy 1993). They have resisted by inventing their own forms which are the result of resistance and dealing with dissonance.³ This is as true of the professional designers and domestic seamstresses whose hybrid, fusion products are a true reflection of their experiences, as it is of the marketers who have brought new products to the marketplace where they continue to develop new ways of selling.

Their innovative stitching approaches and marketing methods have much in common with 'disruptive technologies' (Christensen 1997), the term I used in Chapter 8 to describe the activities of Komal Singh and Mala Rastogi, but which applies equally well to those of the other fashion entrepreneurs. These are the technologies which, used by people on the periphery, are ignored by mainstream markets at their peril. These disruptive innovations have enormous potential to disrupt existing commercial conventions by creating new arenas which are both innovative and subversive to the established ones. Christensen states:

> Disruptive technologies typically enable new markets to emerge. There is strong evidence showing the companies entering these emerging markets early have significant first-mover advantages over later entrants.
>
> (Christensen 1997:3)

I suggest that, for all the women entrepreneurs I have studied, their innovative interventions from their gendered, racialized and therefore peripheral location give them their disruptive capabilities. Paradoxically, their position of apparent disadvantage, doubly marginalized as women members of an ethnic minority, is in fact the source of their economic strength. As diasporic locals, it is their hybridized locations that they are selling (much as the elite Indian and Pakistani designers are selling, less successfully, their inherited national sites). As a Sweden-based British Asian design professional, also from a multiply-migrant background, said to me, 'These British Asians, especially the younger ones, are marketing their attitude and their local experiences ... they are good at "the moment". They can combine really well, trying out the fusions, lots of crossovers. This is their strength.' Even though the marketers of Chapters 7 and 8 are not directly involved in the design process of the clothes they sell, like the designers and domestic seamstresses they have deep-rooted local market knowledge that is a fundamental part of their biographical experiences. Designers, marketers and stitchers alike, they are all super-responsive to the changing demands of their clients/customers among whom they live and work. They are thus quintessential niche- or micro-marketers. In addition, they all either have or have developed extensive knowledge of their production sites in the subcontinent.

But it is the late twentieth-century developments in global communications which enable them to capitalize on their marginality. They are expert at using communication technologies to facilitate their enterprises. I refer here to the use of faxes to size and design garments, the use of couriers to collapse time and space in markets to get outfits to London in under a week. Changes in the clothes and design economies in the subcontinent have also been important, notably the rapid professionalizing of the production of ready-made and designer clothes. The British Asian entrepreneurial women were faster than their male counterparts at picking up these clothes trends and at producing and marketing them through new technologies of transfer.

Necessarily colluding with capitalism, by creating their own novel, non-conformist market spaces, the women do, at the same time, resist capital processes. As Dorinne Kondo states, writing about the performance of race in fashion and theatre in her book, *About Face*:

> ... many people on the margins know from experience, the world of representation and of aesthetics is a site of struggle, where identities are created, where subjects are interpellated, where hegemonies can be challenged. And taking seriously that pleasure, that life-giving capacity of aesthetics, performance, bodies, and the sensuous is, within our regime of power and truth, an indisputably political act.
>
> (Kondo 1997:4)

The designers, marketers and stitchers of suits are agents in the struggle for identity and representation. For them, the market is not only about economic exchange but is also about many other agendas which are facets of their politicization and cultural negotiations and identities of opposition, collision and combat. This, as we have seen, is in fact their market advantage.

They embody so well the significant features of the new capitalism, 'decentralization, networking, flexibility, co-operation, collaboration, customization, getting close to the customer, and small, flexible and local organization' (Gee et al. 1996:39). How close, then, are the stitching, designing, image-making and marketing women I have been writing about to the currents of our times! They have not been to prestigious business schools, nor learnt marketing skills from the professional experts in these fields, nor do they operate with the big budgets of corporations and large companies. But their marginalities, as played out in the cultural and commercial zones in which they operate, have actually given them a close fit with the contemporary market moment. For a change, their locations of racial and gender disadvantage have become sites of cultural and commercial influence in the markets of the new millennium Theirs are markets from the margins succeeding within the fast-changing economies of global capitalism. Local, flexible, close to their customers, they have the edge to succeed in globalized spaces that are fluid, rapidly changing, with multiple movements of information, commodities and peoples; in all these emerging spaces no one power is supreme and no existing power circuits are clearly visible or navigable through existing classificatory frames.

GLOSSARY

* The spellings here are roughly phonetic. I am not using a particular system. There are many regional and urban-rural variations.

achkan a man's closely fitting long jacket with mandarin collar and tight sleeves, the lower part of the jacket flaring gently outwards from waist to knee.

ambi a design motif based on the mango, borrowed and adapted to become the Paisley motif.

angarkha a long tunic tied across the chest with four strings, or a crossover jacket tied on the left.

Benarsi a classic pure silk fabric, taking its name from Benares (now Varanasi) where it was originally made.

choost-pyjama trousers in long leg-hugging style, falling to folds at the ankle.

churidhar sleeves sleeves with bangle-like folds to the wrists.

dupatta (or **chuni**) scarf or stole, 2.25 to 3 metres long.

durree a hand-woven cotton mat used on the floor or on the bed.

galma the neckline.

ghagra (or **kagra**) a woman's skirt of mid-shin to near-ankle length, pleated or gathered into the waistline; it is very full, the hem being up to 5 metres around, and is therefore referred to as 'umbrella style'.

gira a seamstress's informal measurement based on the flat palm of the hand – 3 to 4 inches.

gith equivalent to two giras and defined by the measurement across a spread hand, from thumb point to the end of the little finger.

jhora a co-ordinated set of clothes.

kaaj the slit at the side of the kameez.

kaliyan the panels or gores in a skirt (thus kaliyan-walli – made with panels).

kurta (can also be spelled **kurtha**) – loose garment like a shirt or tunic, with long sleeves.

lachaa a long tunic worn over a ghagra.

lengha (can also be spelled **langha** or **lengah**)   ankle-length skirt cut on the bias.

lungi   a wraparound skirt of 3 metres of so: in some cultures worn by men, in others by both genders.

mul-mul cottons   muslins.

odhini suits   suits with a large dupatta (or scarf).

oongli   the width of one finger, used in particular for measuring seam allowances; two fingers are used if a larger allowance is needed.

plate-wallay suit   plain suit with tapered vertical darts in the kameez, giving a close fit into the waist.

ponchays   trouser cuffs.

salwaar-kameez   an ensemble consisting of kameez (tunic, usually knee-length, gently flared, and with close fitting sleeves), salwaar (or shalwaar) (baggy trousers) and chuni or dupatta (scarf or stole, up to 3 metres long).

shamu satin   a satin with a matt or soft finish.

shararahs   flared trousers.

sina-prona or **seenha-paronha**   literally sewing and beading, but a metaphor for the many skills that consititute the making of a home.

zardozi   elaborate gold coil thread embroidery.

Non-fashion words

angrez   a white woman.

apnay   our people or belonging to us (as people of Indian extraction).

apni   ours, as applied to a feminine object (masculine equivalent is apna).

giddha   a Punjabi folk dance usually performed by women.

gora   a white person.

gurdwara   the Sikh temple.

kirtan   the sung music of the temple.

the ladies' **sangeet**   the gathering of women to sing folk songs and to dance, centred around a wedding celebration (often spread over several days).

satsungs   religious events or celebrations.

NOTES

INTRODUCTION

1   At a deeper level, the fast capitalist world is a semiotic world, a world of signs and symbols, a world where 'design' and life style count more than the materiality of products or the concrete social practices of people and institutions.

(Gee 1996:38)

2 'The buzz of the market' was discussed on the Christopher Lydon's *The Connections*, on WBUR public radio from Boston, 2 August 1999.
3 On the new capitalism, see also Peters (1992 and 1994) and Sennett (1998). On new capitalism and globalization, I have found the following of use: Featherstone (1990), Castells (1993 and 1996a–c), Barnet and Cavanagh (1994), Beck et al. (1994), Friedman (1994), Waters (1995), Appadurai (1996), Scott (1997), Jameson and Miyoshi (1998) and Lechner and Boli (2000).
4 'It is a space of weak power but it is a space of power nonetheless' (Hall 1997a:34) to develop counter politics, resistances and perspectives that are from the localized margins.
5 Gilroy (1993b) writes of diaspora black music:

> ... the circulation and mutation of black musics provide a powerful illustration of how the untidy patterns of differentiation and sameness to which a diaspora gives rise might yield a novel notion of tradition as the medium of exchange and creative development rather than invariant repetition.

(1993b:7)

6 These economies of design are, inevitably, based on the exploitation of poor people on the subcontinent. These are capitalist processes that are exploitative of poverty because these economies are absolutely based on the gap between the rich and poor. I do not want to glorify this fashion economy of designer clothes and ready-made suits but to bear in mind that the exclusivities sold through these clothes do have an exploitative underbelly of sweatshop labour.
7 Thurow is actually writing about changing economic landscapes in the information age:

> New technologies mean change. Change means disequilibrium. Disequilibrium conditions create high-return high-growth opportunities. The winners understand the new technologies, are lucky enough to be in the right place at the right time, and have the skills to take advantage of these new

situations. They become rich ... Disequilibrium situations usually depend upon radical changes in technology, but sometimes entrepreneurs can create disequilibriums by seeing sociological opportunities to change human habits.

(Thurow 1993:3)

Of course, their opportunity and ability to make use of the new technologies of communication are also key to the success of the British Asian women entrepreneurs of whom I am writing.

1 CULTURAL NARRATIVES OF THE SUIT

1 The negative coding of the suit also applied to the turbans worn by Sikh men. The early fights with British employment agencies were around the turban, the fights by Sikhs to be allowed to wear the turban in their places of work and for their sons to have the right to wear a turban in schools. Many Sikh men cut their hair and gave up the turban until the times changed in the 1970s and 1980s when they donned them again as the communities became more culturally confident.

2 Each wedding requires multiple outfits for close relatives of the bride and groom, and at least two each for the guests who attend just the wedding day, for the morning ceremony and the reception in the evening. Women often change thrice in one day, for the morning temple ceremony, for lunchtime and then again in the evening for the wedding reception. There are many pre-wedding functions like the court marriage, the ladies' sangeet, an event for singing folk songs combined with bhangra and gidda dancing, and religious satsungs organized at home and at the temples.

3 Whitney Chadwick describes how Delaunay, inspired by Cubist and other Futurist art movements of the time, in 1913:

> ... began to make 'simultaneous' dresses and fabrics, organizing their patterns of abstract forms to enhance natural movement of the body and produce a moving surface of shimmering color ... In the early twentieth century, women's fashions would become an important medium through which the principles of abstraction were translated to a broad public as the Victorian legacy of clothing as a means of defining class and occupation gave way to the modern preoccupation with clothing as a means of creating identity.
>
> (Chadwick 1991:43–44)

4 Raminder Kaur and Varinder Kalra describe bhangra and the processes that emerged from it:

> Modernized Bhangra of the 1980s filled a demand amongst Asians, enabling them to enjoy a musical genre that was at once modern yet different from mainstream pop in such a way as to express their transmuted identity in innovative ways. However, although initially the Bhangra scene allowed for a Br-Asian identification particular to Britain, by the end of the decade the centrality of Bhangra to this formation began to subside ... Out of these fractures of musical styles came other cultural expressions inspired by a wide range of sources ... Bhangra traits and lyrics have been mixed with the dancehall Rap genre known as Ragga. It is notable that the dynamics of musical interchange in Black and Br-Asian margins has resulted in the likes of Bally Sagoo's remixes with Bhangra tracks, Ragga patois and other dance sounds. This creolization between two musical forms [is] commonly referred

to as Ragga-Bhangra, and the performers aas Ragga/Bhangramuffins. They are an assertion of the meeting of black musics and Bhangra traditions with their own musical histories and reference points'.

(Kaur and Kalra 1996)

5 By 1992, Naseem Khan was able to write: 'The last decade has seen an extraordinary phenomenon – the arrival of commercial fashion, with all that implies' (Khan 1992:62).

6 For a fuller analysis of the Apache Indian phenomenon, see Les Back's 1995 article, 'X Amount of Sat-Siri-Akaal: Apache Indian, Reggae Music and Intermezzo Culture'.

2 ETHNICIZED CONSUMPTION

1 The Euronews report also stated that 15 per cent of the British population choose curries as their favourite meal, surpassing roast beef at 12 per cent and Chinese food at 11 per cent.

2 Some Indian restaurants have difficulty in recruiting personnel. Indian chefs resident in Britain are getting old, while British-born Asians are more reluctant than first-generation immigrants to put in the punishingly long hours necessary to work in the restaurants. The centre seeks to professionalize the running of restaurants, in the Southall area at least, both to overcome recruitment problems and also to aid economic regeneration.

3 Kal Dhaliwal started off by renovating restaurants in Scotland. He was a child migrant who came to Scotland at six years old. He read law at Oxford University and is presented as:

A self-confessed 'child of Thatcher' with an entrepreneurial bug ... Mr Dhaliwal sensed a yearning, both outside London among second generation Asians, for a bit of glamour and for restaurants that looked like they could be in Manhattan.

(*The Economist* 7 August 1999)

According to the restaurant's publicity, its clientele are 'young Indians who are equal in status and prestige to the Sloane Rangers of England' who 'want the latest gadget, the trendiest of designer labels and the smartest residence'. The restaurants have been extremely successful. Forty per cent of the people working at Shimla Pinks are not Asians.

4 Princess Diana wore suits during her visits to Pakistan twice in 1996 and early 1997. She also wore suits a few times in London after these visits, during the last two years before her death. Her salwaar-kameez outfits – three of them in pink, light turquoise blue and creamy pink – were widely covered on the front pages of just about every British newspaper as well as being reported on TV. In the *Daily Express* of 23 February 1996, the headline ran as 'A Touch of Eastern Cool: How to Follow Diana's Example and Spice Your Summer Wardrobe'. Princess Diana wore designer Catherine Walker's version 'of the traditional Punjabi Shalwaar Kameez in the palest pink', reputed to cost around £2,000 (ibid.). This article also had Koo Stark's choices and advice about these Punjabi clothes and information about some of the upmarket retail outlets which sold them. Princess Diana's suits in late 1996 and early 1997 were off-the-peg from Ritu (see Chapter 5 for a full discussion of Ritu, the person and her shop).

5 Other newsworthy non-Asian suit-wearing women include US Senator Hilary Clinton, model Naomi Campbell and Hollywood actress Demi Moore. Recently, too, actress Nicole Kidman wore a mirror-work embroidered kameez in October 1999 to

promote the children's charity NSPCC with the Duke of York in London. Lisa Leeson, air hostess for Virgin Atlantic and the former wife of the rogue trader who bought Barings Bank down with his derivative markets dealings in Singapore, wore a cream kameez with parallel trousers suit for her second marriage in 1998.

6   Fashion Week hails capital's many cultures. At the London Fashion Week yesterday, streetwear label *Red or Dead* paid homage to multi-racial London. Wayne Hemingway scoured the streets for Asian and black models who strode down the runway beside the fairest blue-eyed blondes to the sound-track from Kula Shaker, whose album, a mix of East and West, is top of the pops this week.

(*Guardian* 27 September 1996)

7 *Goodness Gracious Me* is the popular, award-winning BBC sketch show produced by Anil Gupta which takes a lighthearted look at the British Asian community in the 1990s. Its performers are Sanjeev Bhaskar, Kulvinder Ghir, Meera Syal and Nina Wadia. First broadcast on radio in 1996, it has subsequently had several successful series on TV.

3 PIONEERING FASHION ENTREPRENEUR: GEETA SARIN

1 The Hindujas are the wealthiest Indians in Britain and ranked the eighth wealthiest people in Britain (*The Times* 8 November 1999). They are currently being investigated for corruption in India and in 2001 caused a political scandal in the UK (resulting in the ministerial resignation, for a second time, of Peter Mandelson) when granted citizenship shortly after donating money to fund the religious zone of the ill-fated Millennium Dome.

2 Carol Tulloch's study of domestic dressmaking and creativity in the Jamaican community of the 1940s to 1960s is relevant here, as well as to the domestic seamstresses of Chapter 10. She argues that while the negotiating of style and identity that goes on within the designing process is not consciously subversive, it is 'a means to integrate [the accepted values of British dress codes and fashions] with ... [Jamaican] idiosyncratic inflection, that advocated *their* cultural values, *their* "colouredness", *their* "Jamaicanness".' Geeta Sarin (and the other British Asian designers/seamstresses I discuss) are similarly negotiating an identity for themselves and their clients. What Tulloch says within the British Jamaican context also holds true for the British Asian: the design process facilitates '... the subliminal emotions and meanings in being a Jamaican woman in Britain and the assertion of her own aesthetic-self and by extension a collective identity' (Tulloch 1999:122). Cosgrove (1989) makes a similar point about clothes and identity in his analysis of the 'zoot suit' worn by young black men in 1930s New York as 'an emblem of ethnicity and a way of negotiating identity' (Cosgrove 1989:4).

4 SECOND-GENERATION GLOBALIZER: BUBBY MAHIL

1 Bubby thinks she dressed Cherie Booth because Cherie's fashion consultant knows the beautician, Bharati Vyas, who has a salon in Chiltern Street in central London. Bharati Vyas knows of Bubby's shop and clothes.

2   Diaspora space is the intersectionality of diaspora, border, and dis/location as a point of confluence of economic, political, cultural and psychic processes. It is where the multiple subject positions are juxtaposed, contested, proclaimed

or disavowed; where the permitted and the prohibited perpetually interrogate; and where the accepted and the transgressive imperceptibly mingle even while these syncretic forms may be disclaimed in the name of purity and tradition ... Diaspora space is the point at which boundaries of inclusion and exclusion, of belonging and otherness, of 'us' and 'them' are contested.

(Brah 1996:208–9)

5 SELLING THE NATION: REVIVALIST INDIAN DESIGNER RITU KUMAR

1 The leitmotif of Ritu Kumar's reign has been revivalism and the eponymous Ritu London will stock her trademark zardozis [gold coil thread embroidery], along with a range of rare printed suedes and casual clothes. Once popular with the fabulous Moghul empresses, the art of zardozi was dying on its feet when Ritu revived it and made it fashionable to the point where it's become de rigueur for Indian brides.

(*Galazee International* May–June 1996:14)

Zardozi embroidery was part of court life and royal garb, introduced by the Moghuls and considered an Indo-Persian skill practised by craftsmen in Bengal.
2 Pierre Bourdieu (1977) writes about 'disinterestedness' in profits from art and cultural products which are symbolically highly charged.
3 In the Indian fashion magazine *La Mode* September–November 1994 there is a black and white picture of *Tree of Life*, with a caption that says, 'Searching for Life is reflective of the ancient lineage and rich cultural traditions that affirm our past and give impetus to the future'. The accompanying article, by Gopika Nath, states that, '... the *Tree of Life* ... is perhaps reflective of the insecurity of the invasion of investment, tending towards a desire to return to our roots, trace our antecedents, formulate our standing today, in relation to the Indian Tree of Life'.
4 Emma Tarlo (1996:322) refers to what Ritu said in greater detail:

In 1952 the All India Handicraft Board was established with the idea that urban Indians had a moral duty to support Indian handicrafts ... Many of the people involved in this movement were highly dedicated individuals with a genuine interest in appreciating and reviving indigenous craft skills. In particular it was prominent women like Kamaladevi Chattopadhyaya and Pupul Jayankar, not to mention Indira Gandhi herself, who tried to popularise handloom fabrics of different regions by actually wearing them.

6 SELLING ART CLOTHES IN CLASSED MARKETS

1 Yazz's publicity in *Libas* (1995, 8.3:45) lists collections by Tarun Tahiliani, Pallavi Jaikishen, Abu Jani and Sandeep Khosla. Tarun Tahiliani is best known to a British white audience as the designer of Jemima Goldsmith's outfit for her wedding to Imran Khan in 1995.
2 This was a fashion show organized by suit entrepreneur Mala Rastogi, in collaboration with Zee TV, as a showcase for local fashion houses and a charity fundraiser. I tell Mala Rastogi's story in detail in chapter 8.
3 Tarun Tahiliani's shop in Bombay has:

Fine Clothing for Discerning Men and Women. Stocking the clothes of many of the well-known designers like Ashish Soni, Bobby and Manju

Grover, Gitanjali Kashyap, JJ Valaya, Kotwara – the label produced by Meera and Muzaffar Ali, Madheu Jain, Monisha Jaisingh, Rohit Bal, Rohit Khosla and Tarun Tahiliani's own label and Angor, the label produced by the Ensemble design studio amongst other designers.

(Advertisement, Libas International 1994, 7:1)

7 DAMINIS: A COMMERCIAL COMMUNITY MAMA'S SHOPS

1 In an article in *Libas* called 'The Green Revolution', Green Street is portrayed as:

> ... a derelict, crime-ridden, frightening place in the seventies ... nobody would even go through it during the day. And even up to 1978–9, three quarters of the street was boarded up ... Then Asians started moving in during the early eighties from the surrounding areas, and now the overwhelming majority of businesses are Asian. Due to the prosperity, this area has seen tremendous development especially in the last five years. The growth has also affected the local Asian fashion scene with new, trendy and sophisticated fashion houses and designer labels opening alongside basic fabric stores and ready made garment shops ... Bubs Mahil of Chiffons thought that Green Street was unique, as 'it is the only place that combines the lower end of the market with the highest'. But Mani Kohli of Khubsoorat boutique summed it up best: 'Southall is a very Punjabi place and Wembley is a very Gujarati place. Here (on Green Street) you find Gujaratis, Pakistanis and Indians. We are working hand in hand and offering the best we can.'

(Libas Vol 7 1994: 119 and 139)

2 In 1996, these were in the shops and were further popularized in the mainstream media by Cherie Booth, the British Prime Minister's wife, who wore one designed by Bubby of Chiffons in a cream colour in April 1998.

8 NETWORKING MARKETERS OF READY-MADE SUITS

1   I come back to the deadly seriousness of intellectual work ... I come back to the difficulty of instituting genuine cultural practice, which is intended to produce some kind of organic intellectual political work, which does not try to inscribe itself in the overarching meta-narrative of achieved knowledges, within the institutions. I come back to theory and politics, the politics of theory. Not theory as the will to truth, but theory as a set of contested, localized conjunctural knowledges, which have to be debated in a dialogical way. But also as a practice which always thinks about its intervention in a world in which it would make some difference, in which it would have some effect.

(Gramsci 1971:274)

See also David Morley and Kuan-Hsing Chen's (1996) discussion of Stuart Hall as an organic intellectual and Hall's essays, *Cultural Studies and its Theoretical Legacies* (1992) and *Gramsci's Relevance for the Study of Race and Ethnicity* (1996b).

2 *Stardust*, like *Libas*, is a fashion magazine aimed at the Asian market.

9 DIASPORA SINA-PRONA: SEWING AND PATTERNING CULTURES

1 I learnt from the New York *Dreams on Paper* exhibition that:

> The democratization of American fashion was in large part a product of popular success of the sewing machine and the parallel development of the paper pattern industry. In combination, sewing machines and patterns promised easily attainable fashions at reasonable prices to women across the country. Further, an accomplished seamstress could supplement the family income; democracy in action, even on the domestic front.
>
> (*Dreams on Paper: Home Sewing in America* exhibition brochure, 1997)

Dreams on Paper: Home Sewing in America traces this important chapter in the history of American enterprise. In 1864, Ebenezer Butterick, drawing upon his experience as a tailor, assured the growth of the commercial pattern industry with his innovation of patterns in graded sizes. In 1872, James McCall entered the field as his chief competitor. The other two major companies were *Vogue*, a New York society magazine which introduced patterns in 1899 and later, in 1927, Simplicity patterns.

Betty Williams, who was the driving force behind the Fashion Institute of Technology exhibition and also the main force behind the *Dreams on Paper* exhibition, writing in her article, 'On the Dating of Tissue Paper Patterns', states:

> The earliest mass produced commercial patterns were made and sold by Mr. and Mrs. Demorest, Ebenezer Butterick and James McCall in the mid-19th century. At first they sold them from their homes or small shops but it quickly dawned on them there was a better way to market their products, women's magazines ... This being a period when the entrepreneurial spirit was virtually a national mania, the Demorests, Mr Butterick and Mr MacCall didn't settle for space in existing publication. Each started their own 'fashion' Magazine ... Mme Demorest's *Mirror of Fashion*, Butterick's *Metropolitan Report* and McCall's *The Queen* offered news of the latest fashions from Paris, London and New York, beauty tips, household hints and, more importantly, advertisements for mail order patterns ...
>
> (Williams 1996/7)

We are also told that:

> Early patterns, unsized and unscaled, were intended as guides for professional tailors and dressmakers. Tailors patterns appeared in print as early as the 16th century ... By the late 18th century, instruction books for making clothing had become available, both for the professional tailor and the home seamstress. Women's magazines and tailors journals were publishing garment designs as both unscaled diagrams and full-size patterns by the mid-19th century ... The birth of the American pattern industry occurred in 1854 when Madame Demorest established her design company. Several forces contributed to the popularity of the paper pattern. Most important was the invention and swift spread of the sewing machine, priced for the domestic market. Women's periodicals which provided regular news of changing fashions, often included affordable patterns as supplements or by mail order. As the nation expanded and the postal system was improved, circulation of these magazines rose rapidly. The democratization of fashion was becoming a reality.
>
> (*Dreams on Paper: Home Sewing in America* exhibition brochure 1997)

2 'Freehand dressmaking is the creation of individualized designs which may be inspired by a variety of sources, not predetermined by a bought paper pattern' (Tulloch 1999:114). Tulloch proposes the term 'designer–maker' for seamstresses who work in this way (Ibid.:116).

3 See Shapiro (1986) for a discussion of the dynamics of home science and domesticity, some of which are supremely oppressive, and the institionalization of domesticity as a science in institutionalized frames.

10 DESIGNING DIASPORAS THROUGH SKETCHES

1 We discussed her measurement methods, which are very commonly used, especially by the older women. I myself use these hand measures all the time. Hand and finger measures are giras, gith and oonglis. The middle part of a flat hand, the four fingers area, is called a gira (roughly three to four inches). A spread stretched hand from the thumb point to the little pinky finger point is a gith, about eight inches. Two giras make a gith. The first two fingers together, anponglian, constitute approximately an inch, used for measuring seam allowance in particular.

2 Carla Freeman (2000) writes about informatic workers in data processing office jobs, who create 'a professional feminine look' by designing and sewing tailored skirt suits. They do this themselves during the weekend or get needleworkers and dressmakers to sew this 'professionalizing' garb for them and their fellow workers. They fashion a professional identity through the complex semiotics of these tailored suits that distinguish them from the non-office workers who traditionally worked in agricultural and manufacturing sectors.

3 Cheryl Buckley makes a similar point. Her family in 1960s Yorkshire were dressed in home-made clothes by choice rather than financial necessity: 'it was due to the apparent shoddiness of much shop-bought clothing which were turned inside out before buying, to check that the seams were well sewn' (Buckley 1999:60).

4 Tulloch describes a very similar way of working in her account of 'designer-maker' Anella James:

> In Britain, Anella had access to a wealth of inspiration – shop windows, magazines, television, mail order catalogues – but in rural Slygoville [in Jamaica] of the 1940s and 1950s … Anella relied very much on her own ideas and observation of the city and its people when she visited Spanish Town and the capital of Jamaica, Kingston.
>
> (Tulloch 1999:115)

5 The established designer created a sketch that was later translated into the industrially produced garments. In explaining the move from the emphasis on dressmaking to 'budding dress designers' at the Barrett Street Technical College which became the London School of Fashion, McRobbie states:

> While there are no official definitions available, 'design' in these contexts appears to be based on the practice of the established designers in Paris to describe work based on an original sketch, drawing or a set of drawings and translated into a model or prototype garment. After this had been revised or reworked on a foile (or dummy), a pattern provided the basis of the garment itself. When the patterns were sized and graded the collection was ready to go into production.
>
> (McRobbie 1998:29)

CONCLUSION

1   'The emergence of new subjects, new genders, new ethnicities, new regions, new communities, hitherto excluded from the major forms of cultural representation, unable to locate themselves except as decentered and subaltern, have acquired through struggle, sometimes in very marginalized ways, the means to speak for themselves for the first time. And the discourses of power in our society, the discourses of the dominant regimes, have certainly been threatened by this de-centered cultural empowerment of the marginal and the local.

(Hall 1997b:34)

2 Mort (1996) develops really well the masculine commercial scenarios that emerged through the sexual politics in a masculinized arena where a varied range of personnel had produced over a long period the spaces in which men's markets, a 'masculine world of goods', could flourish:

London, along with most of the other western metropolitan centers, has a burgeoning homosexual quarter, where commerce, community and sexual politics co-exist alongside more mainstream practices of city life ... The commercial experiments in masulinity appear to have been long-term, not merely transient.

He goes on to say:

... One result of this process was the expanding number of social identities offered to young men. Far from existing as advertising texts, consumption scripts shaped the interiority of experience of those who participated in the drama of contemporary city life. Commercial signposts have come to occupy a prominent place in young men's narrative about themselves and their place in the world.

3 Tulloch makes a similar point about style as resistance in black culture:

There is no attempt at delusion here as to the origins of Britain's black culture ... it was manufactured as a form of survival against the unnecessary barbarism of the African slave trade ... It was a culture of resistance ... its style became a rather ostentatious armour to order and create an exclusive identity for a people who desperately wanted to achieve a sense of community following the abolition of slavery and acceptance into the free world

(Tulloch 1992:85)

BIBLIOGRAPHY

Adburgham, A. (1975) *Liberty's: A Biography of a Shop*, London and Sydney: Unwin Hyman.

Alund, A. and Granqvist, R. (eds) Negotiating Identities: Essays on Immigration and Culture in Present-Day Europe, Amsterdam: Rodopi.

Appadurai, A. (1986) *The Social Life of Things: Commodities in Cultural Perspective*, Cambridge and New York: Cambridge University Press.

—— (1996) *Modernity at Large: Cultural Dimensions of Globalization*, Minneapolis, Minn. and London: University of Minneapolis Press.

Ash, J. and Wilson, E. (eds) (1992) *Chic Thrills: a Fashion Reader*, London: Pandora.

Back, L. (1995) 'X Amount of Sat-Siri-Akaal: Apache Indian, Reggae Music and Intermezzo Culture', in R. Sunquist (ed.) *Cultural Studies and Discourses on Ethnicity*, Amsterdam: Rodopi.

Barnet, R. J. and Cavanagh, J. (1994) *Global Dreams: Imperial Corporations and the New World Order*, New York: Simon and Schuster.

Barthes, R. (1990) 'Written Clothing', in *Fashion System*, Berkeley and Los Angeles, Calif.: University of California Press.

—— (1990) *Fashion System*, Berkeley and Los Angeles, Calif.: University of California Press.

Beck, U., Giddens, A. and Lash, S. (1994) *Reflexive Modernization: Politics, Tradition and Aesthetics in the Modern Social Order*, Palo Alto, Calif.: Stanford University Press.

Bernstein, B. (1996) *Pedagogy, Symbolic Control and Identity: Theory, Research, Critique*, London: Taylor & Francis.

Bhachu, P. (1985) *Twice Migrants: East African Sikh Settlers in Britain*, London and New York: Tavistock.

—— (1986) 'Work, Dowry and Marriage among East African Sikh Women in the UK', in C. B. Bretell and R. J. Simon (eds), *International Migration: The Female Experience*, Totowa, N.J.: Rowman and Allanheld.

—— (1988) *Enterprising Women: Ethnicity, Economy and Gender Relations*, London and New York: Routledge.

—— (1991) 'East African Sikh Settlers in Britain. Twice versus Direct Migrants', in C. Peach et al. (eds) *The Modern Western Diaspora*, Oxford and Delhi: Oxford University Press.

—— (1993a) 'Identities Constructed and Reconstructed: Representations of Asian

Women in Britain', in G. Buijs (ed.) *Migrant Women: Crossing Boundaries and Changing Identities*, Oxford and New York: Berg Publishers Limited.

—— (1993b) 'Twice Versus Direct Migrants', in I. Light and P. Bhachu (eds) *Immigration and Entrepreneurship*, Rutgers, N.J.: Transactions Press.

—— (1996) 'Multiple Migrants and Multiple Diasporas', in P. Singh and S. Singh Thandi (eds) *Globalization and the Region: Explorations in Punjabi Identity*, Coventry: APS Press.

—— (1997) 'Dangerous Designs: Asian Women and the New Landscapes of Fashion', in A. Oakley and J. Mitchell (eds) *Who's Afraid of Feminism? Seeing Through the Backlash*, London: Hamish Hamilton.

Bourdieu, P. (1977) 'The Production of Belief: Contribution to an Economy of Symbolic Goods', reprinted in R. Collins et al. (eds) (1986) *Media, Culture and Society: A Critical Reader*, Newbury Park, Calif.: Sage Publications.

Brah, A. (1996) *Cartographies of Diaspora: Contesting Identities*, London and New York: Routledge.

Bretell, C. B. and Simon, R. J. (1986) *International Migration: The Female Experience*, Totowa, N.J.: Rowman and Allanheld Publishers.

Buckley, C. (1999) 'On the Margins: Theorizing the History and Significance of Making and Designing Clothes at Home', in B. Burman (ed.) *The Culture of Sewing*, Oxford and New York: Berg.

Buijs, G. (1993) *Migrant Women: Crossing Boundaries and Changing Identities*, Oxford and New York: Berg Publishers.

Burman, B. (1999) *The Culture of Sewing: Gender, Consumption and Home Dressmaking*, Oxford and New York: Berg.

Carnoy, M., Castells, M., Cohen, S. and Cardoso, F. M. (1993) *The New Global Economy in the Information Age: Reflections on Our Changing World*, University Park, Pa.: Pennsylvania State University Press.

Castells, M. (1993) 'The Information Economy and the New International Division of Labor', in Carnoy, M. et al. (eds) *The New Global Economy in the Information Age: Reflections on Our Changing World*, University Park, Pa.: Pennsylvania State University Press.

—— (1996a) *The Information Age: Economy, Society and Culture Volume I: The Rise of Network Society*, Oxford and Malden, Mass.: Blackwell Publishers.

—— (1996b) *The Information Age: Economy, Society and Culture Volume II: The Power of Identity*, Oxford and Malden, Mass.: Blackwell Publishers.

—— (1996c) *The Information Age: Economy, Society and Culture Volume III: End of Millennium*, Oxford and Malden, Mass.: Blackwell Publishers.

Chadwick, W. (1991) 'Living Simultaneously: Sonia and Robert Delaunay', in *Significant Others: Creativity and Intimate Partnership*, London and New York: Thames & Hudson.

Christensen, C. M. (1997) *The Innovator's Dilemma: When New Technologies Cause Great Firms to Fail*, Boston, Mass.: Harvard Business School Press.

Collins, R., Garnham, N., Scannell, P., Schlesinger P. and Sparks, C. (1986) *Media, Culture and Society: A Critical Reader*, Newbury Park, Calif.: Sage Publications.

Cosgrove, S. (1989) 'The Zoot Suit and Style Warfare', in A. McRobbie (ed.) *Zoot Suits and Secondhand Dresses: An Anthology of Fashion and Music*, Basingstoke and London: Macmillan.

Craik, J. (1994) *The Face of Fashion*, London and New York: Routledge.

Featherstone, M. (ed.) (1990) *Global Culture: Nationalism, Globalization and Modernity*, London and Newbury Park, Calif.: Sage Publications.

Freeman, C. (2000) *High Tech and High Heels in the Global Economy*, Durham and London: Duke University Press.

Friedman, J. (1990) 'Being in the World: Globalization and Localization', in M. Featherstone (ed.) *Global Culture: Nationalism, Globalization and Modernity*, London and Newbury Park, Calif.: Sage Publications.

—— (1994) *Cultural Identities and Global Processes*, London and Newbury Park, Calif.: Sage Publications.

Gaskell, E. (1855) *North and South*, Oxford: Oxford Paperbacks (1998 edition).

Gee, J. P. (1996) 'Fast Capitalism: Theory and Practice', in J. P. Gee, G. Hull and C. Lankshear (eds) *The New Work Order: Behind the Language of the New Capitalism*, Boulder, Colo.: Westview Press.

—— (2001) 'New Capitalism and New Kinds of People', in M. Kalantzis and B. Cope (eds) *Transformations in Language and Learning: Perspectives on Multi-Literacies*, Melbourne: Common Ground Publishers.

Giddens, A. (1991) *Modernity and Self Identity: Self and Society in the Modern Age*, Palo Alto, Calif.: Stanford University Press.

Gilroy, P. (1987) *There Ain't No Black in the Union Jack*, London: Hutchinson.

—— (1993a) *The Black Atlantic: Modernity and Double Consciousness*, London and New York: Verso Press.

—— (1993b) *Small Acts: Thoughts on the Politics of Black Cultures*, London: Serpent Tail Press.

Goldstein, J. (1995) 'The Female Aesthetic Community', in G. E. Marcus and F. R. Myers (eds) *The Traffic in Culture: Refiguring Art and Anthropology*, Los Angeles and Berkeley, Calif: University of California Press.

Gramsci, A. (1971) *Selections from the Prison Notebooks*, (eds) G. Nowell Smith and Q. Hoare, New York: International Publishers.

Grossberg, L. et al. (eds) (1992) *Cultural Studies*, London: Routledge.

Hall, S. (1992) 'Cultural Studies and its Theoretical Legacies', in L. Grossberg et al. (eds) *Cultural Studies*, London: Routledge.

—— (1996a) 'New Ethnicities', in D. Morley and Kuan-Hsing Chen (eds) *Stuart Hall: Critical Dialogues in Cultural Studies*, London and New York: Routledge.

—— (1996b) 'Gramsci's Relevance for the Study of Race and Ethnicity', in D. Morley and Kuan-Hsing Chen (eds) *Stuart Hall: Critical Dialogues in Cultural Studies*, London and New York: Routledge.

—— (1997a) 'The Local and the Global: Globalization and Ethnicity', in A. King (ed.) *Culture, Globalization and the World-System: Contemporary Conditions for Representation of Identity*, Minneapolis, Minn.: University of Minnesota Press.

—— (1997b) 'Old and New Identities, Old and New Ethnicities', in A. King (ed.) *Culture, Globalization and the World-System: Contemporary Conditions for Representation of Identity*, Minneapolis, Minn.: University of Minnesota Press.

Jalan, R. (1997) 'As Asian Orientalism? *Libas* and the Textures of Postcolonialism', in A. Scott (ed.) *The Limits of Globalization: Cases and Arguments*, London: Routledge.

James, L. (1997) *Raj: the Making and Unmaking of British India*, London: Abacus (Little, Brown & Company).

Jameson, F. and Miyoshi M. (1998) *The Cultures of Globalization*, Durham and London: Duke University Press.

Kalantzis, M. and Cope, B. (2001) *Transformations in Language and Learning: Perspectives on Multi-Literacies*, Melbourne: Common Ground Publishers.

Kaur, R. and Kalra, V. (1996) 'Resounding (Anti)Racism, or Concordant Politics?', in S. Sharma, J. Hutnyk and A. Sharma (eds) *Disorienting Rhythms: The Politics of the New Asian Dance Music*, London and Totowa, N.J.: Zed Books.

Keay, J. (1993) *The Honourable Company: a History of the English East India Company*, London: Harper Collins.

Khan, N. (1992) 'Asian Women's Dress From Joe Bloggs: Changing Clothes for Changing times', in J. Ash and E. Wilson (eds) *Chic Thrills: a Fashion Reader*, London: Pandora.

Kidwell, C. and Chrismas, M. (1974) *Suiting Everyone: The Democratization of Clothing in America*, Washington, D.C.: Smithsonian Institute Press.

Kondo, D. (1997) *About Face: Performing Race in Fashion and Theater*, New York and London: Routledge.

Lash, S. and Urry, J. (1994) *Economy of Signs and Space*, London and Newbury Park, Calif.: Sage Publishers.

Lechner, F. and Boli, J. (2000) *The Globalization Reader*, Oxford: Blackwell Publishers.

Light, I. and Bhachu, P. (1993) *Immigration and Entrepreneurship*, Rutgers, N.J.: Transactions Press.

Marcus, G. and Myers, F. (1995) *The Traffic in Culture: Refiguring Art and Anthropology*, Los Angeles and Berkeley, Calif.: University of California Press.

McRobbie, A. (1989) *Zoot Suits and Second-hand Dresses: An Anthology of Fashion and Music*, Basingstoke and London: Macmillan.

—— (1998) *British Fashion Design: Rag Trade or Image Industry?* London and New York: Routledge.

Mercer, K. (1994) *Welcome to the Jungle: New Positions in Black Cultural Studies*, New York and London: Routledge.

Mitchell, J. and Oakley, A. (1997) *Who's Afraid of Feminism? Seeing Through the Backlash*, London: Hamish Hamilton.

Montgomery, L. M. (1925) *Anne of Green Gables*, London: Puffin Books (1994 edition).

Morley, D. and Kuan-Hsing Chen (eds) (1996) *Stuart Hall: Critical Dialogues in Cultural Studies*, London and New York: Routledge.

Mort, F. (1996) *Cultures of Consumption: Masculinities and Social Space in Late Twentieth-Century Britain*, London and New York: Routledge.

Nath, G. (1994) 'Originality and Creativity in the "Art" of Indian Fashion – A Reflection of the National Identity', in *La Mode*, 5.2:72.

Nava, M. (1995) 'Modernity Tamed? Women Shoppers and the Rationalization of Consumption in the Interwar Period', in *Australian Journal of Communication* 22:2, pp. 1–19.

Ogren, K. (1989) *The Jazz Revolution: Twenties America and the Meaning of Jazz*, New York: Oxford University Press.

Peters, T. (1992) *Liberation Management: Necessary Disorganization for the Nanosecond Nineties*, New York: Fawcett.

—— (1994) *The Tom Peters Seminar: Crazy Times Call for Crazy Organizations*, New York: Vintage Books.

Rose, P. (1994) *Rap Music and Black Culture in Contemporary America*, Hanover, Ind. and London: Wesleyan University Press.

Scott, A. (1997) *The Limits of Globalization: Cases and Arguments*, London: Routledge.

Sennett, R. (1998) *The Corrosion of character: The Personal Consequences of Work in the New Capitalism*, New York and London: W. W. Norton and Company.

Shapiro, L. (1986) *Perfection Salad: Women and Cooking at the Turn of the Century*, New York: North Point Press.

Sharma. S., Hutnyk, J. and Sharma, A. (1996) *Disorienting Rhythms: The Politics of the New Asian Dance Music*, London and Totowa, N.J.: Zed Books.

Singh, T. (1998) 'It's about Clubwear Meeting the Salwaar Kameez ...', *Eastern Eye*, 17 July 1998.

Tarlo, E. (1996) 'Fashion Fables of an Urban Village', in E. Tarlo *Clothing Matters: Dress and Identity in India*, London: Hurst & Company.

—— (1996) *Clothing Matters: Dress and Identity in India*, London: Hurst & Company.

Thackeray, W. M. (1848) *Vanity Fair*, London: Penguin Books (1994 edition).

Thurow, L. (1999) *Building Wealth: The New Rules for Individuals, Companies, and Nations in a Knowledge-based Economy*, New York: HarperCollins Publishers.

Tulloch, C. (1992) 'Rebel Without a Pause: Black Street Style and Black Designers', in J. Ash and E. Wilson (eds) *Chic Thrills: a Fashion Reader*, London: Pandora Press.

—— (1999) 'There's No Place Like Home: Home Dressmaking and Creativity in the Jamaican Community of the 1940s to the 1960s', in B. Burman (ed.) *The Culture of Sewing*, London and New York: Berg.

Urry, J. (1990) 'The Semiotic Work of Transformation', in J. Urry *The Tourist Gaze*, London: Sage.

Walsh, M. (1979) 'The Democratization of Fashion: the Emergence of the Women's Dress Pattern Industry', in *Journal of American History*, 2 September, 66:299–313.

Waters, M. (1995) *Globalization: Key Ideas*, London and New York: Routledge.

Williams, B. (1996/7) 'On the Dating of Tissue Paper Patterns', in *Cutters' Research Journal* VIII.3.

Newspapers, magazines, TV and catalogues

Asian Age
Bombay Connections Catalogue
Daily Star, 26 March 1996
East
The Economist, 7 August 1999
Euro News, Zee TV
Galazee International, May–June 1996
Glad Rags
The Guardian
Hello!
Image
India Abroad, 28 August 1998
Libas International
La Mode
New York Times
Observer Newspaper, The Week 6 November 1999
Outlook, 20 April 1998
Talking Points
This Week
Vogue

INDEX